STOP! This is the back of the book!

This manga collection is translated into English, but arranged in right-to-left reading format to maintain the artwork's visual orientation as originally drawn and published in Japan. If you've never read comics this way before, take a look at the diagram below to give yourself an idea of how to go about it. Basically, you'll be starting in the upper right-hand corner, and will read each word balloon and panel moving right-to-left. It may take a little getting used to, but you should get the hang of it very quickly. Have fun! If this is the millionth manga you've read this way, never mind. ^_^

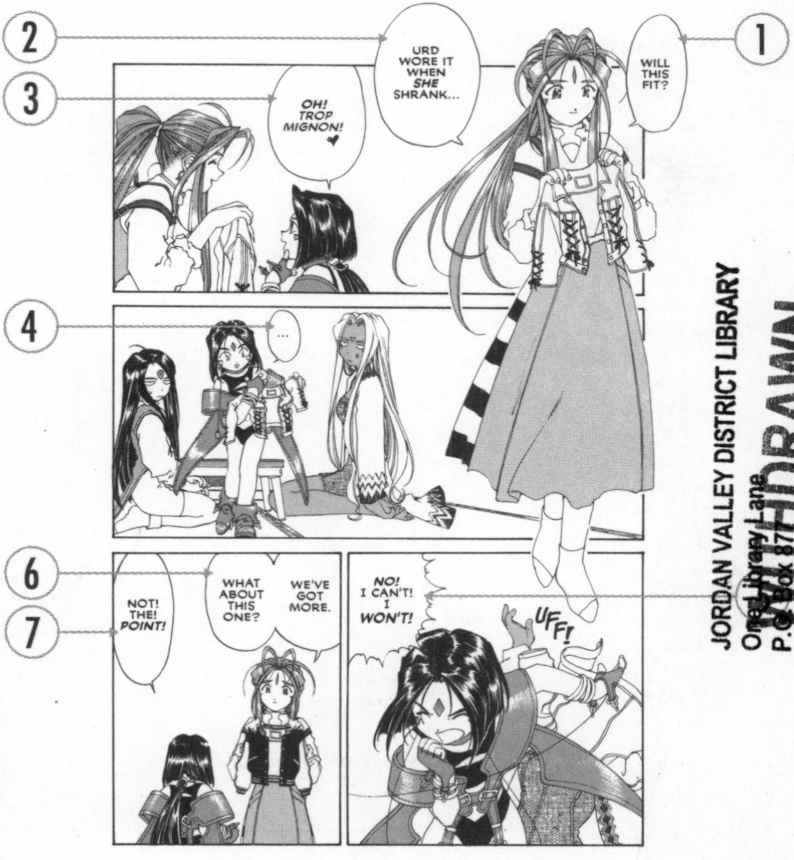
1
WILL THIS FIT?
2
URD WORE IT WHEN SHE SHRANK...
3
OH! TROP MIGNON!
4
...
NO! I CAN'T! I WON'T!
UFF!
6
WE'VE GOT MORE.
WHAT ABOUT THIS ONE?
7
NOT! THE! POINT!

EDITOR
Carl Gustav Horn

DESIGNER
Debra Bailey

ART DIRECTOR
Lia Ribacchi

PUBLISHER
Mike Richardson

English-language version
produced by Dark Horse Comics

Published by Dark Horse Manga
A division of Dark Horse Comics, Inc.
10956 SE Main Street
Milwaukie, OR 97222
www.darkhorse.com

To find a comics shop in your area,
call the Comic Shop Locator Service
toll-free at 1-888-266-4226

First edition: April 2006
ISBN-10: 1-59307-463-8
ISBN-13: 978-1-59307-463-0

1 3 5 7 9 10 8 6 4 2

Printed in Canada

Oh My Goddess!

ああっ女神さまっ 23

STORY AND ART BY

Kosuke Fujishima

TRANSLATION BY

Dana Lewis
and Lea Hernandez

LETTERING AND TOUCH-UP BY

Susie Lee AND Betty Dong
WITH Tom2K

DARK HORSE MANGA™

CHAPTER 142

Bell and Keiichi and the Terrible Guest

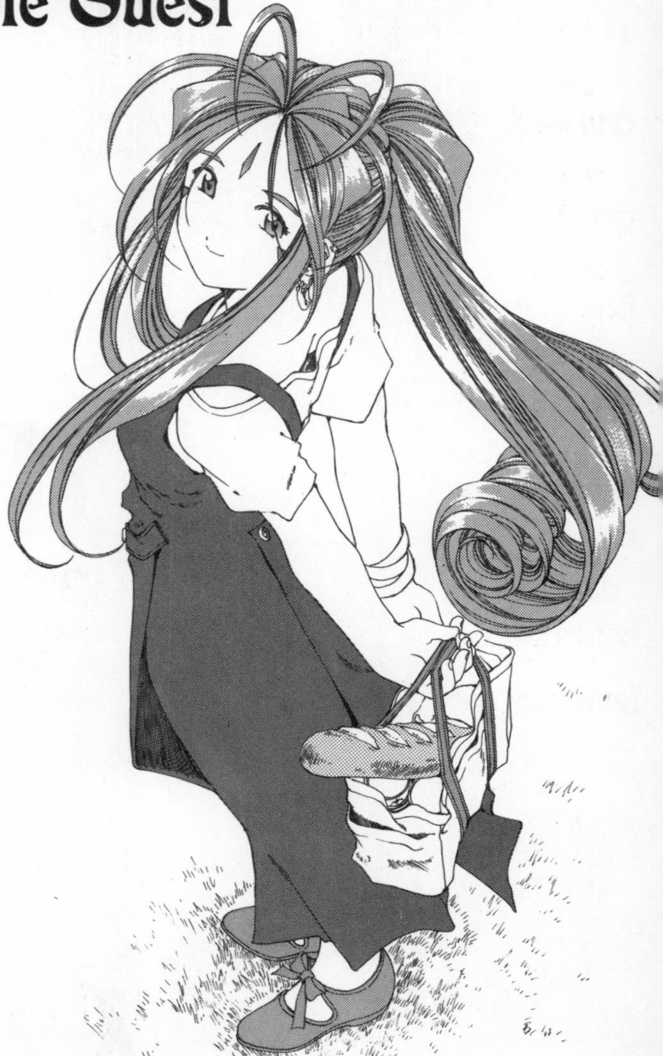

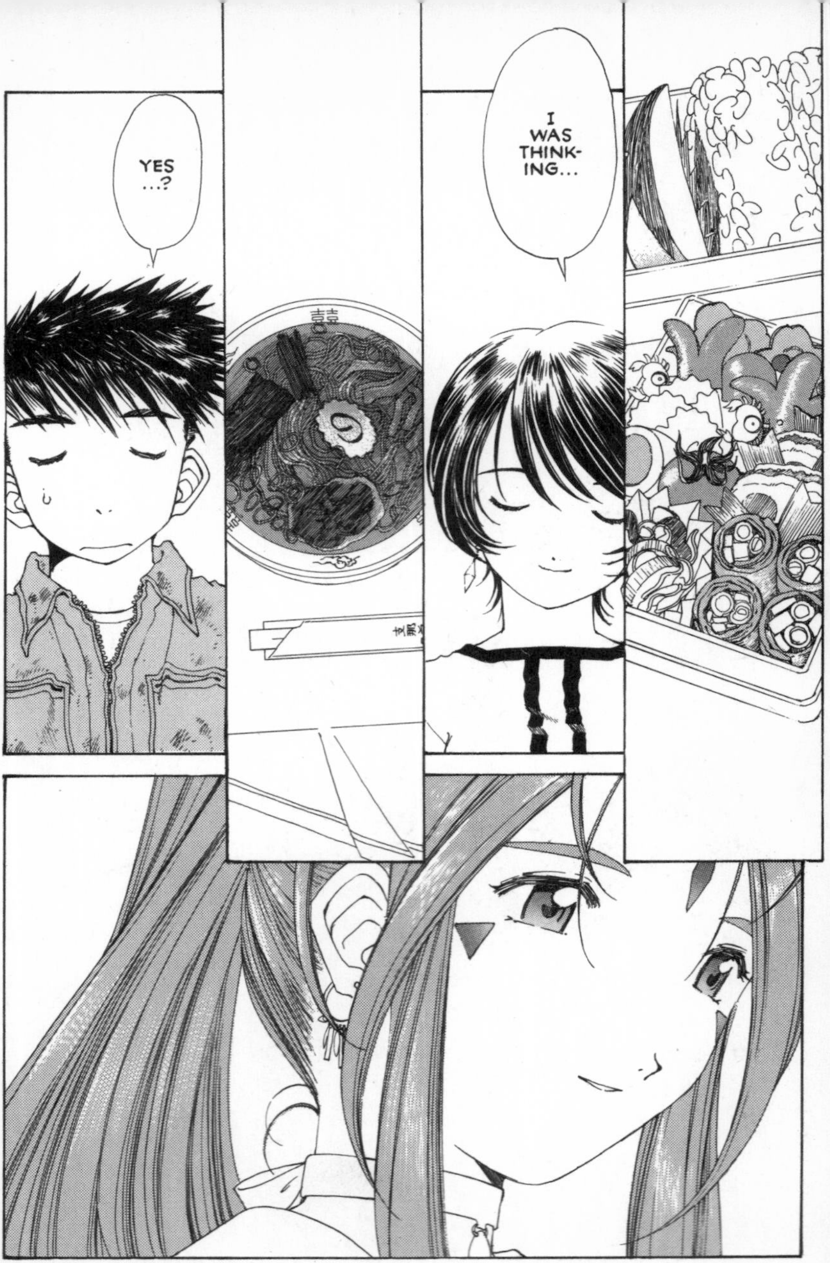
I WAS THINK-ING...
YES ...?

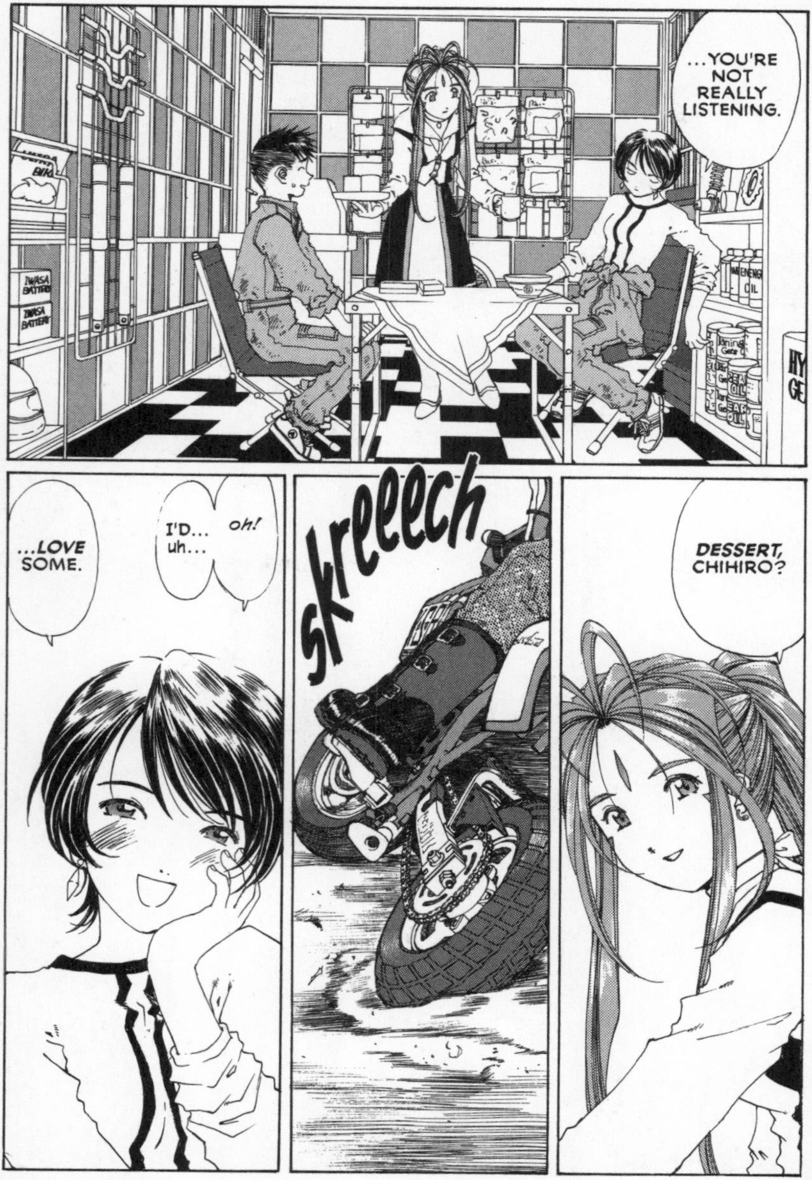
...YOU'RE NOT REALLY LISTENING.
DESSERT, CHIHIRO?
skreeech
oh!
I'D... uh...
...LOVE SOME.

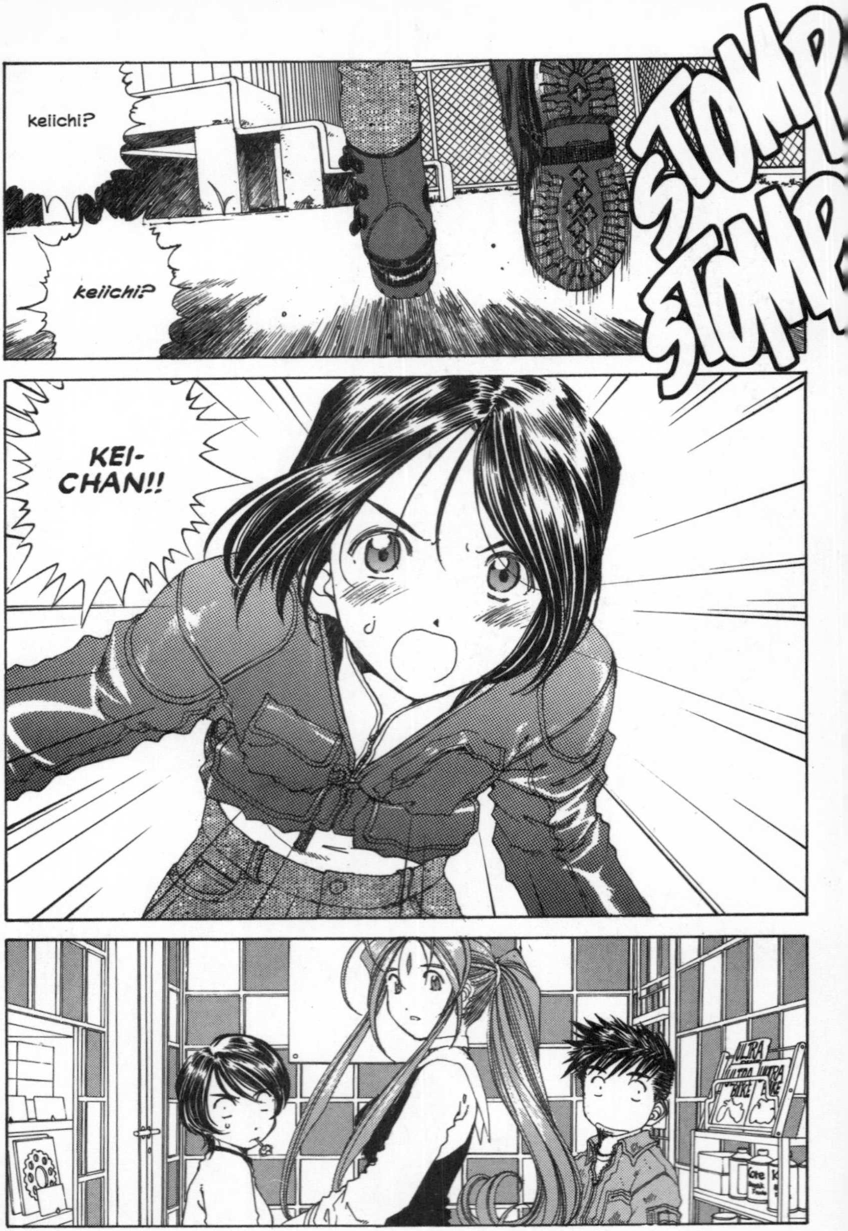
STOMP STOMP
keiichi?
keiichi?
KEI-CHAN!!

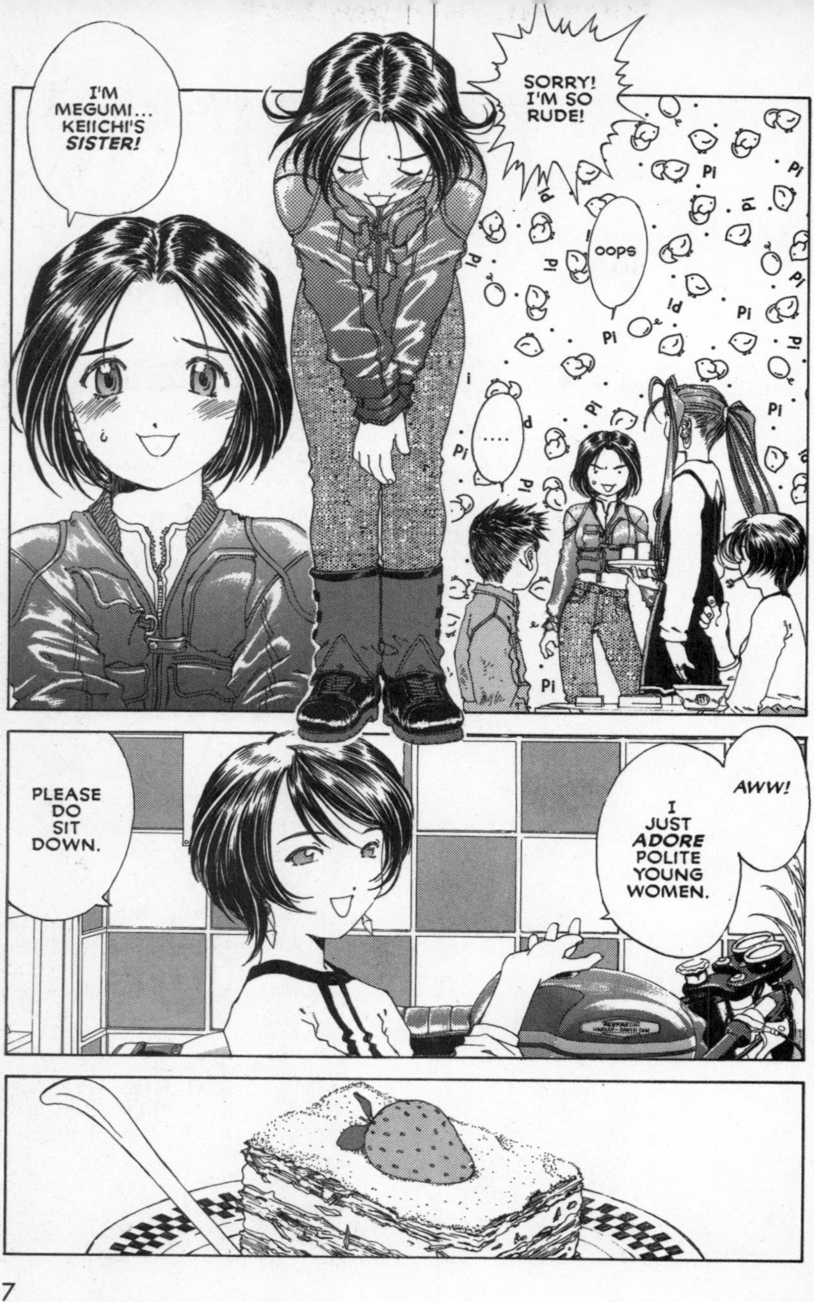
SORRY! I'M SO RUDE!
oops
Pi Pi Pi
.....
I'M MEGUMI... KEIICHI'S *SISTER!*
AWW!
I JUST *ADORE* POLITE YOUNG WOMEN.
PLEASE DO SIT DOWN.

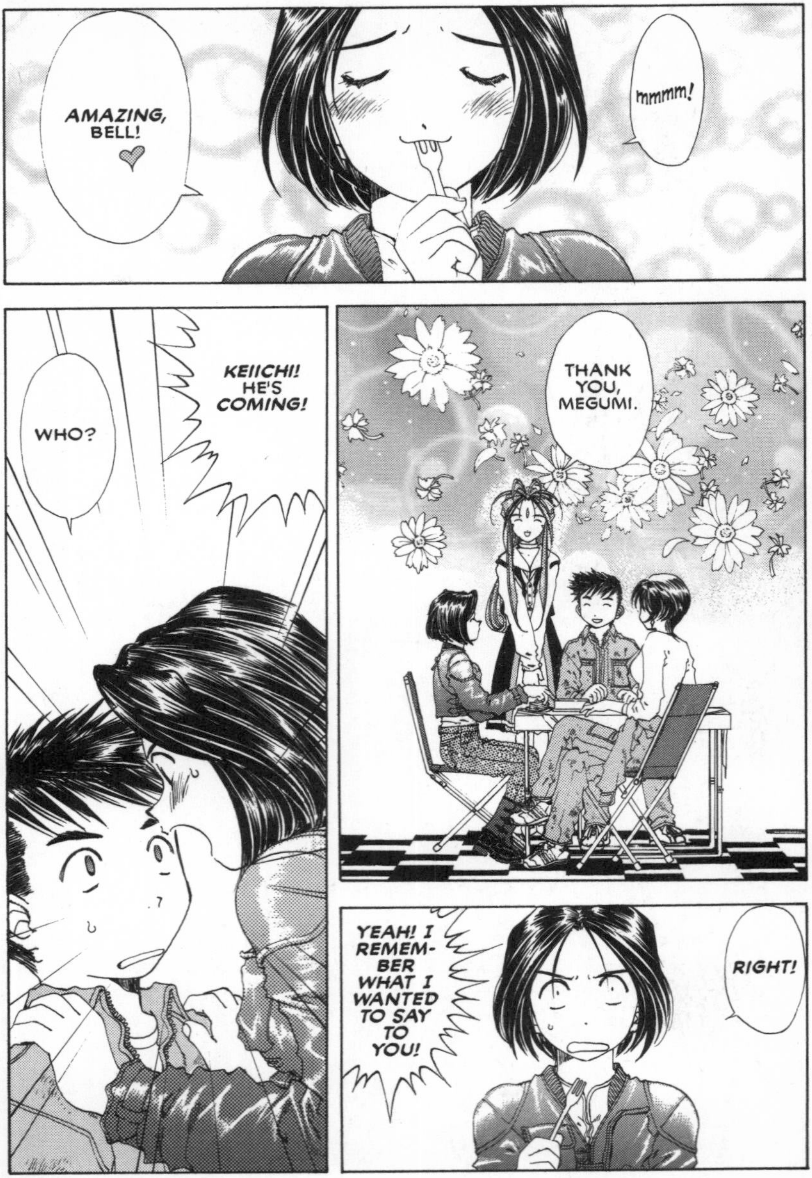
mmmm!
AMAZING, BELL!
THANK YOU, MEGUMI.
RIGHT!
YEAH! I REMEMBER WHAT I WANTED TO SAY TO YOU!
KEIICHI! HE'S COMING!
WHO?

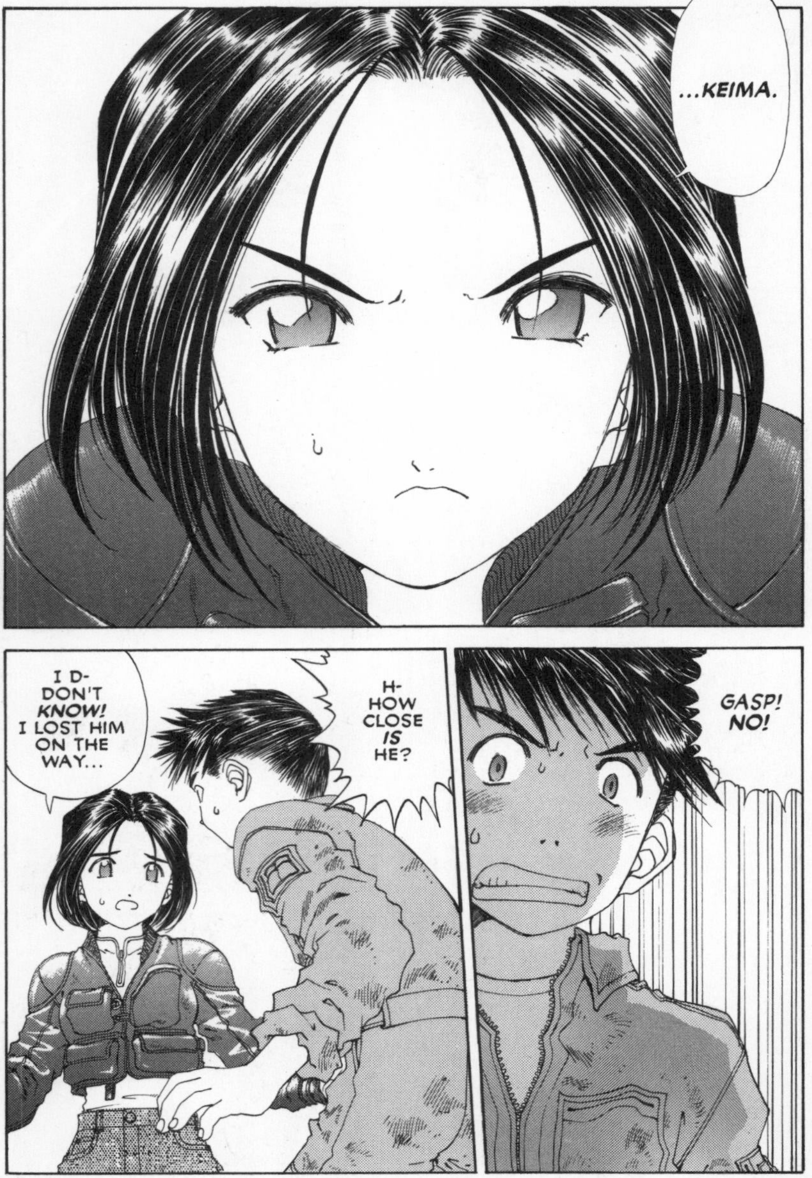
...KEIMA.
GASP! NO!
H-HOW CLOSE *IS* HE?
I D-DON'T *KNOW!* I LOST HIM ON THE WAY...

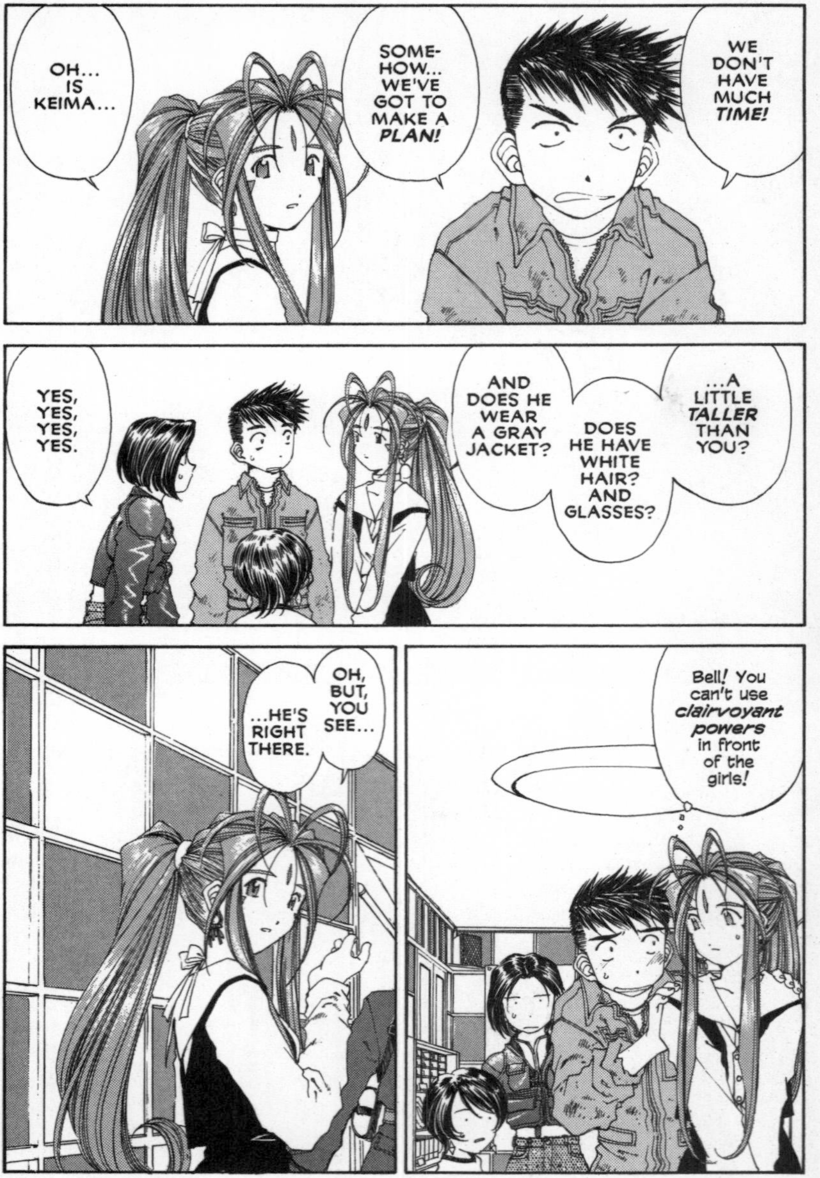

WE DON'T HAVE MUCH TIME!
SOME-HOW... WE'VE GOT TO MAKE A PLAN!
OH... IS KEIMA...
...A LITTLE TALLER THAN YOU?
DOES HE HAVE WHITE HAIR? AND GLASSES?
AND DOES HE WEAR A GRAY JACKET?
YES, YES, YES, YES.
Bell! You can't use clairvoyant powers in front of the girls!
OH, BUT, YOU SEE...
...HE'S RIGHT THERE.

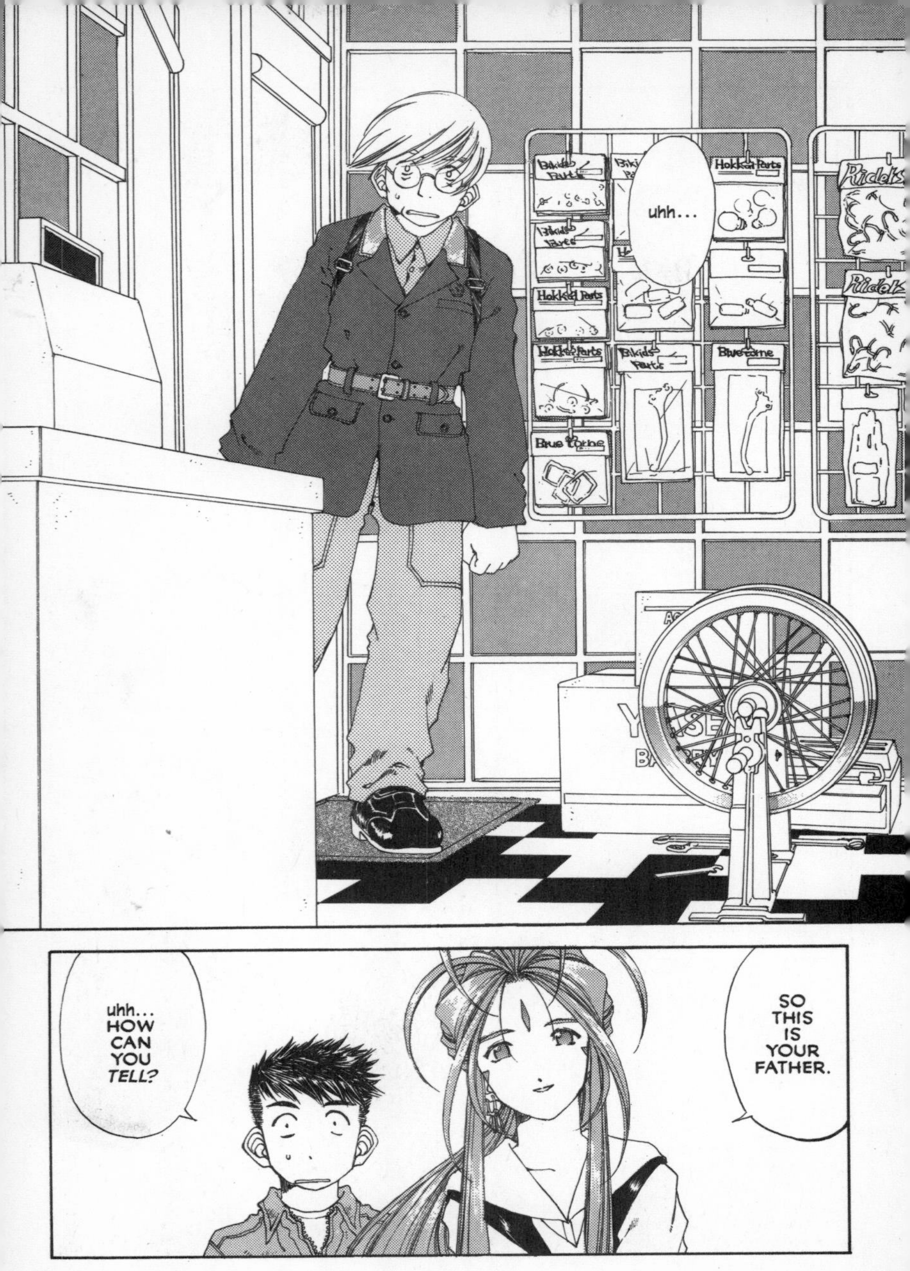
uhh...
SO THIS IS YOUR FATHER.
uhh... HOW CAN YOU *TELL?*

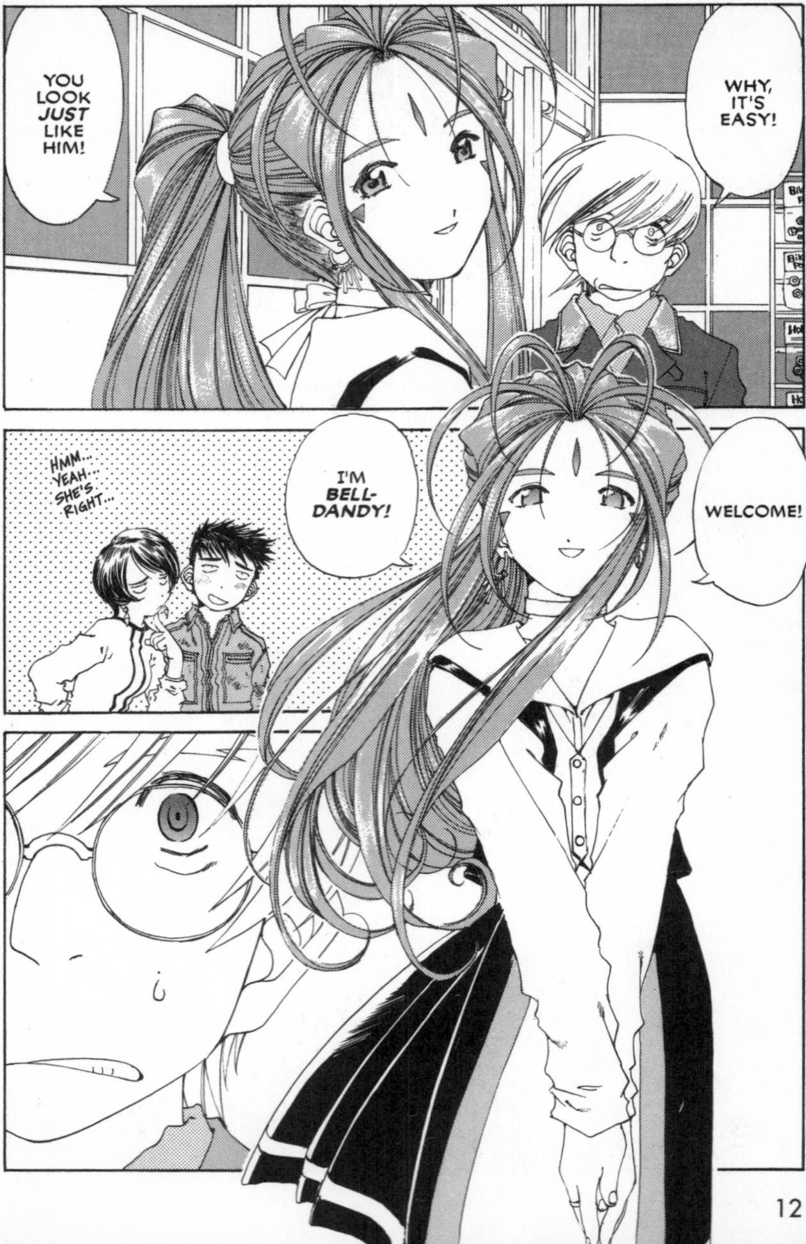
WHY, IT'S EASY!
YOU LOOK JUST LIKE HIM!
WELCOME!
I'M BELL-DANDY!
HMM... YEAH... SHE'S RIGHT...

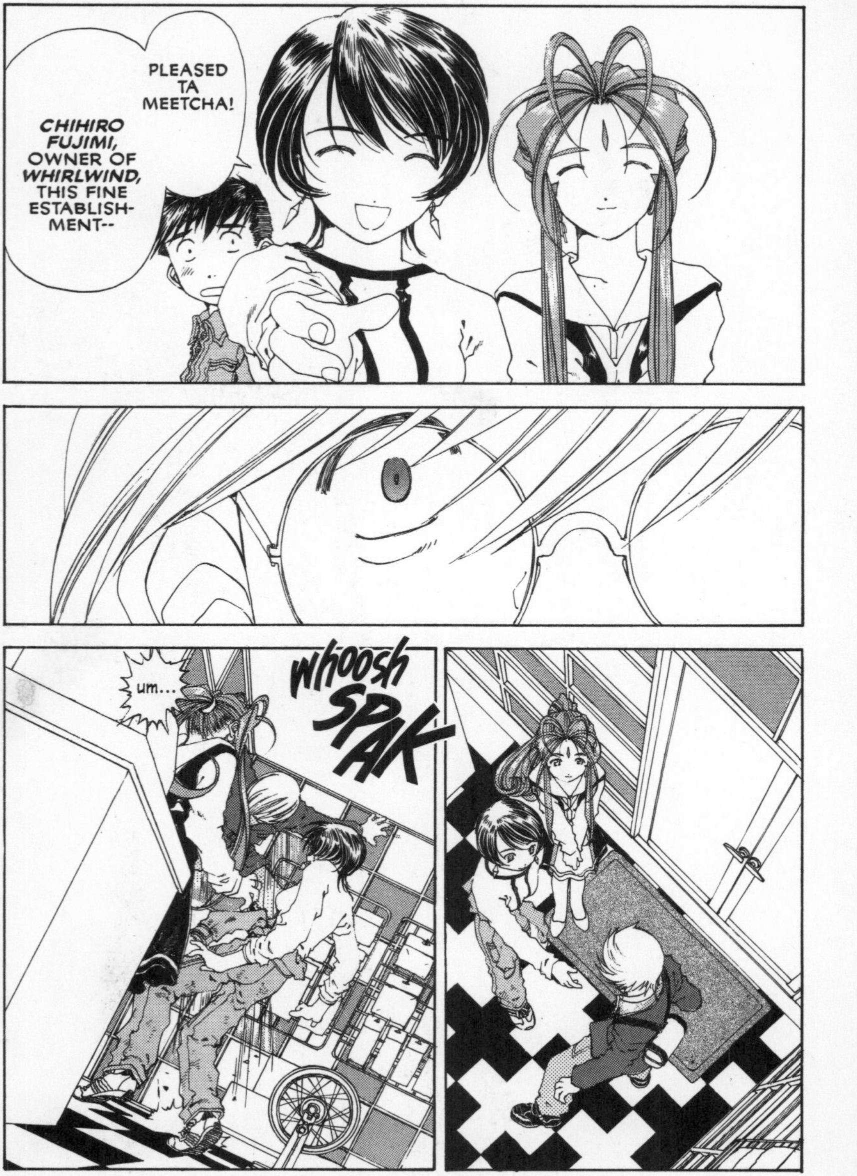
PLEASED TA MEETCHA! CHIHIRO FUJIMI, OWNER OF WHIRLWIND, THIS FINE ESTABLISH-MENT--
whoosh
SPAK
um...

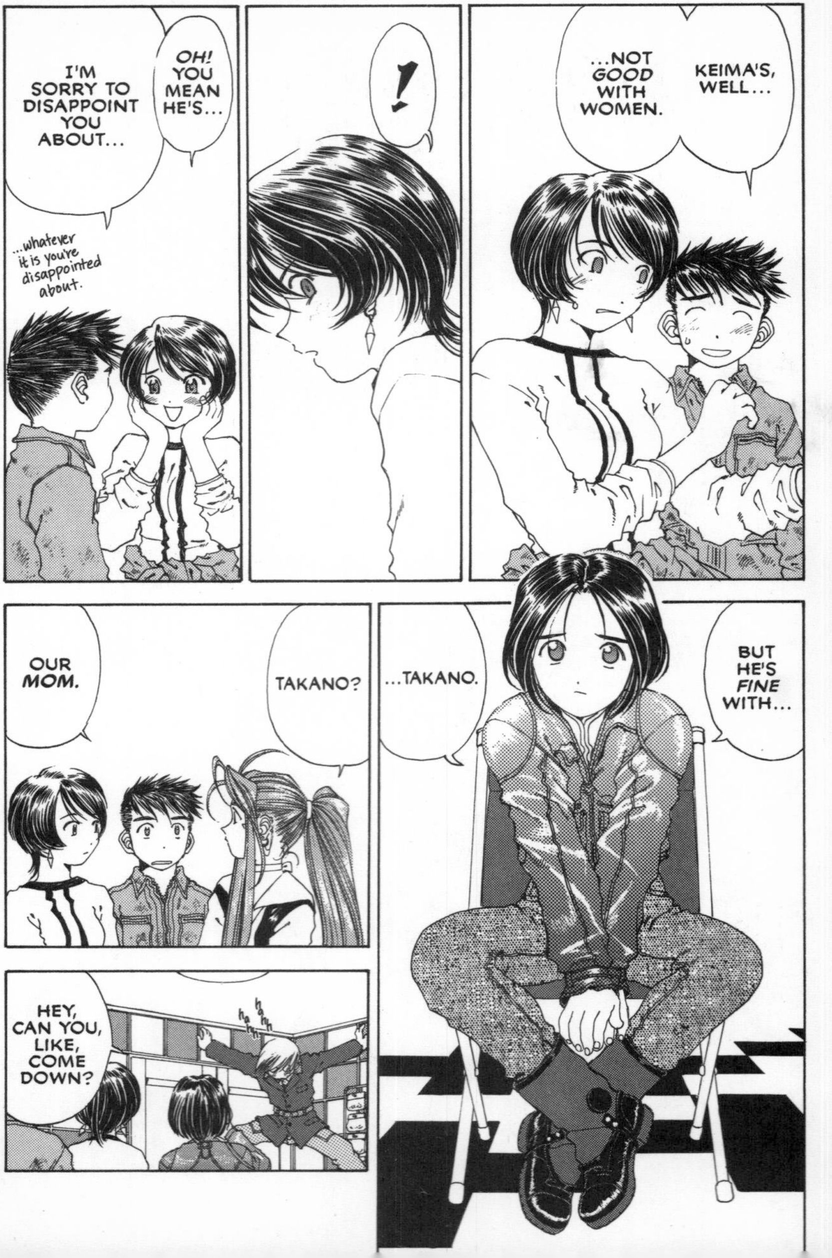
KEIMA'S, WELL...
...NOT *GOOD* WITH WOMEN.
!
OH! YOU MEAN HE'S...
I'M SORRY TO DISAPPOINT YOU ABOUT...
...whatever it is you're disappointed about.
BUT HE'S *FINE* WITH...
...TAKANO.
TAKANO?
OUR *MOM.*
HEY, CAN YOU, LIKE, COME DOWN?

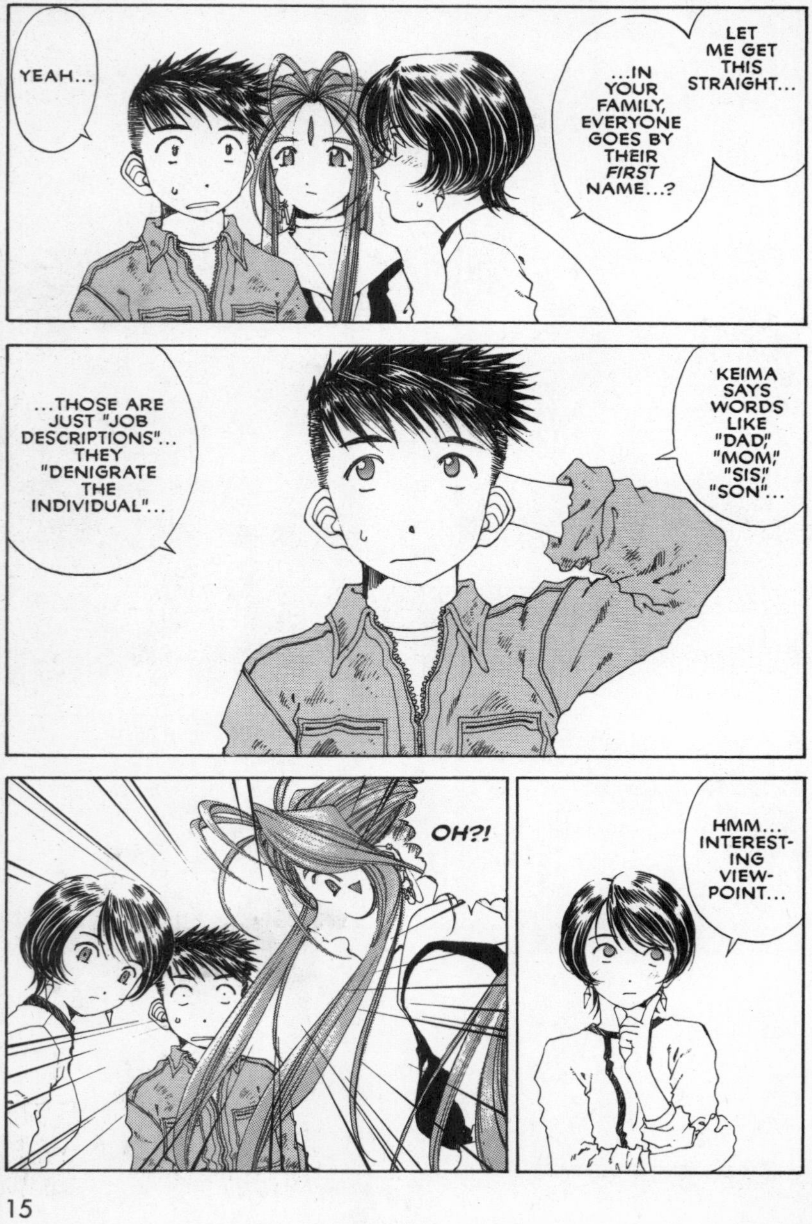
LET ME GET THIS STRAIGHT...
...IN YOUR FAMILY, EVERYONE GOES BY THEIR *FIRST* NAME...?
YEAH...
KEIMA SAYS WORDS LIKE "DAD," "MOM," "SIS," "SON"...
...THOSE ARE JUST "JOB DESCRIPTIONS"... THEY "DENIGRATE THE INDIVIDUAL"...
HMM... INTEREST-ING VIEW-POINT...
OH?!

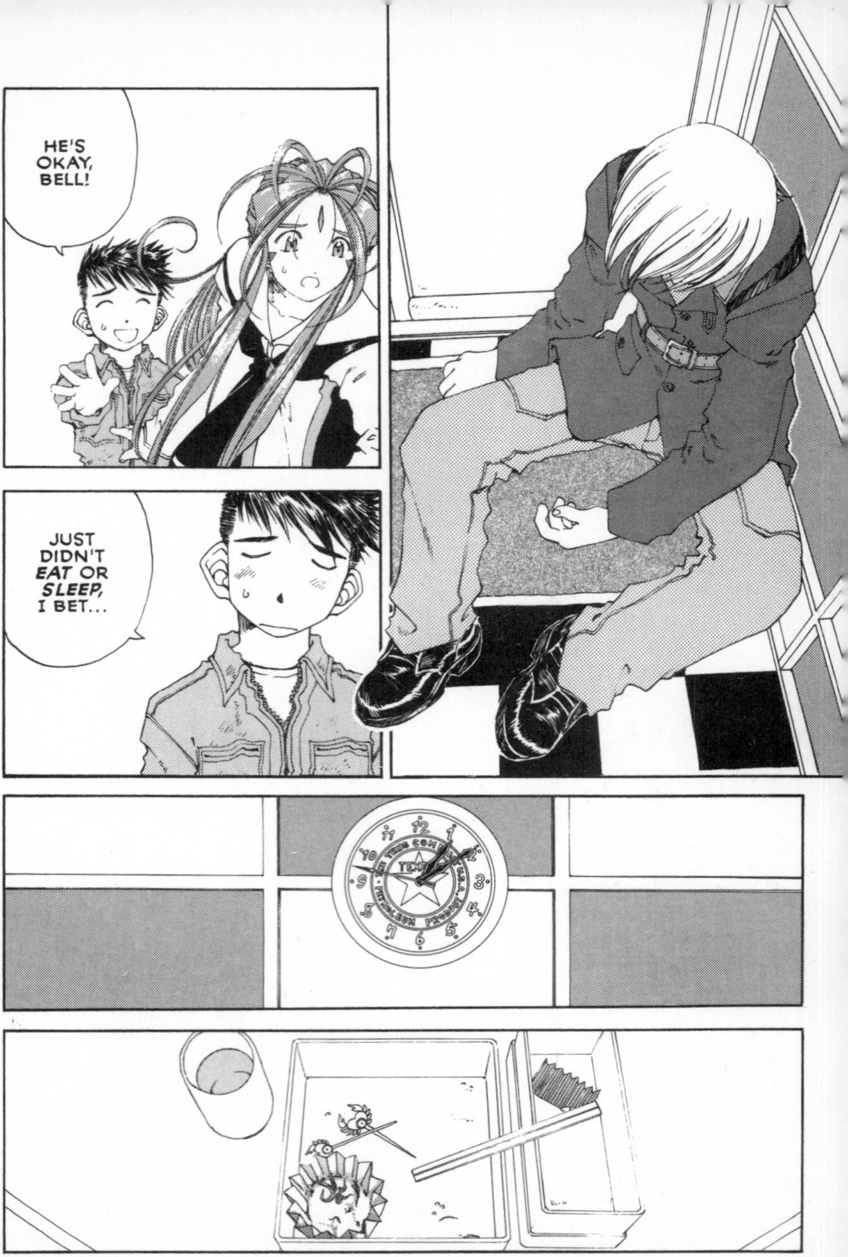
HE'S OKAY, BELL!
JUST DIDN'T EAT OR SLEEP, I BET...

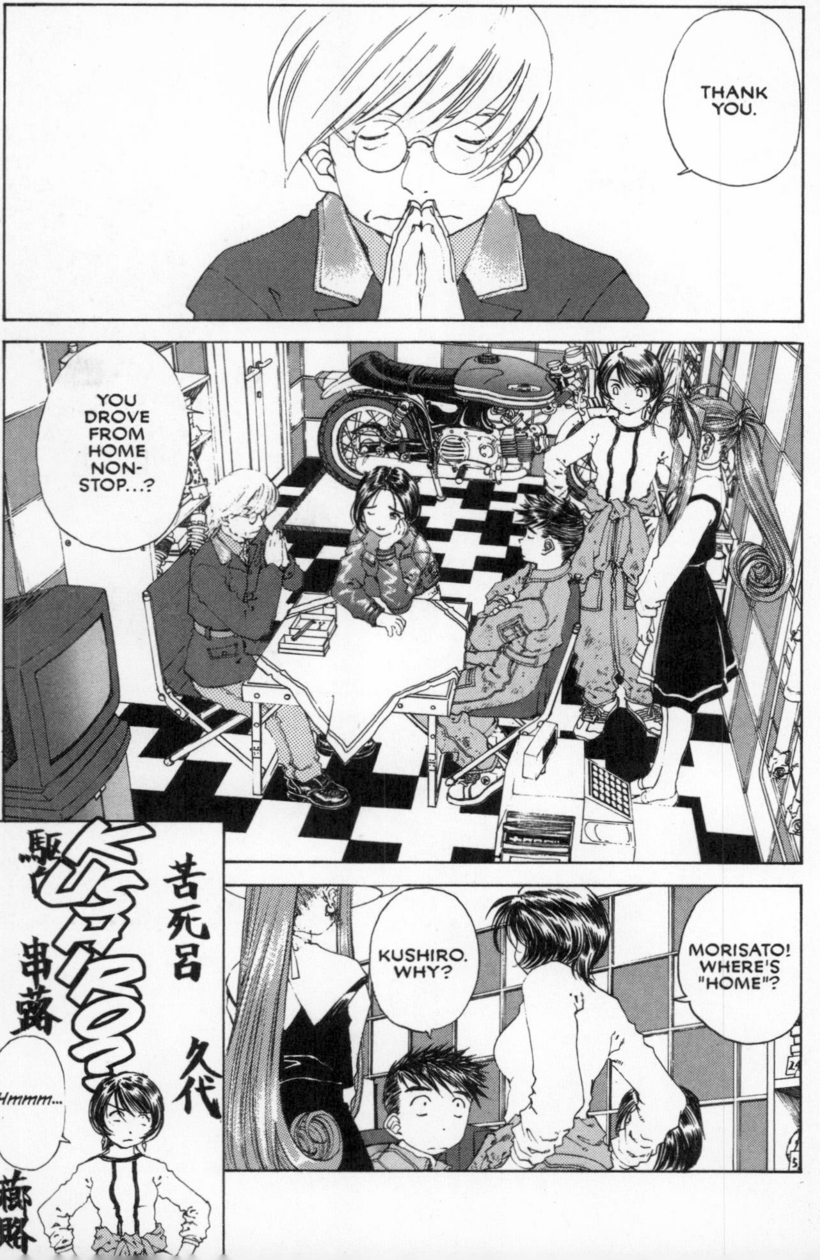
THANK YOU.
YOU DROVE FROM HOME NON-STOP...?
MORISATO! WHERE'S "HOME"?
KUSHIRO. WHY?
KUSHIRO!
苦死呂
久代
駆
串露
櫛賂
Hmmm...

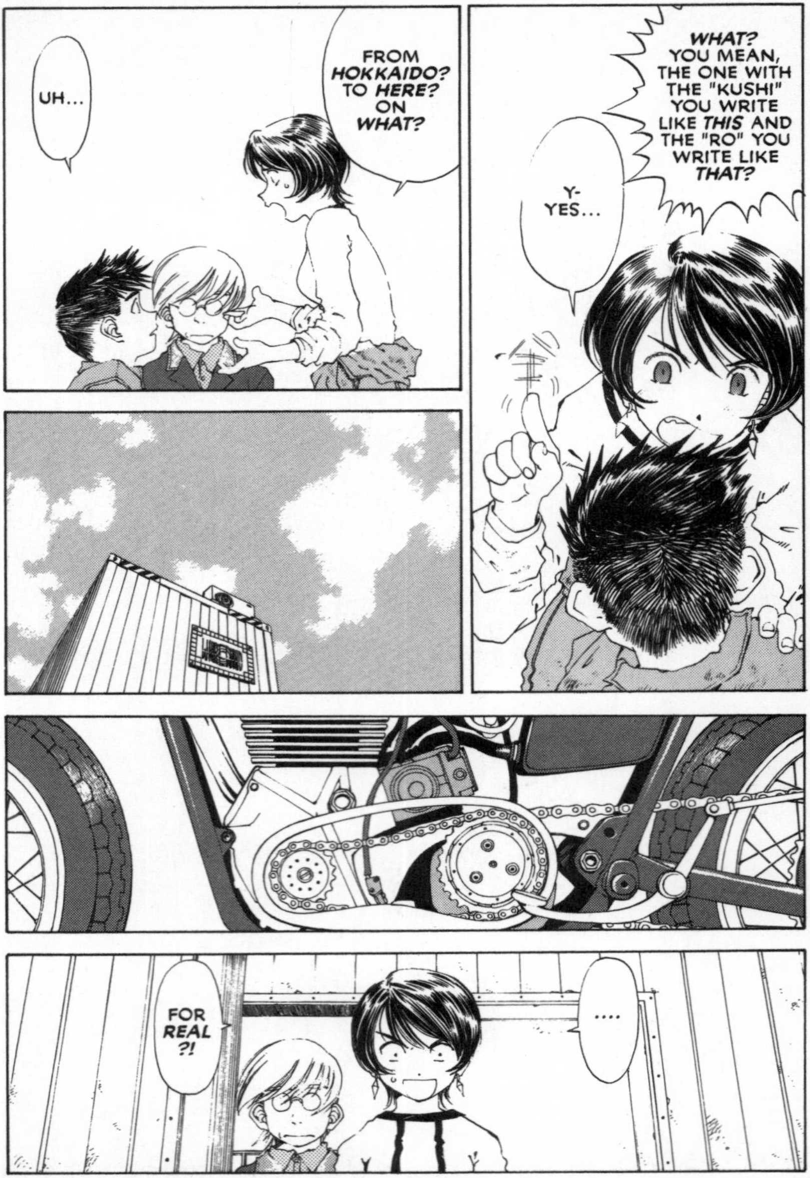
WHAT? YOU MEAN, THE ONE WITH THE "KUSHI" YOU WRITE LIKE THIS AND THE "RO" YOU WRITE LIKE THAT?
Y-YES...
FROM HOKKAIDO? TO HERE? ON WHAT?
UH...
....
FOR REAL?!

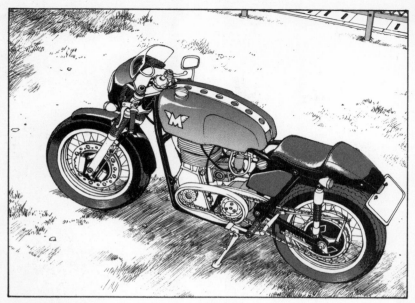

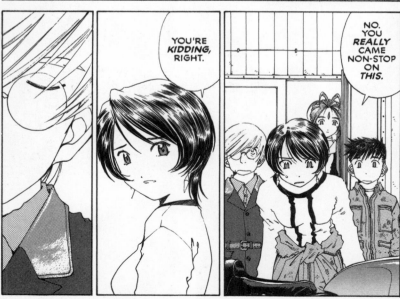

NO. YOU *REALLY* CAME NON-STOP ON *THIS.*
YOU'RE *KIDDING,* RIGHT.

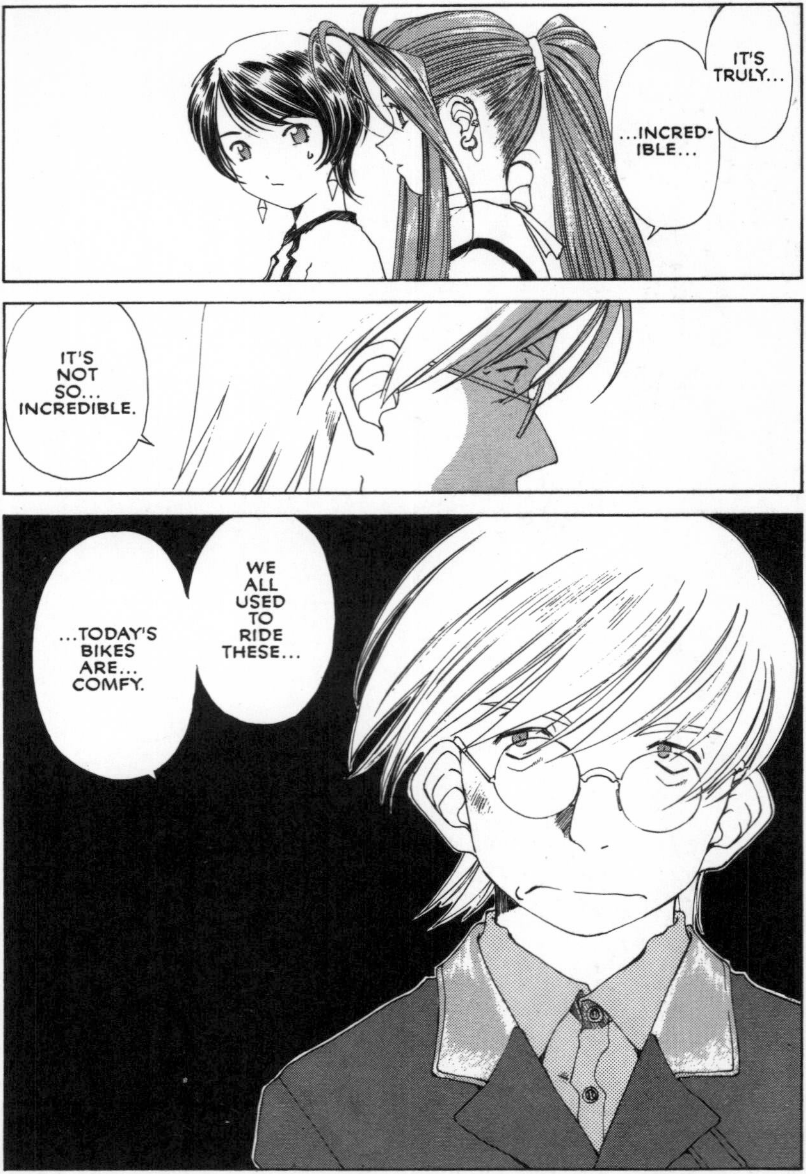
IT'S TRULY...
...INCREDIBLE...
IT'S NOT SO... INCREDIBLE.
WE ALL USED TO RIDE THESE...
...TODAY'S BIKES ARE... COMFY.

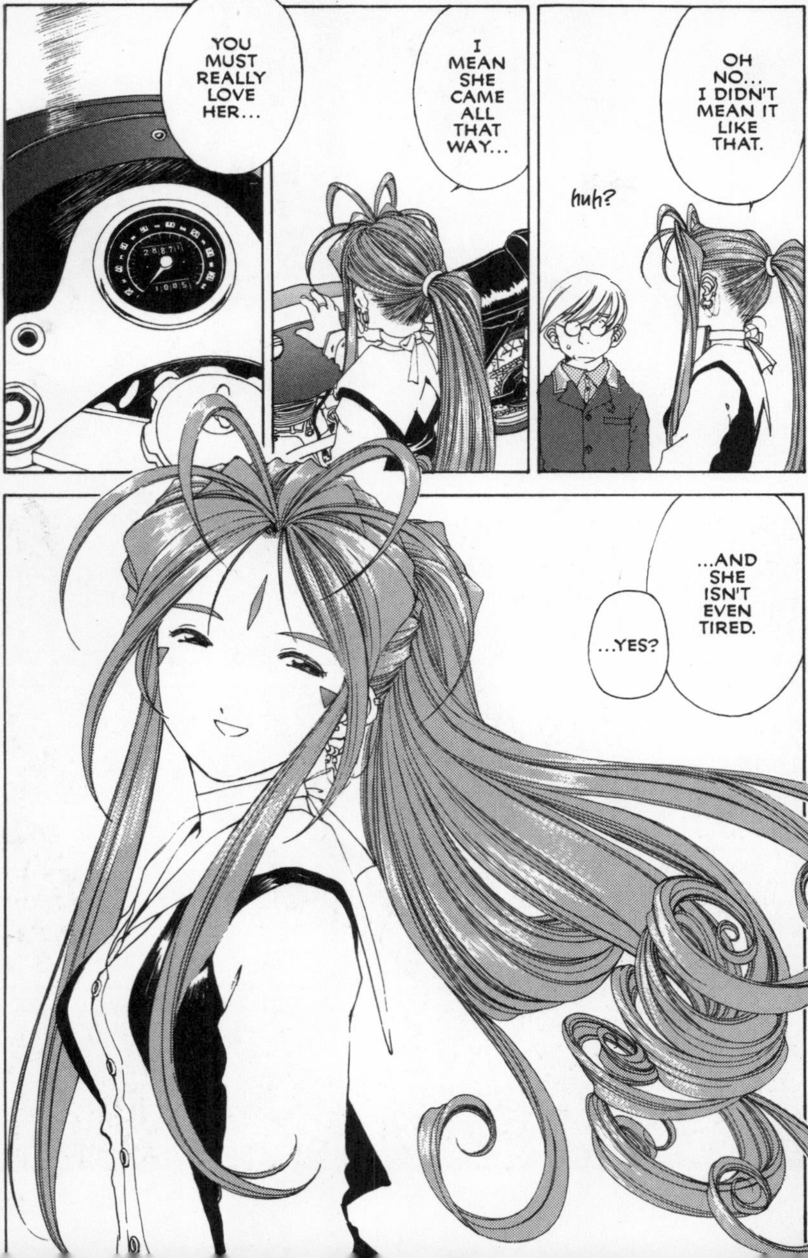
OH NO... I DIDN'T MEAN IT LIKE THAT.
huh?
I MEAN SHE CAME ALL THAT WAY...
YOU MUST REALLY LOVE HER...
...AND SHE ISN'T EVEN TIRED.
...YES?

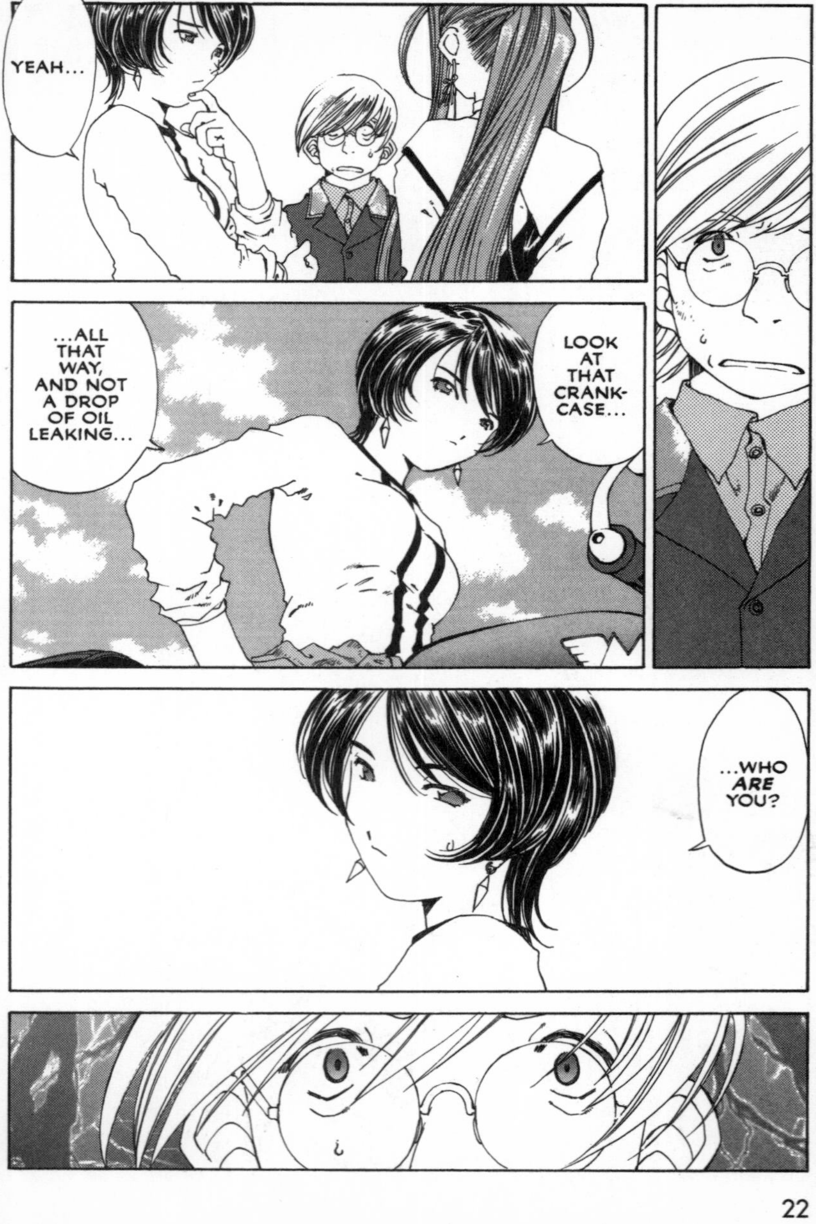
YEAH...
LOOK AT THAT CRANK-CASE...
...ALL THAT WAY, AND NOT A DROP OF OIL LEAKING...
...WHO *ARE* YOU?

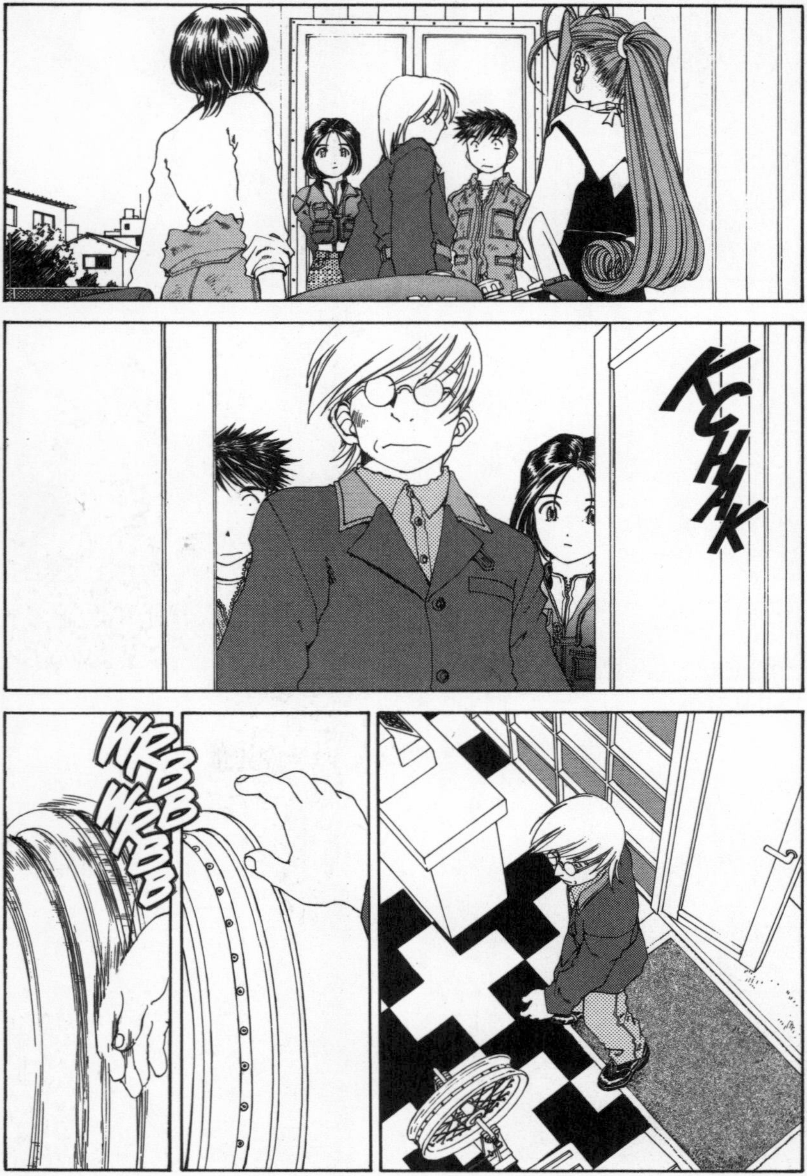
KCHAK
WRBB WRBB

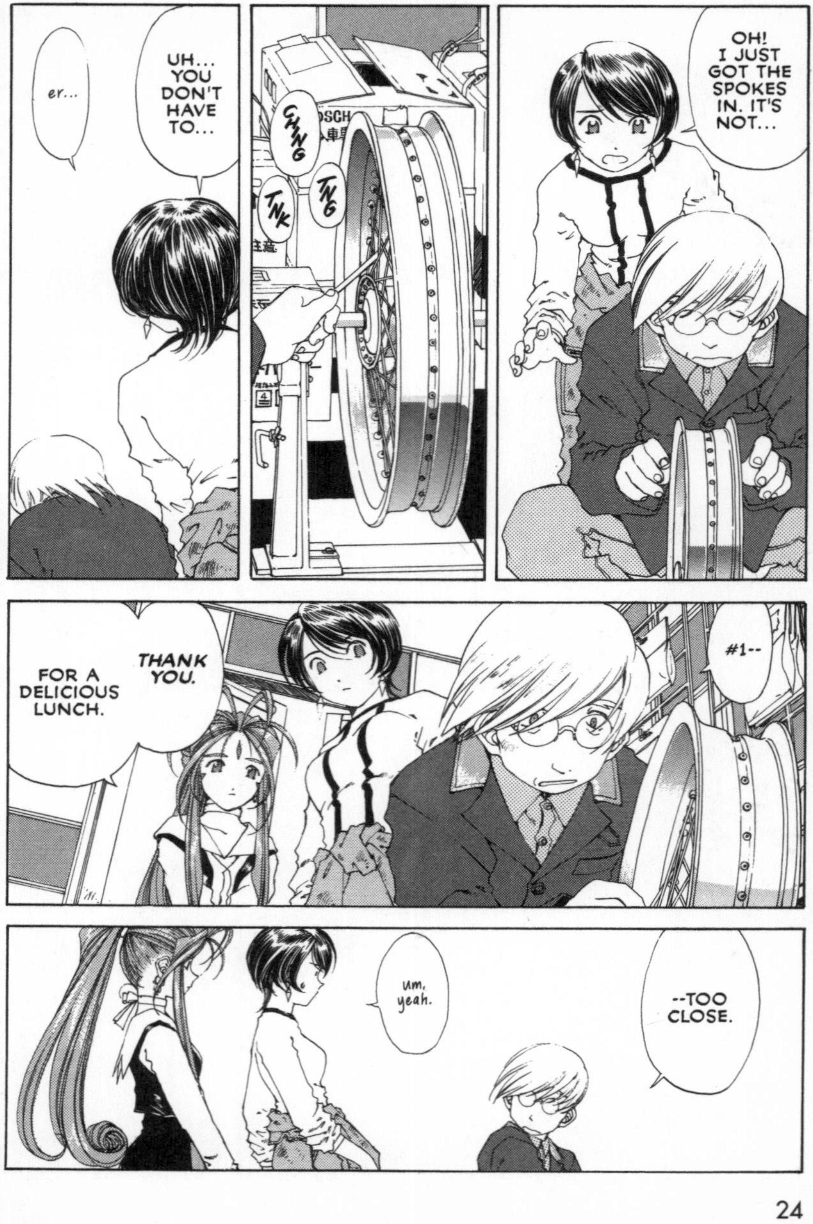
OH! I JUST GOT THE SPOKES IN. IT'S NOT...
CHING
TNG
TNK
UH... YOU DON'T HAVE TO...
er...
#1--
THANK YOU.
FOR A DELICIOUS LUNCH.
--TOO CLOSE.
um, yeah.

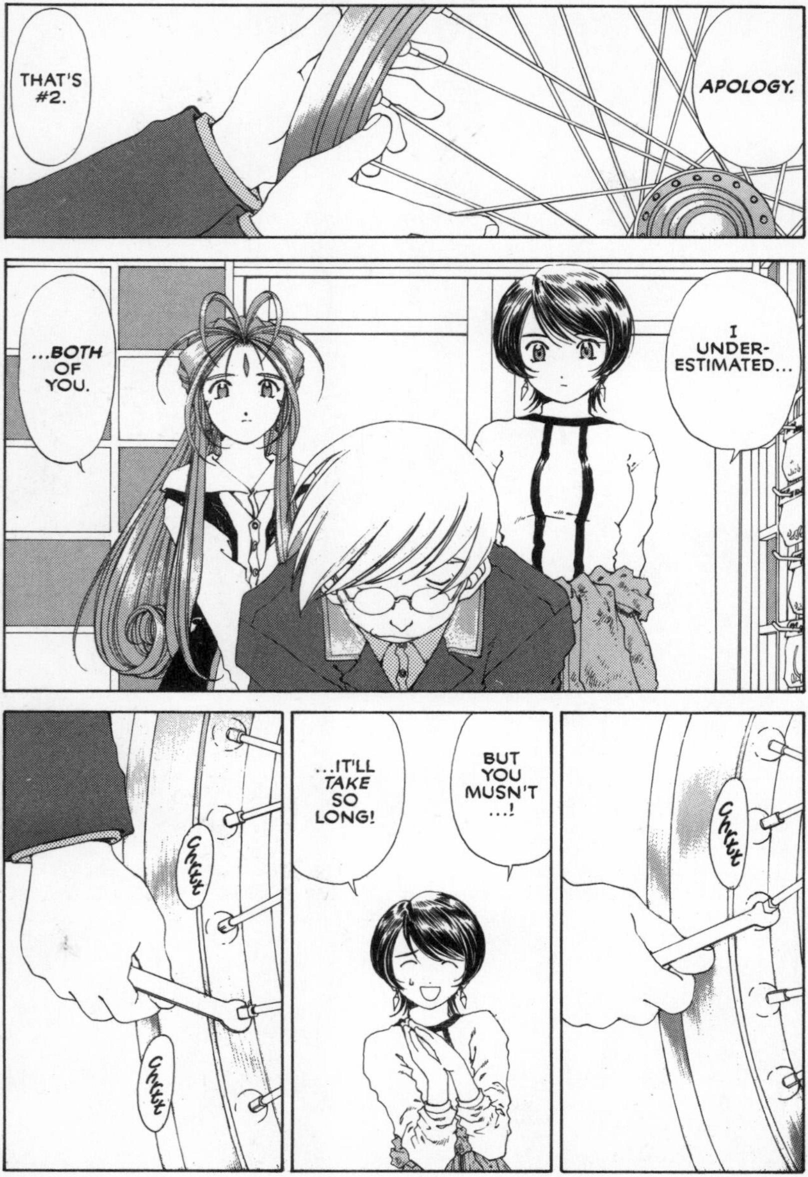
APOLOGY.
THAT'S #2.
I UNDER-ESTIMATED...
...BOTH OF YOU.
BUT YOU MUSN'T ...!
...IT'LL TAKE SO LONG!

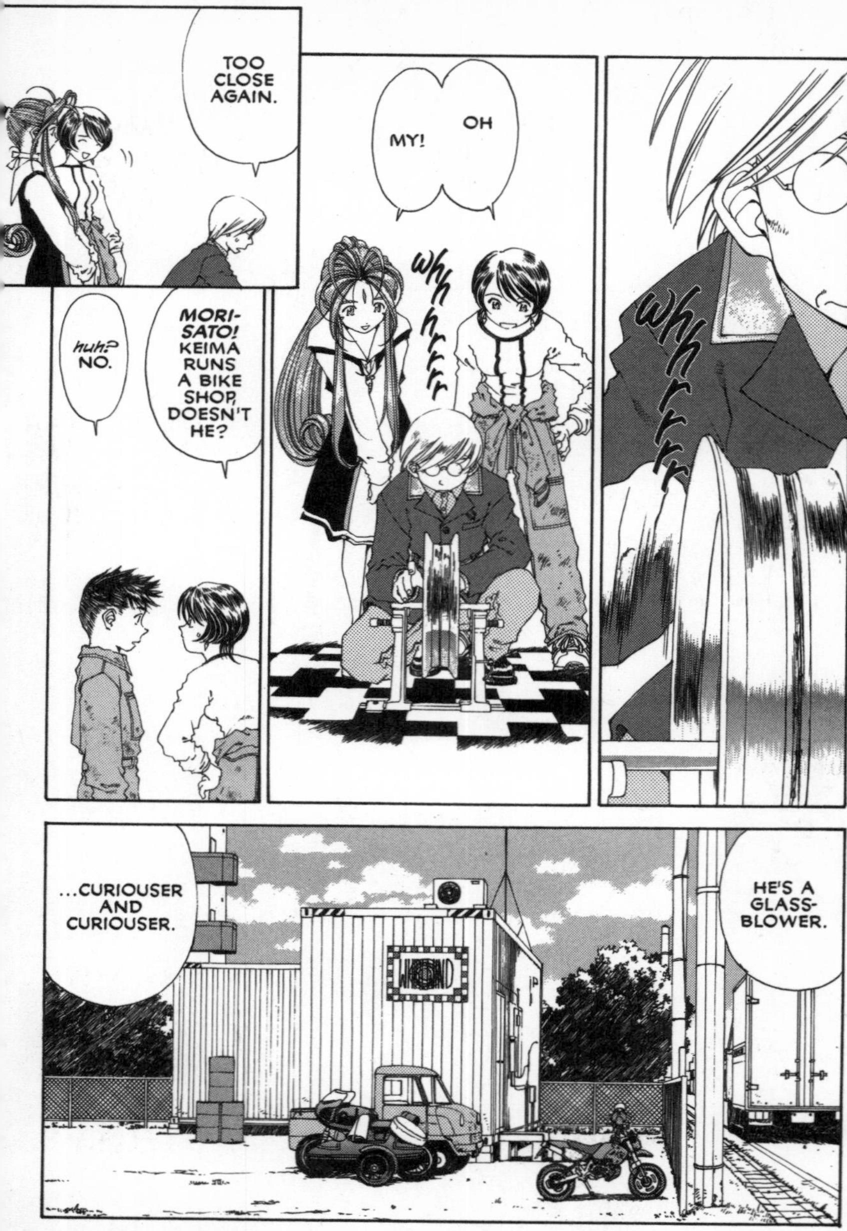
whhrrrrr
OH MY!
whhrrrr
TOO CLOSE AGAIN.
MORI-SATO! KEIMA RUNS A BIKE SHOP, DOESN'T HE?
huh? NO.
HE'S A GLASS-BLOWER.
...CURIOUSER AND CURIOUSER.

CHAPTER 143

Dad on the Run

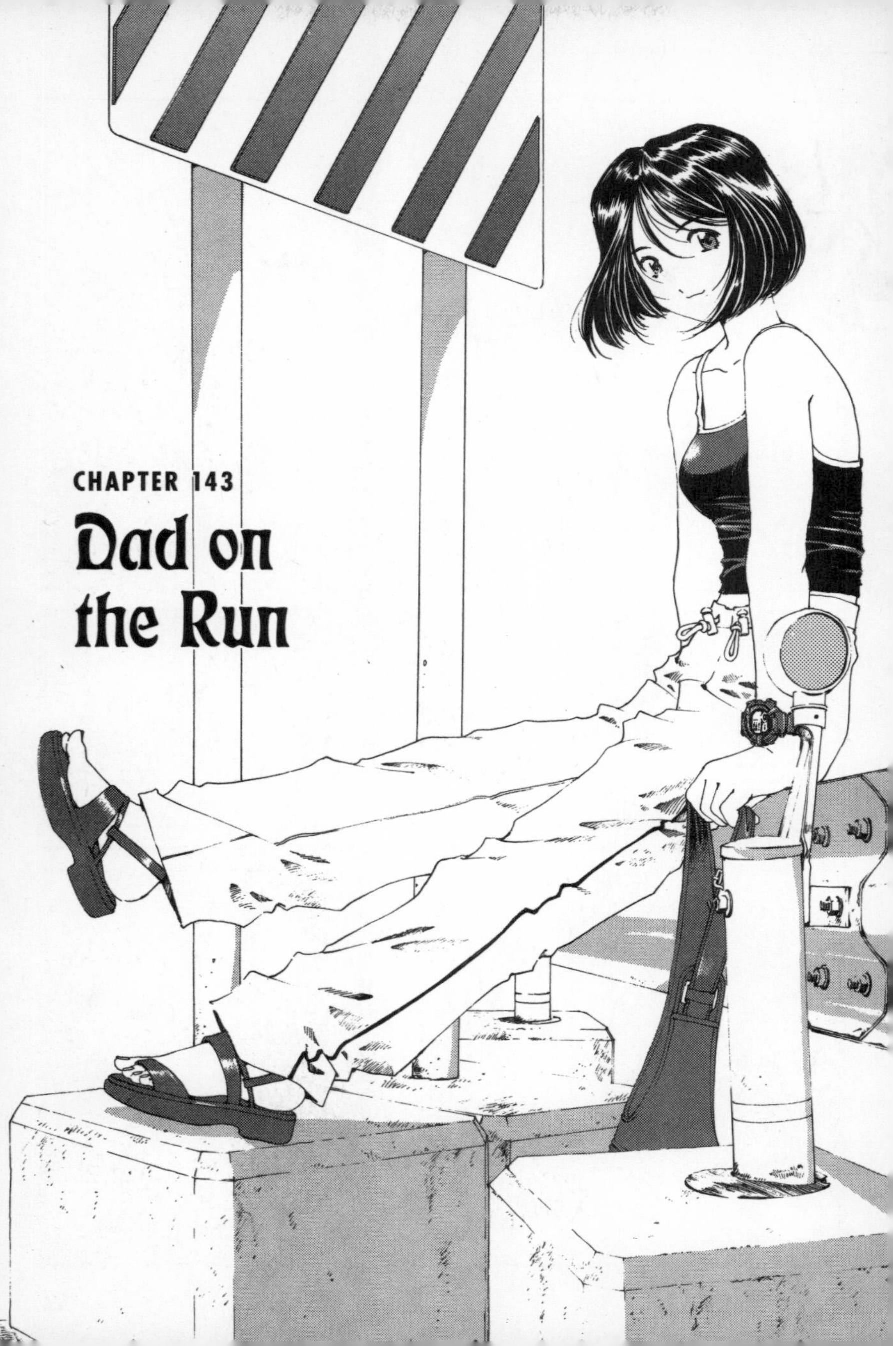

READY!

THREE!

TWO!

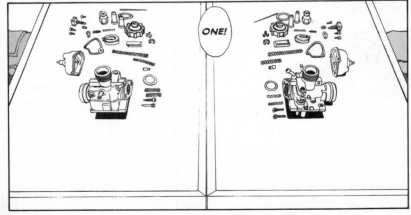

ONE!

28

GO!!

AND!

MORI-SATO.

YEH?

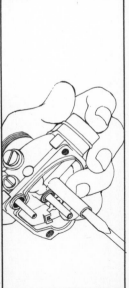

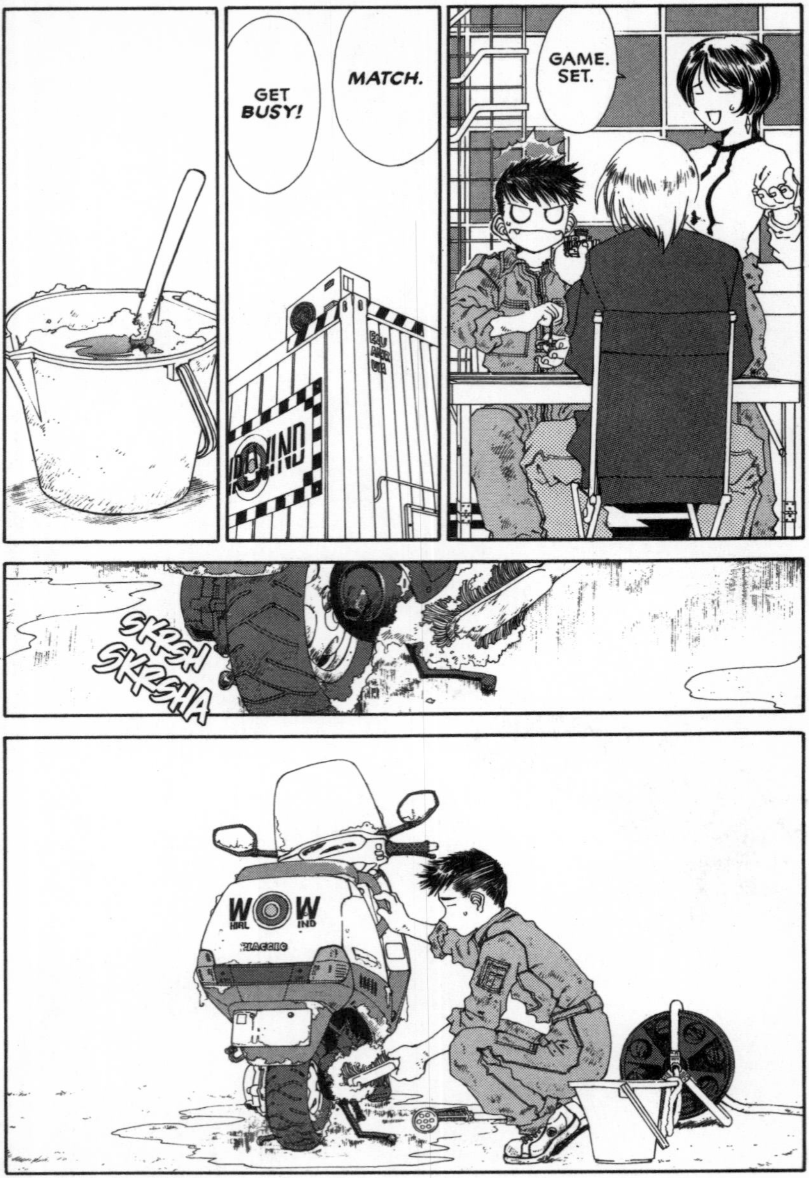
GAME. SET.
MATCH.
GET BUSY!
SKRSH SKRSHA
WOW

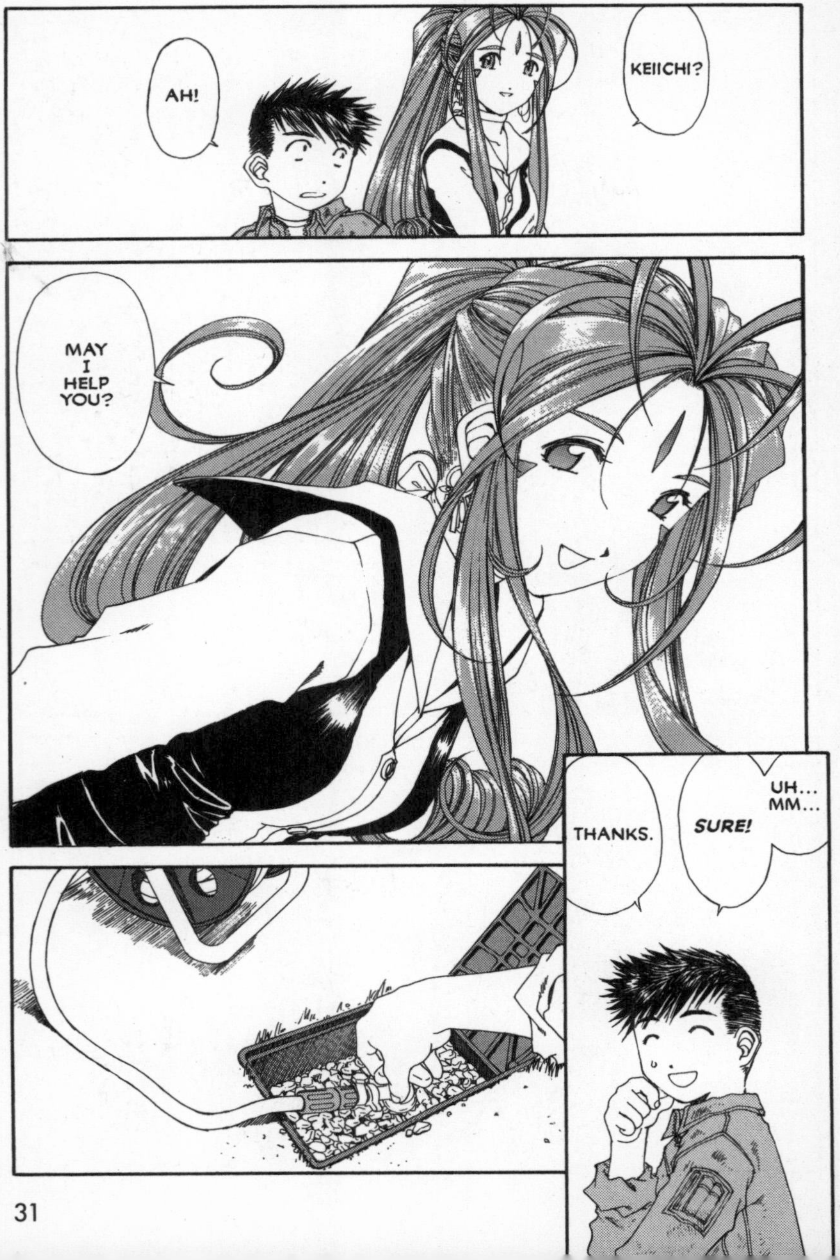
KEIICHI?
AH!
MAY I HELP YOU?
UH... MM...
SURE!
THANKS.

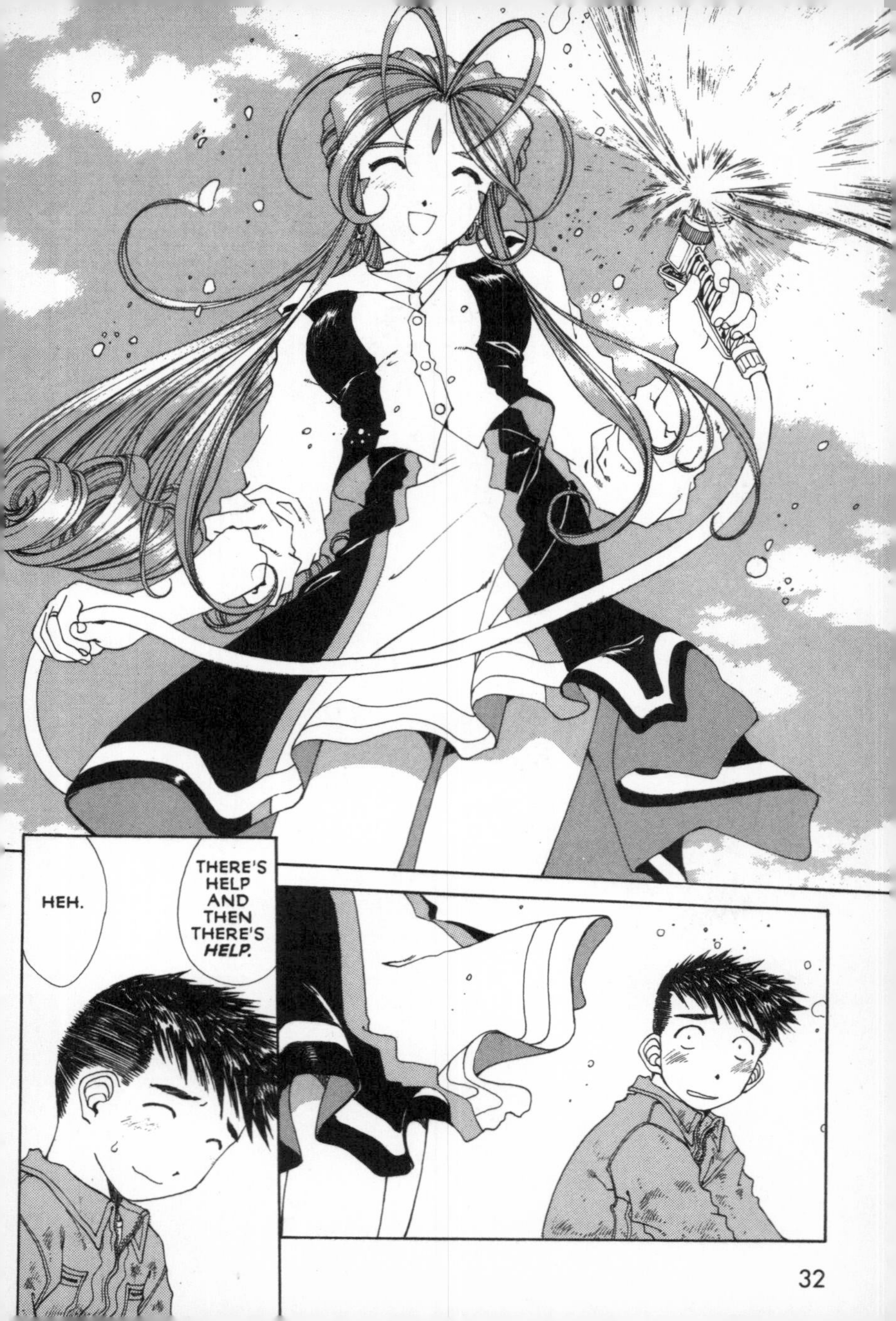
THERE'S HELP AND THEN THERE'S ***HELP.***
HEH.

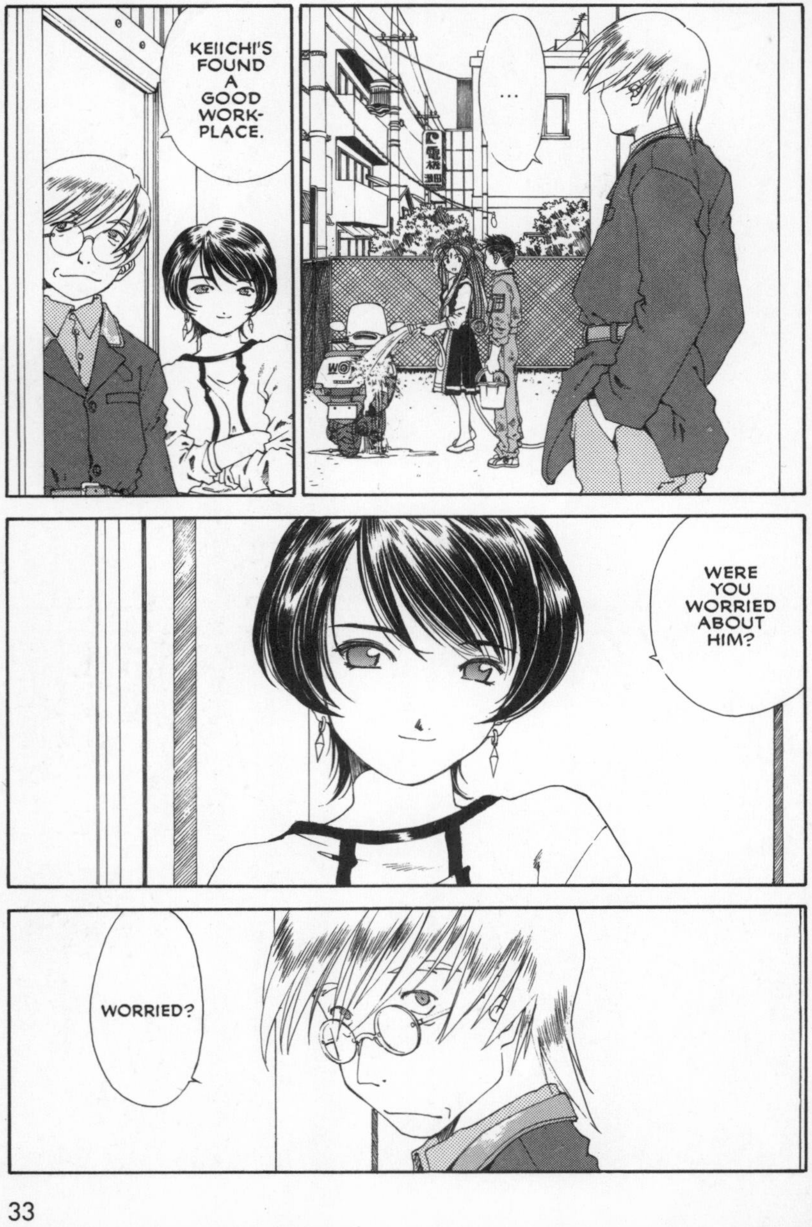
...
KEIICHI'S FOUND A GOOD WORK-PLACE.
WERE YOU WORRIED ABOUT HIM?
WORRIED?

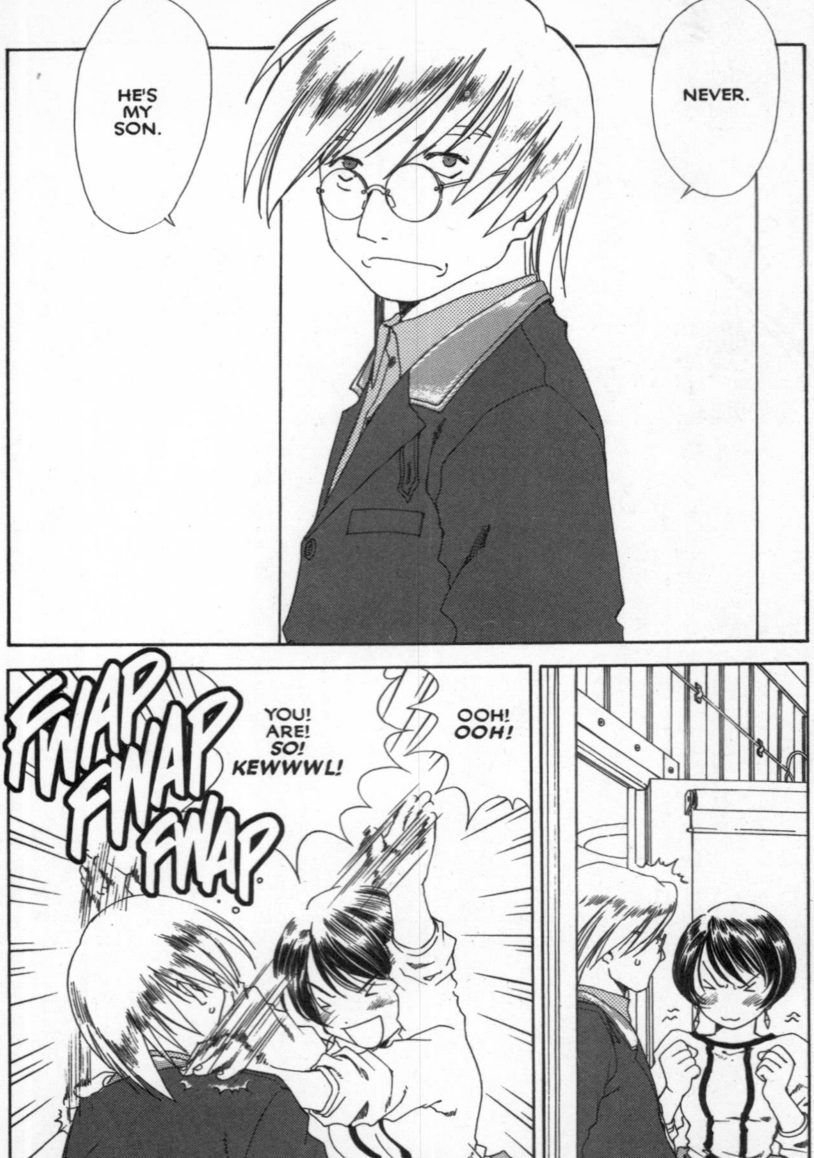
NEVER.
HE'S MY SON.
OOH! OOH!
YOU! ARE! SO! KEWWWL!
FWAP FWAP FWAP

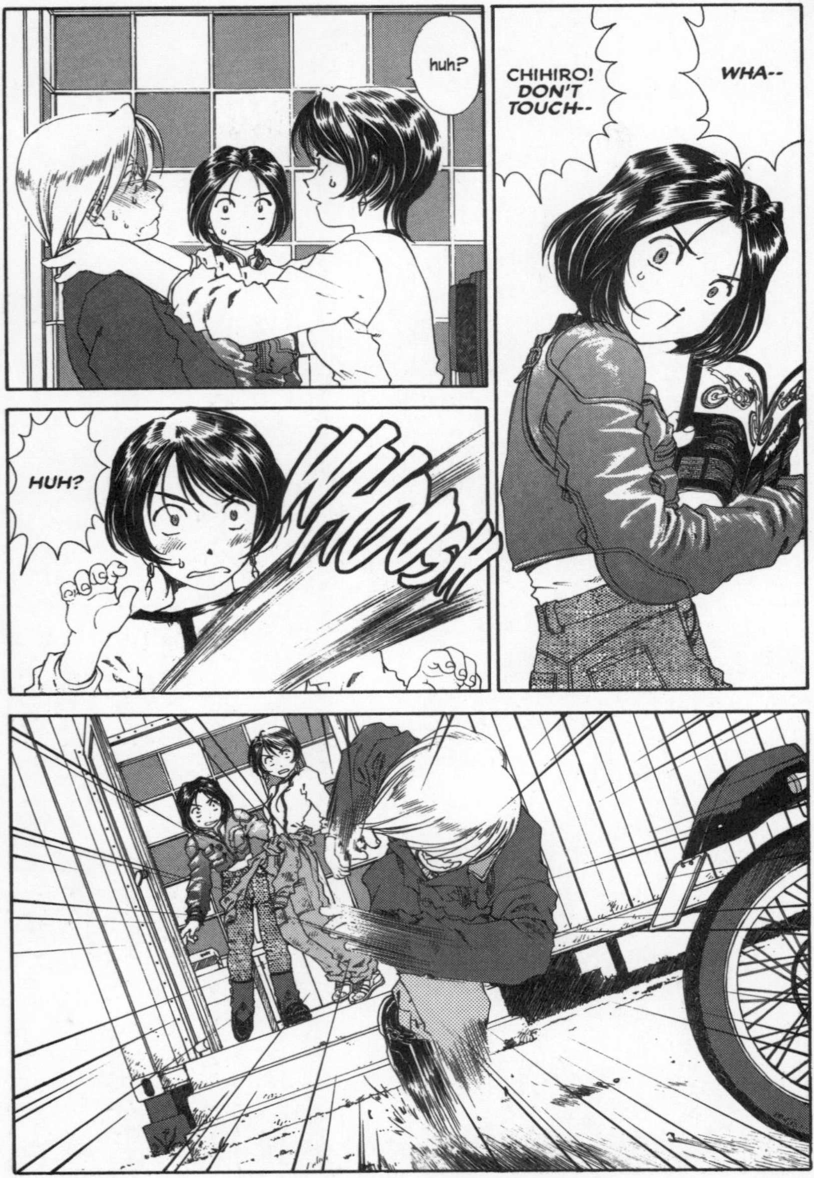
WHA--
CHIHIRO! DON'T TOUCH--
huh?
HUH?
WHOOSH

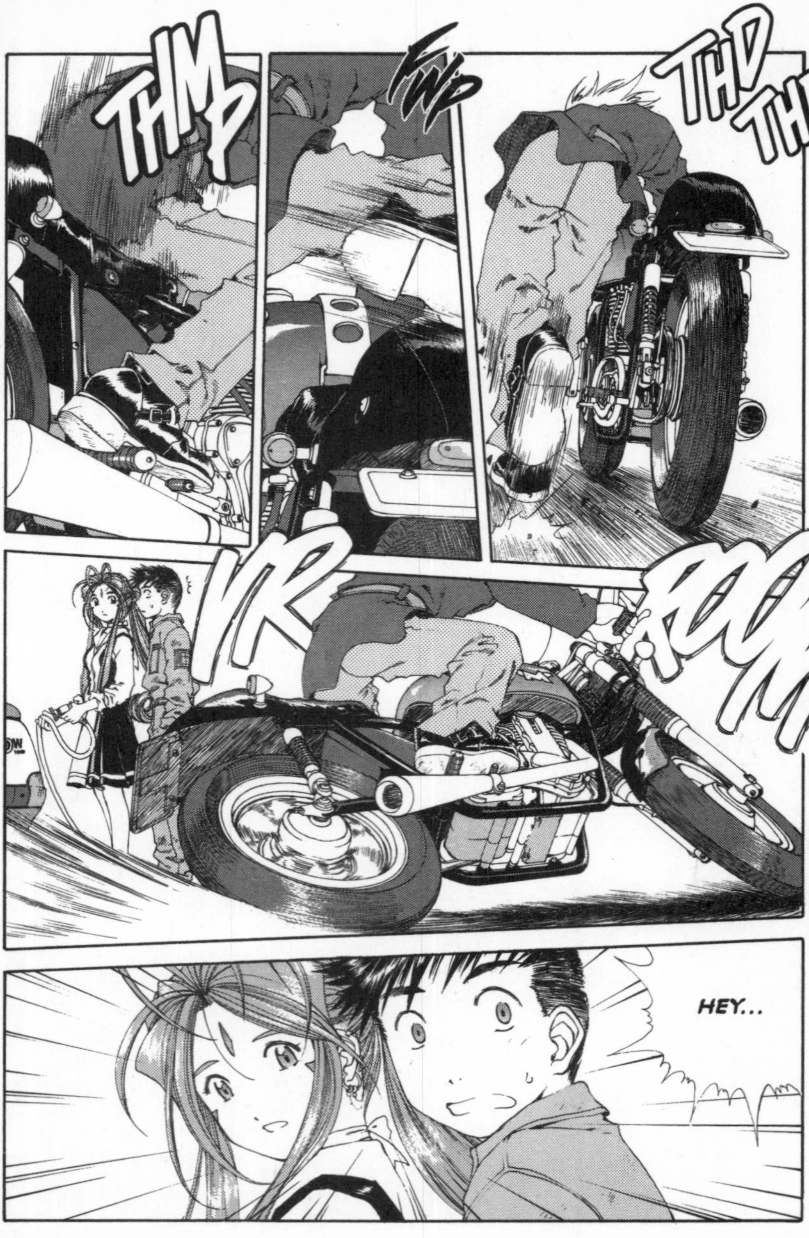
THD THD
FWP
THMP
VRROOM
HEY...

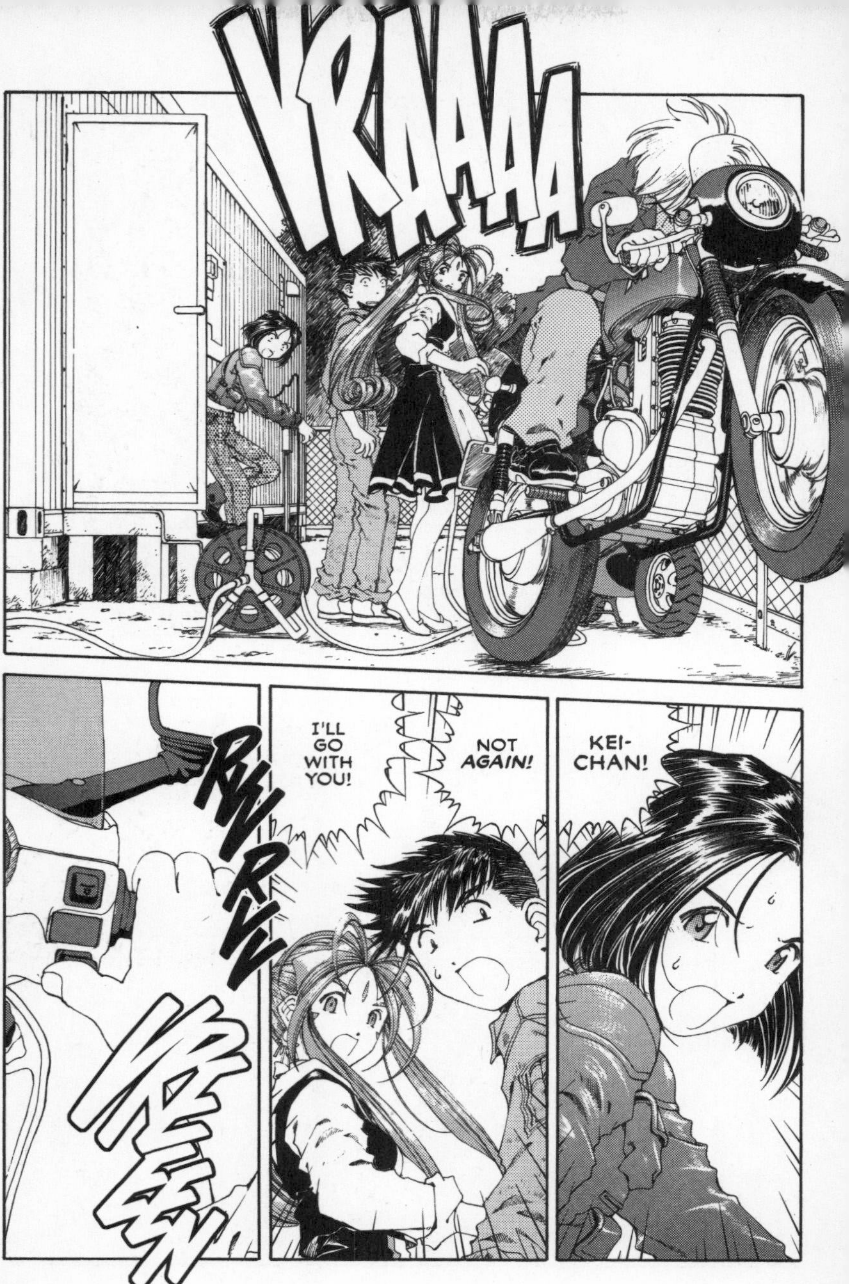
VRAAAA
KEI-CHAN!
NOT AGAIN!
I'LL GO WITH YOU!
VREEEN

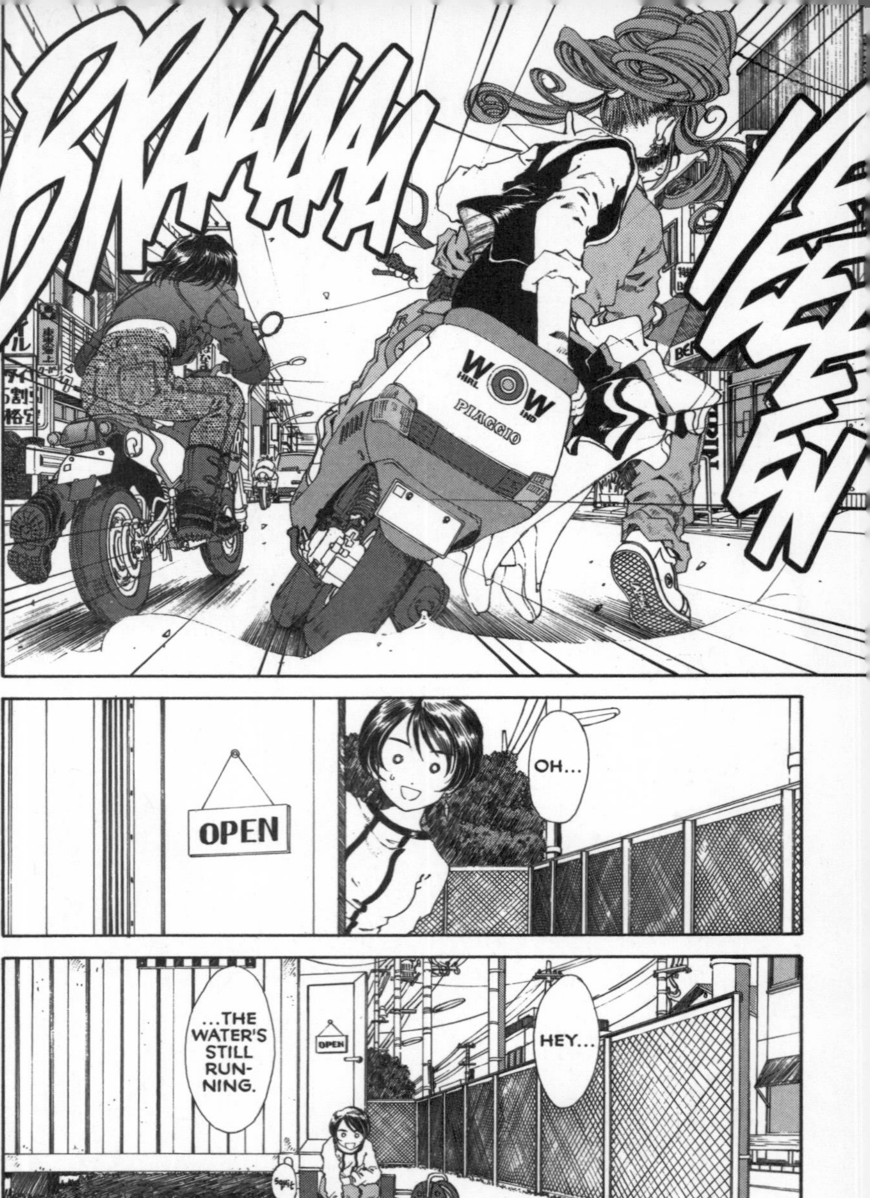
WOW
PIAGGIO
OH...
OPEN
HEY...
...THE WATER'S STILL RUN-NING.
OPEN

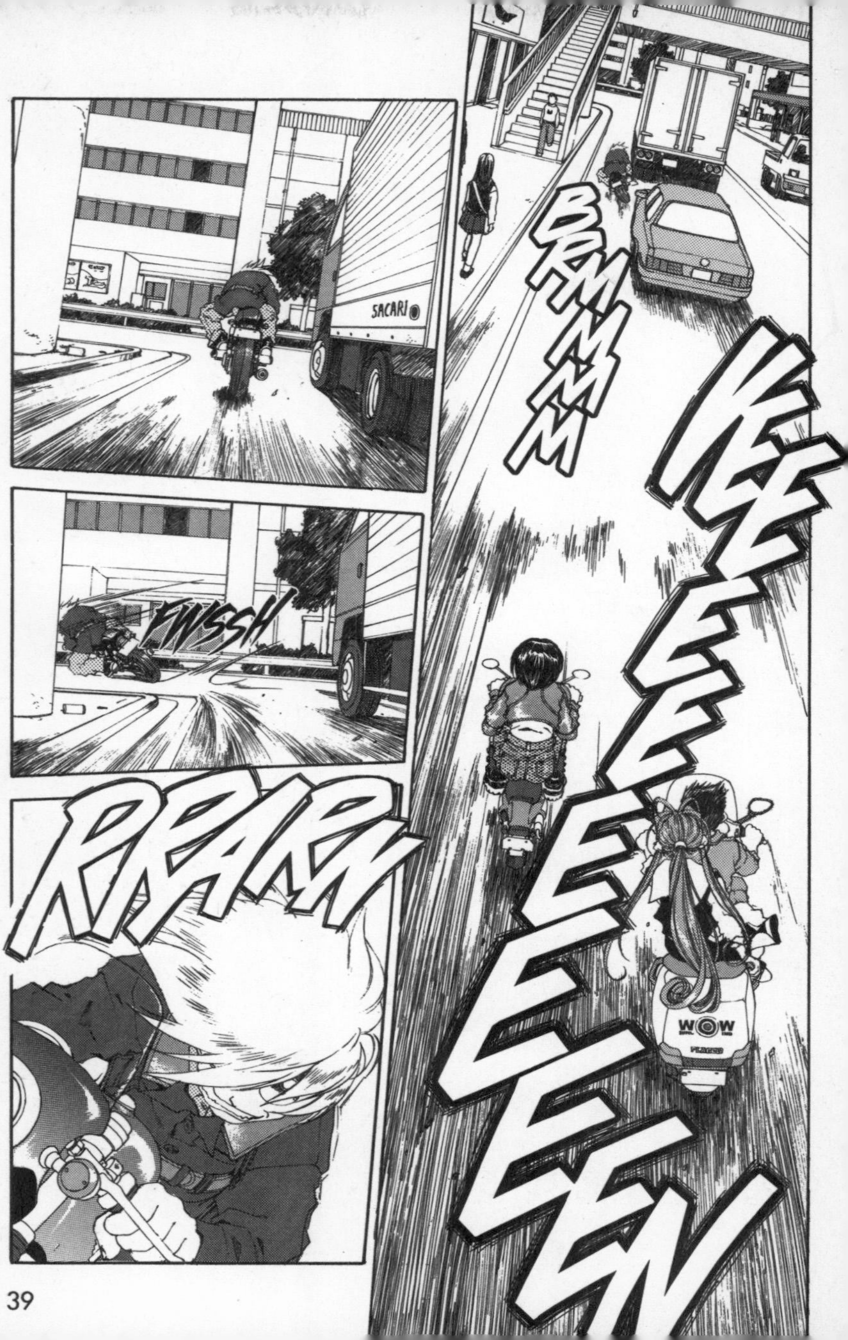
BRMMMMM
KYEEEEEEEEN
SACARI
FWSSH
RRARN
WOW

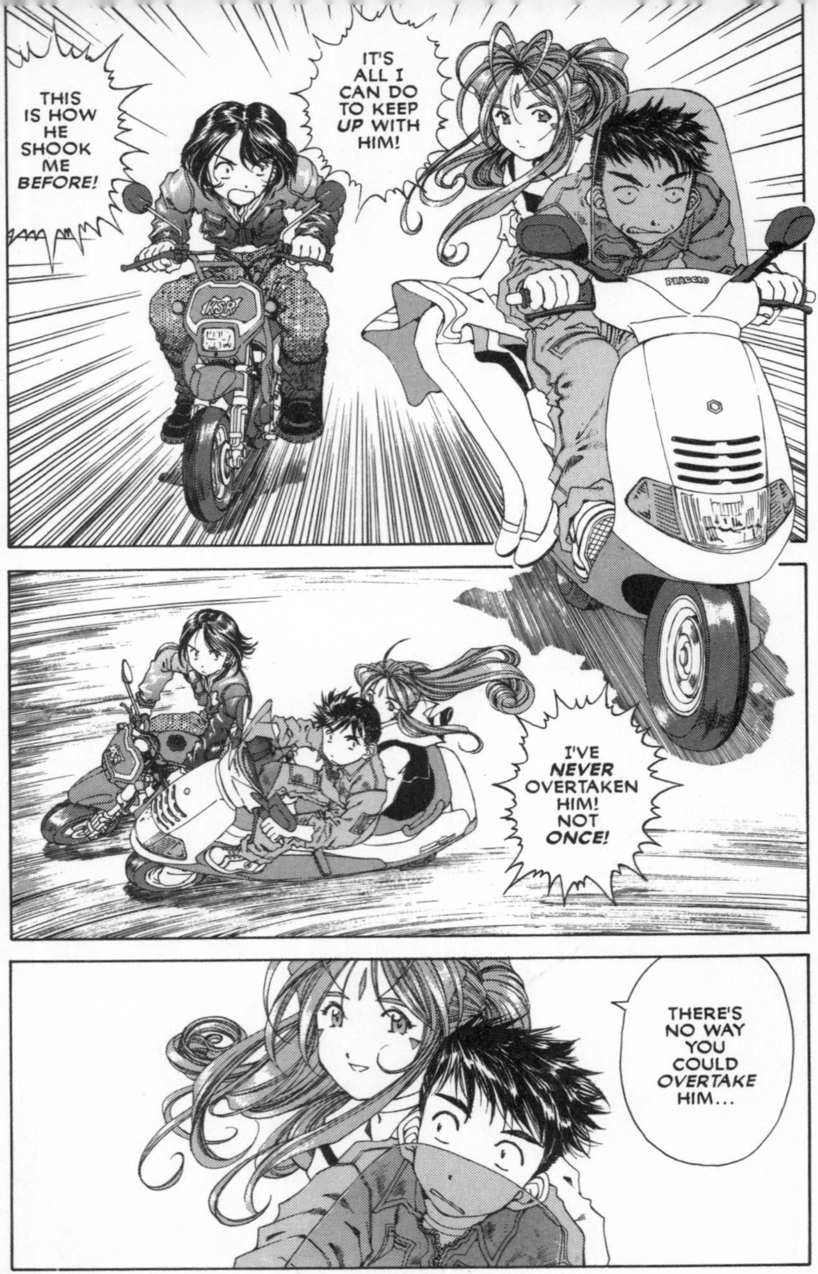
IT'S ALL I CAN DO TO KEEP UP WITH HIM!
THIS IS HOW HE SHOOK ME BEFORE!
I'VE NEVER OVERTAKEN HIM! NOT ONCE!
THERE'S NO WAY YOU COULD OVERTAKE HIM...

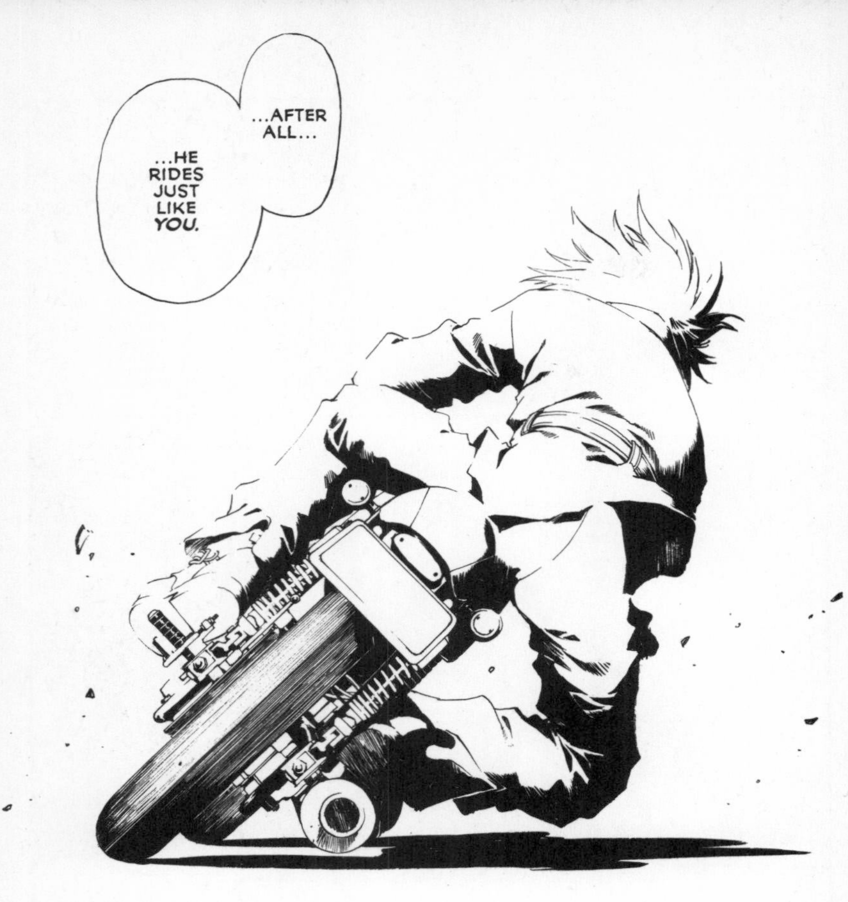
...AFTER ALL...
...HE RIDES JUST LIKE *YOU.*

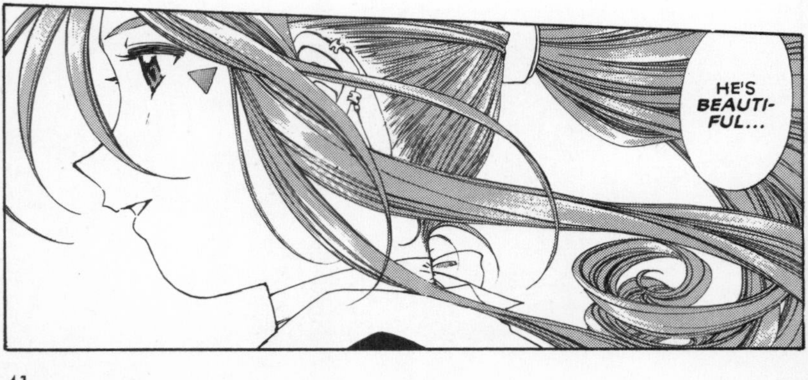
HE'S *BEAUTIFUL...*

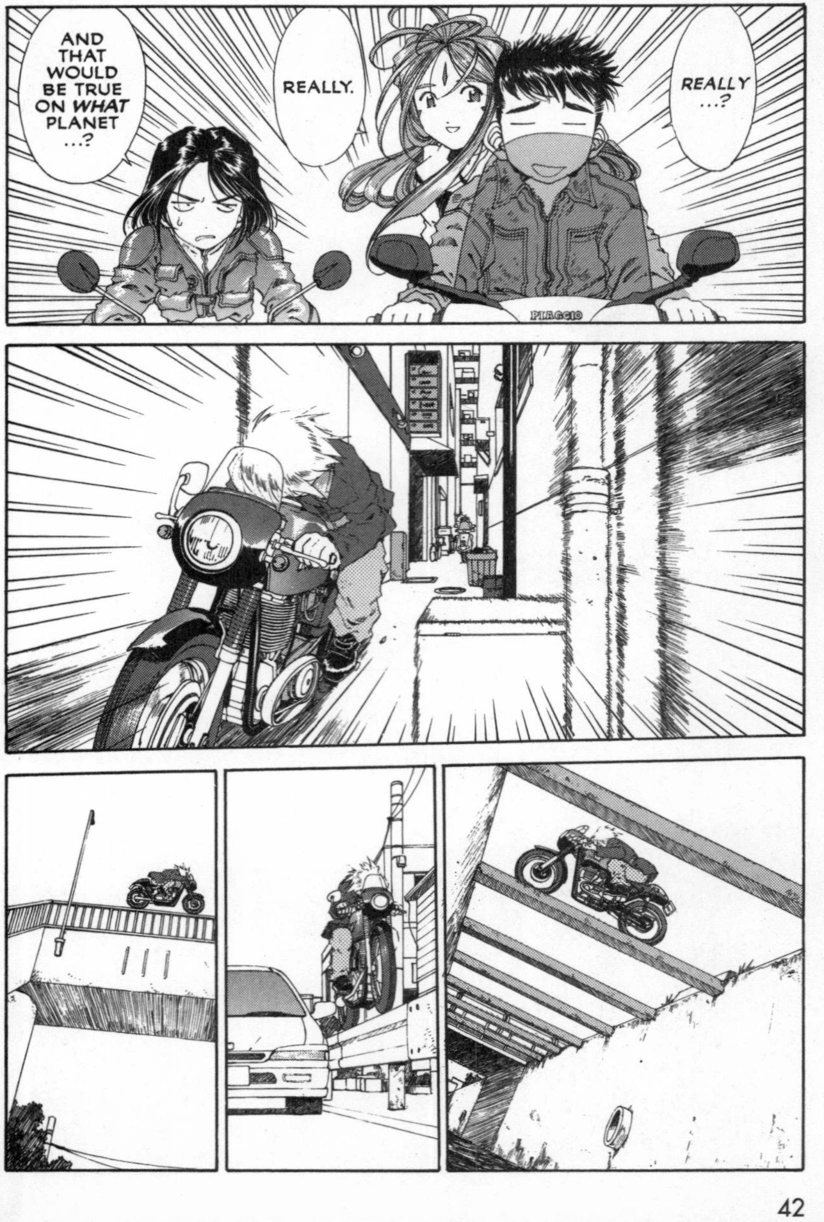
REALLY ...?
REALLY.
AND THAT WOULD BE TRUE ON *WHAT* PLANET ...?
PIAGGIO

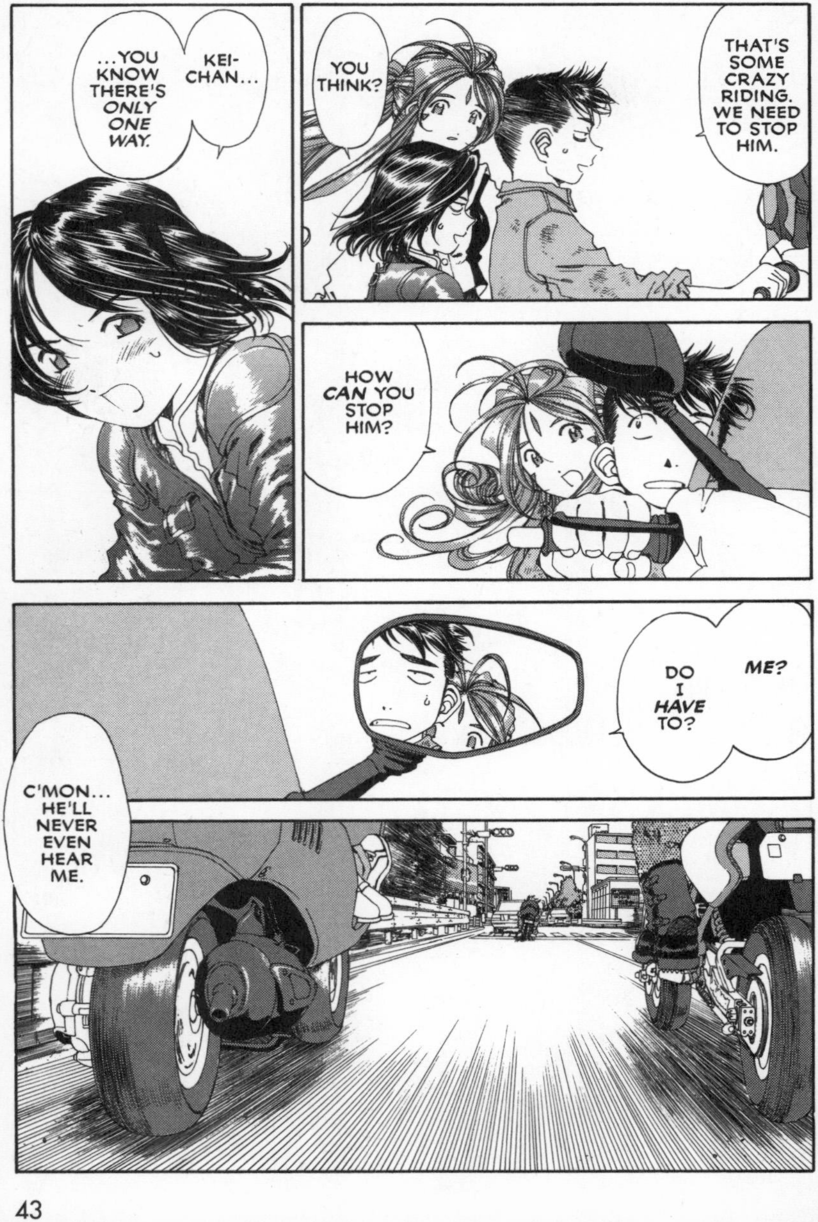
THAT'S SOME CRAZY RIDING. WE NEED TO STOP HIM.
YOU THINK?
HOW CAN YOU STOP HIM?
KEI-CHAN...
...YOU KNOW THERE'S ONLY ONE WAY.
ME? DO I HAVE TO?
C'MON... HE'LL NEVER EVEN HEAR ME.

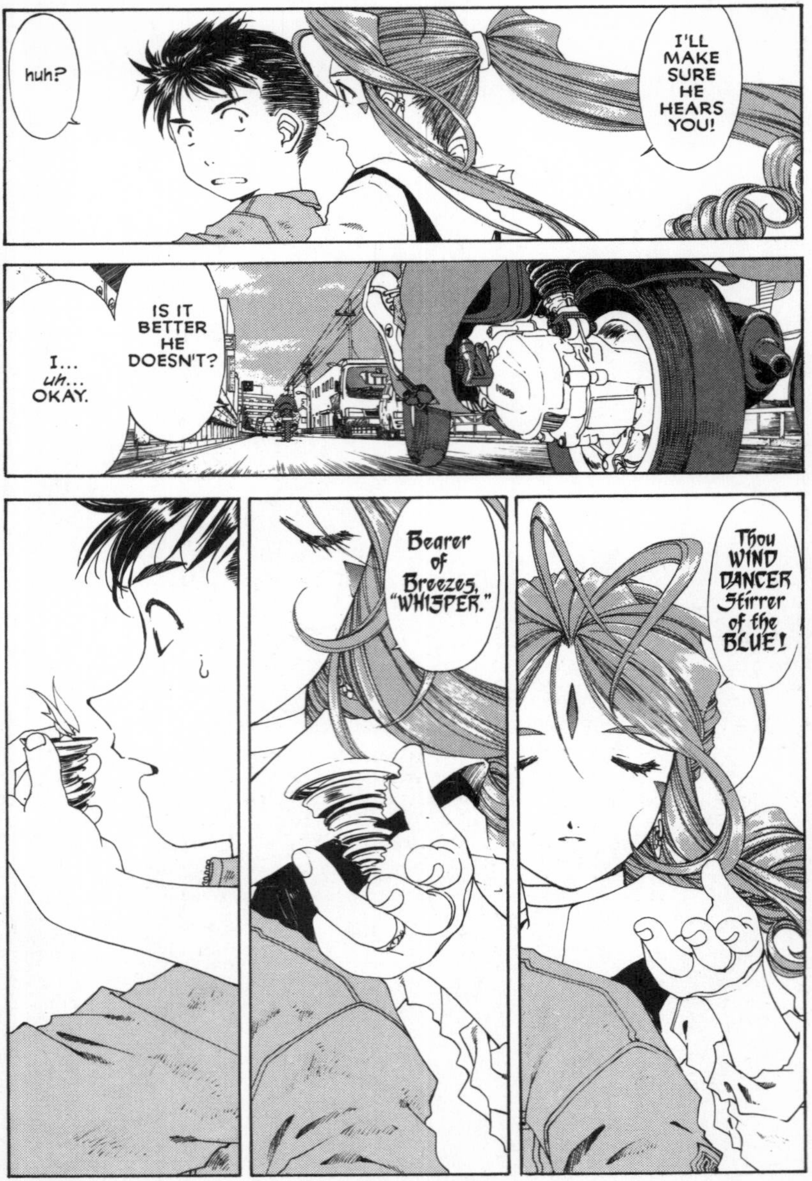
I'LL MAKE SURE HE HEARS YOU!
huh?
IS IT BETTER HE DOESN'T?
I... uh... OKAY.
Thou WIND DANCER Stirrer of the BLUE!
Bearer of Breezes, "WHISPER."

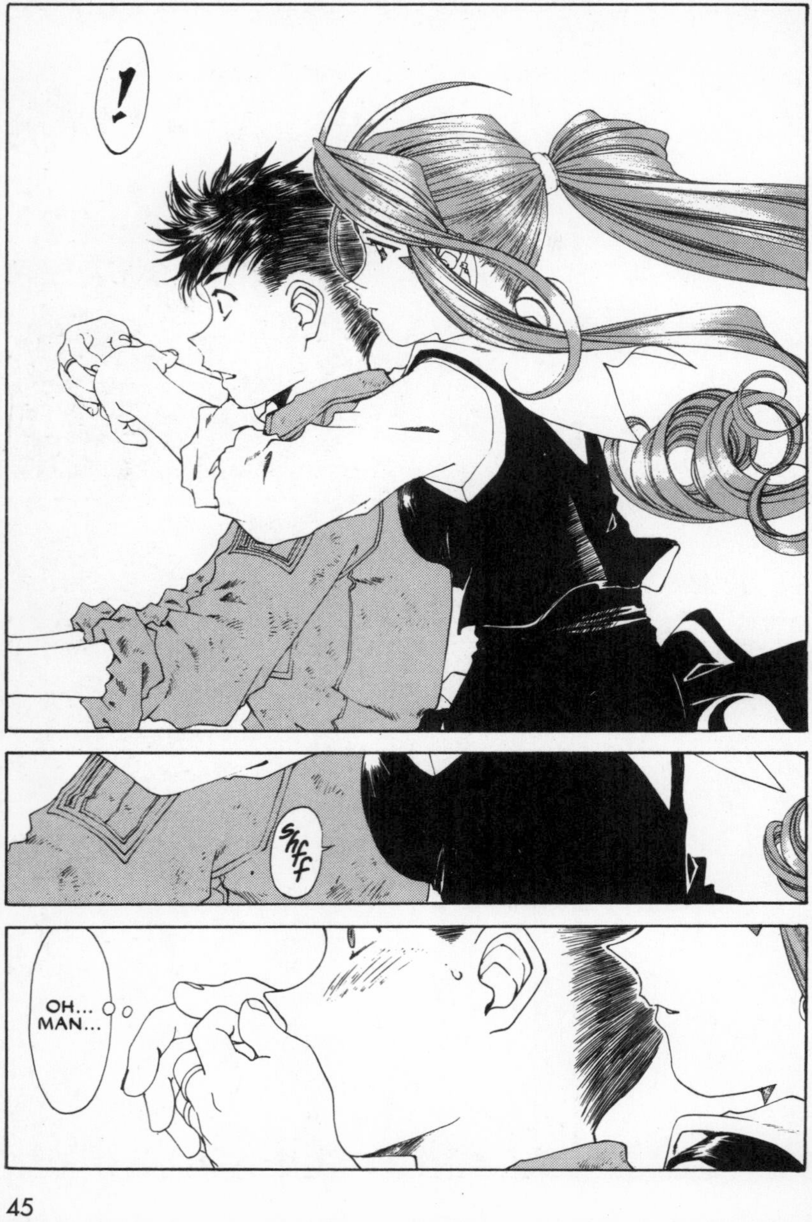
!
SHFF
OH... MAN...

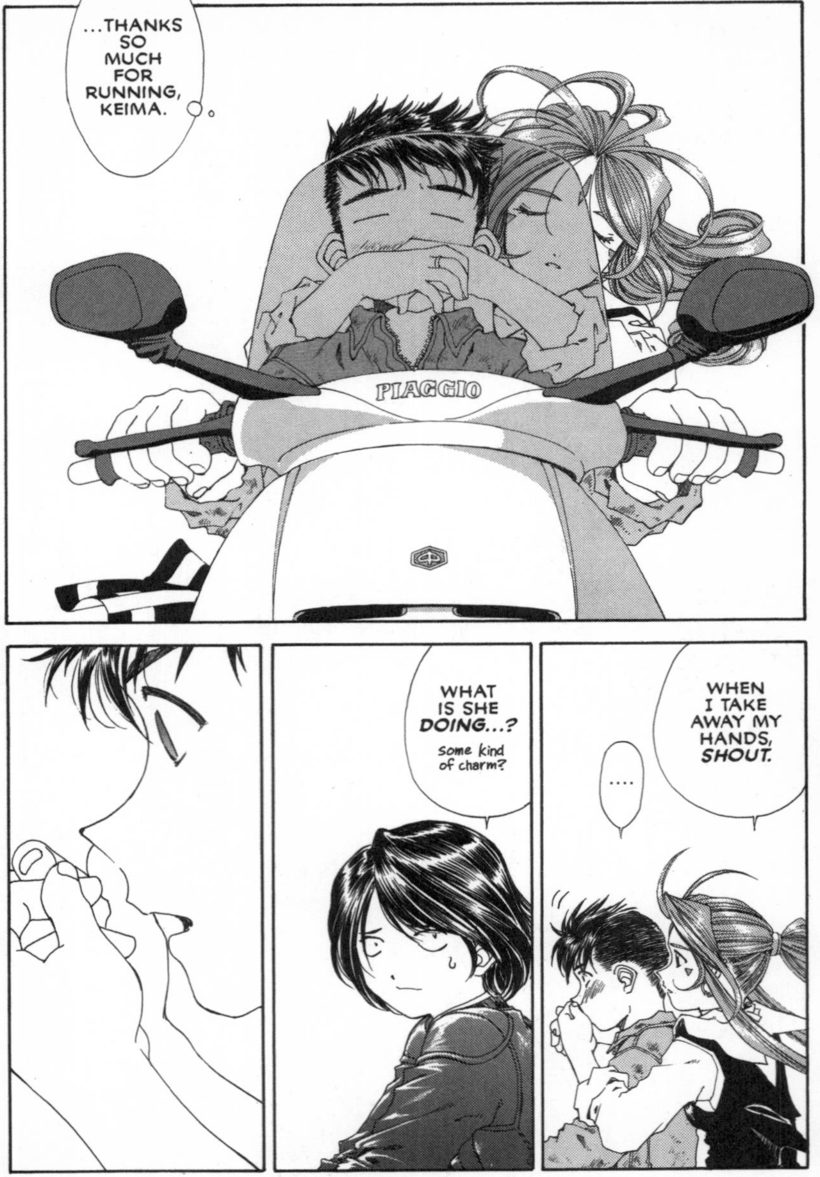
...THANKS SO MUCH FOR RUNNING, KEIMA.
PIAGGIO
WHEN I TAKE AWAY MY HANDS, *SHOUT.*
....
WHAT IS SHE *DOING...?*
some kind of charm?

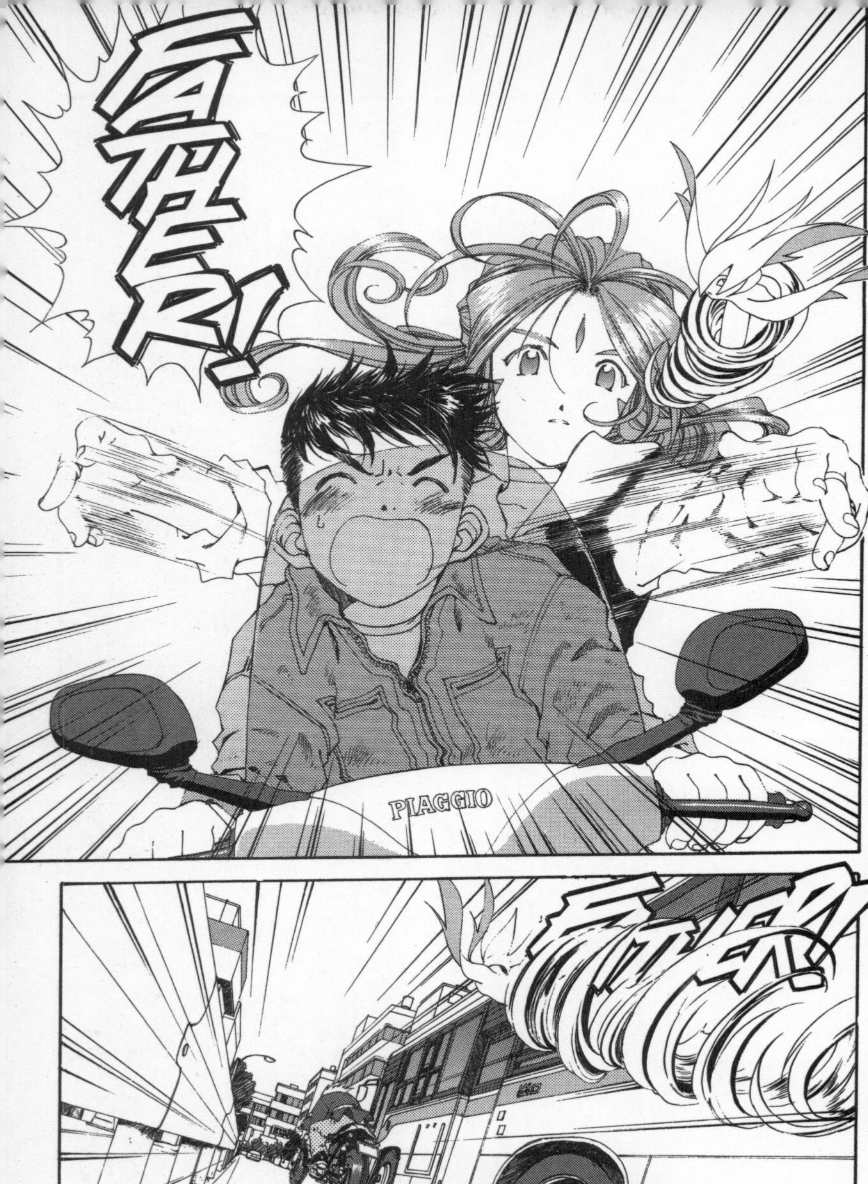
FATHER!
FATHER!

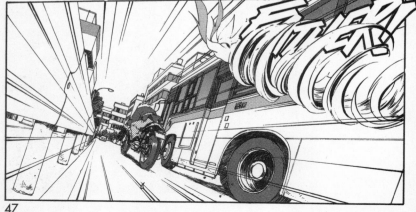

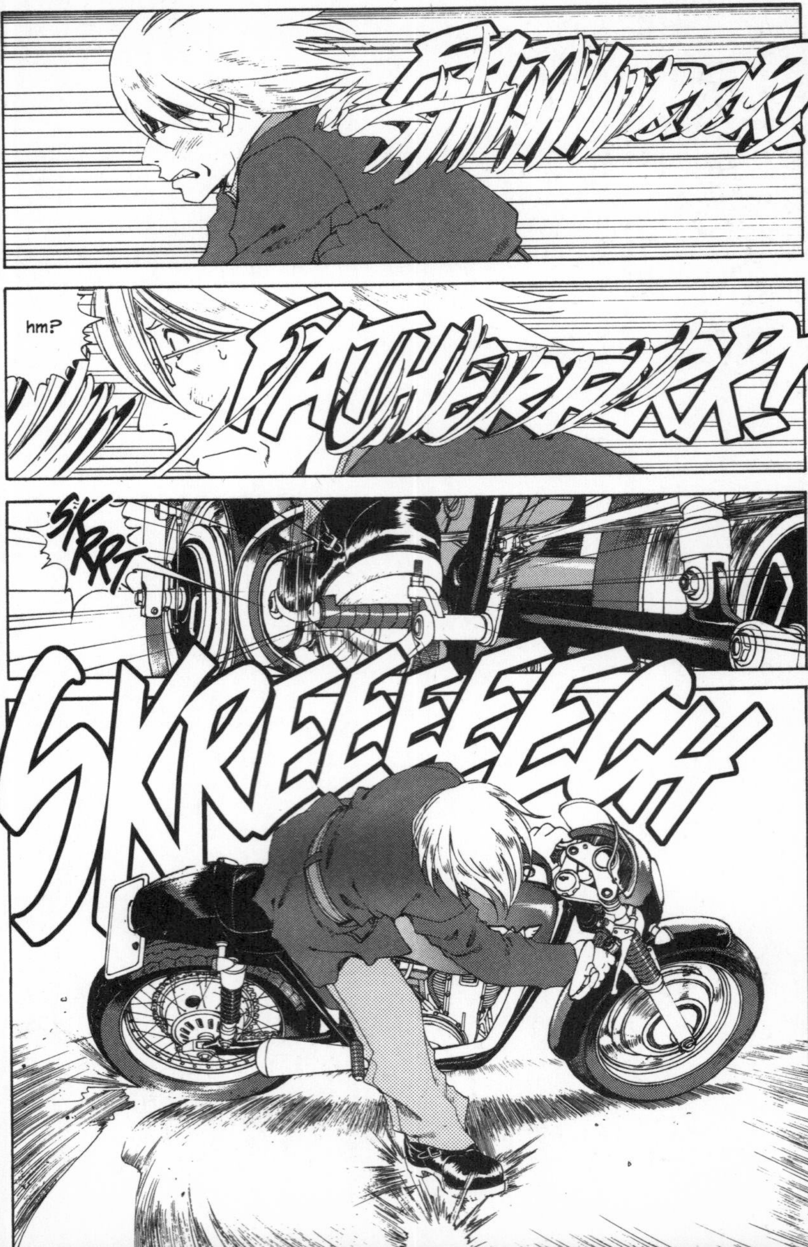
hm?
FATHERRRRR!
SKRRT
SKREEEEECH

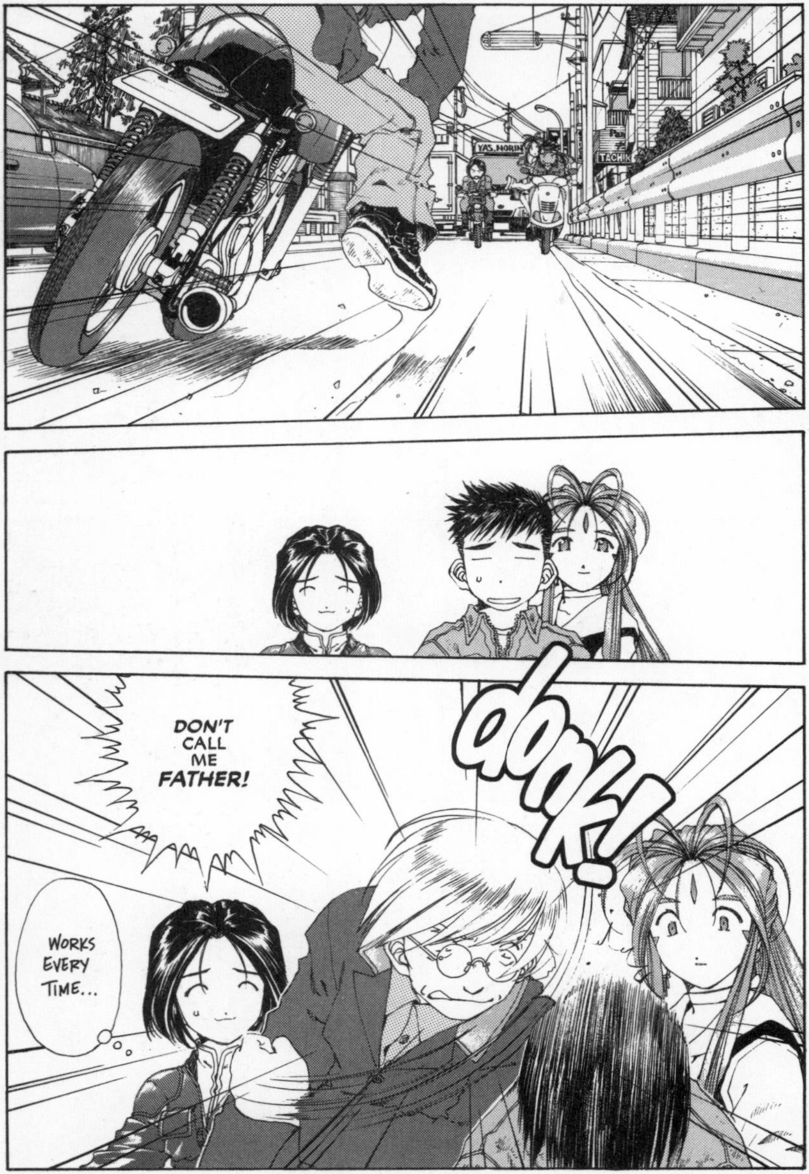
dok!
DON'T CALL ME FATHER!
WORKS EVERY TIME...

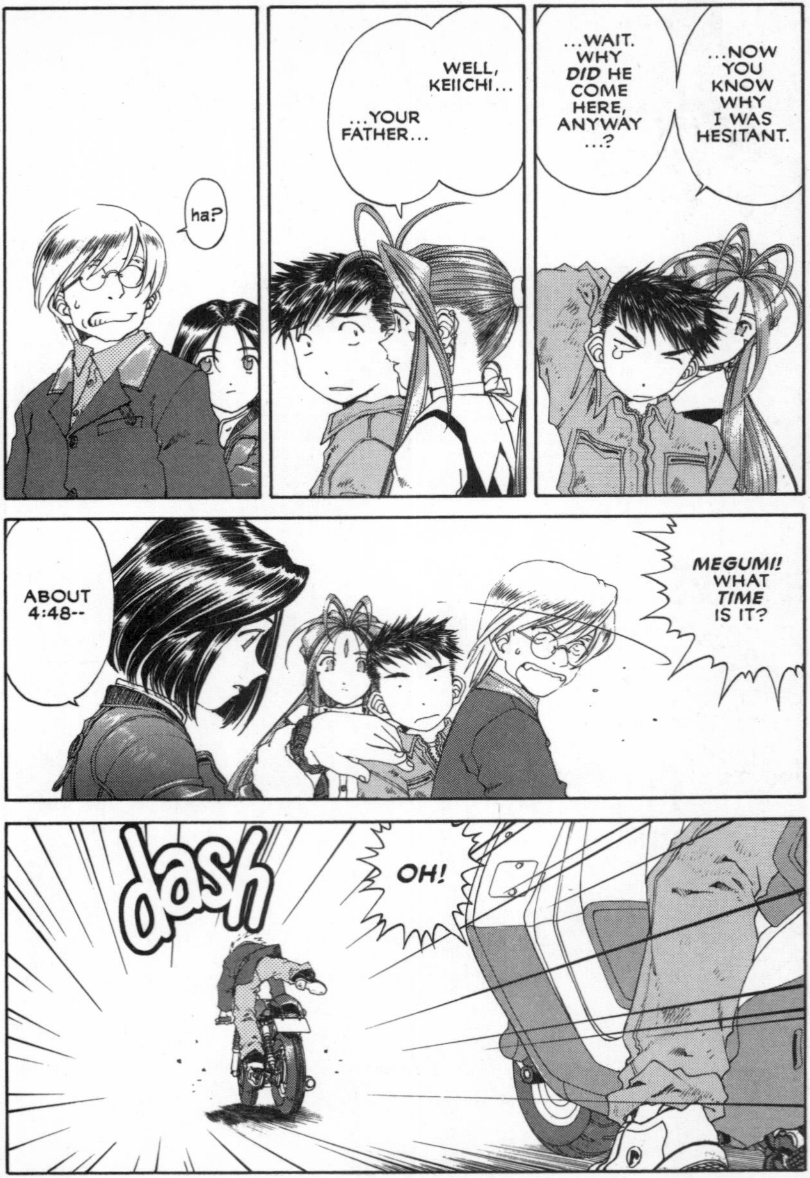
...NOW YOU KNOW WHY I WAS HESITANT.
...WAIT. WHY *DID* HE COME HERE, ANYWAY ...?
WELL, KEIICHI...
...YOUR FATHER...
ha?
MEGUMI! WHAT *TIME* IS IT?
ABOUT 4:48--
OH!
dash

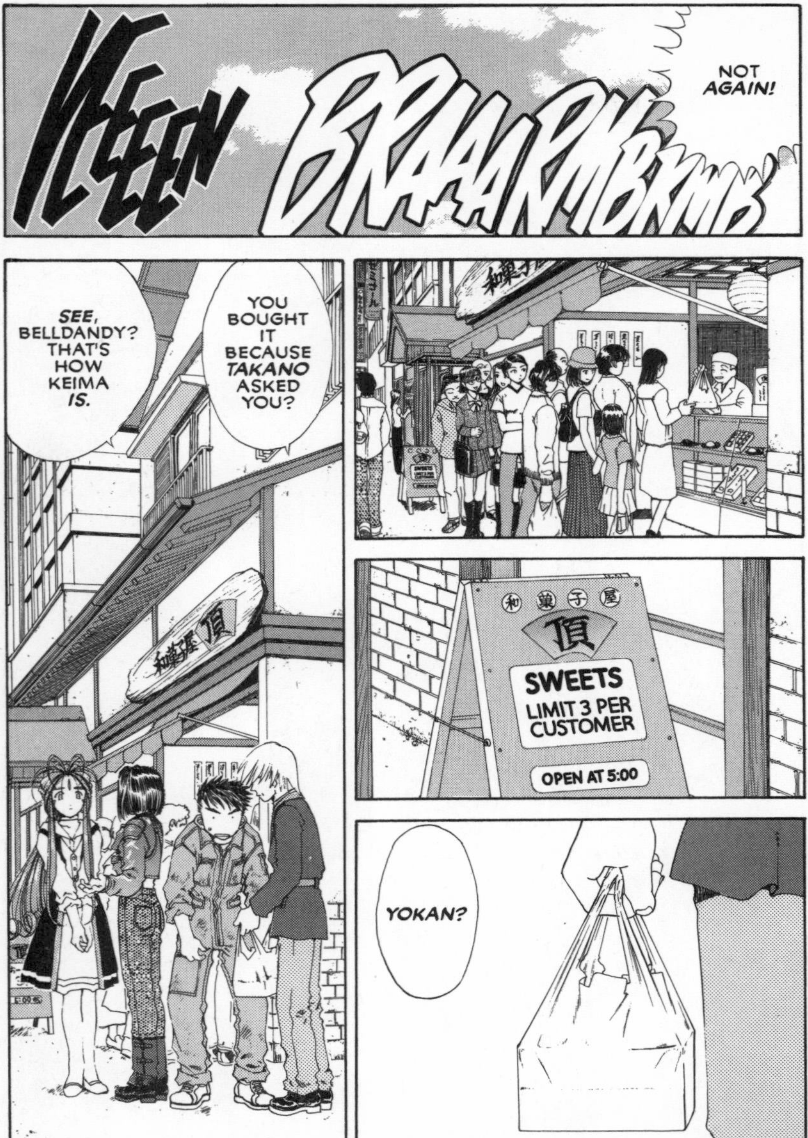
NOT AGAIN!
SWEETS
LIMIT 3 PER CUSTOMER
OPEN AT 5:00
YOKAN?
YOU BOUGHT IT BECAUSE TAKANO ASKED YOU?
SEE, BELLDANDY? THAT'S HOW KEIMA IS.

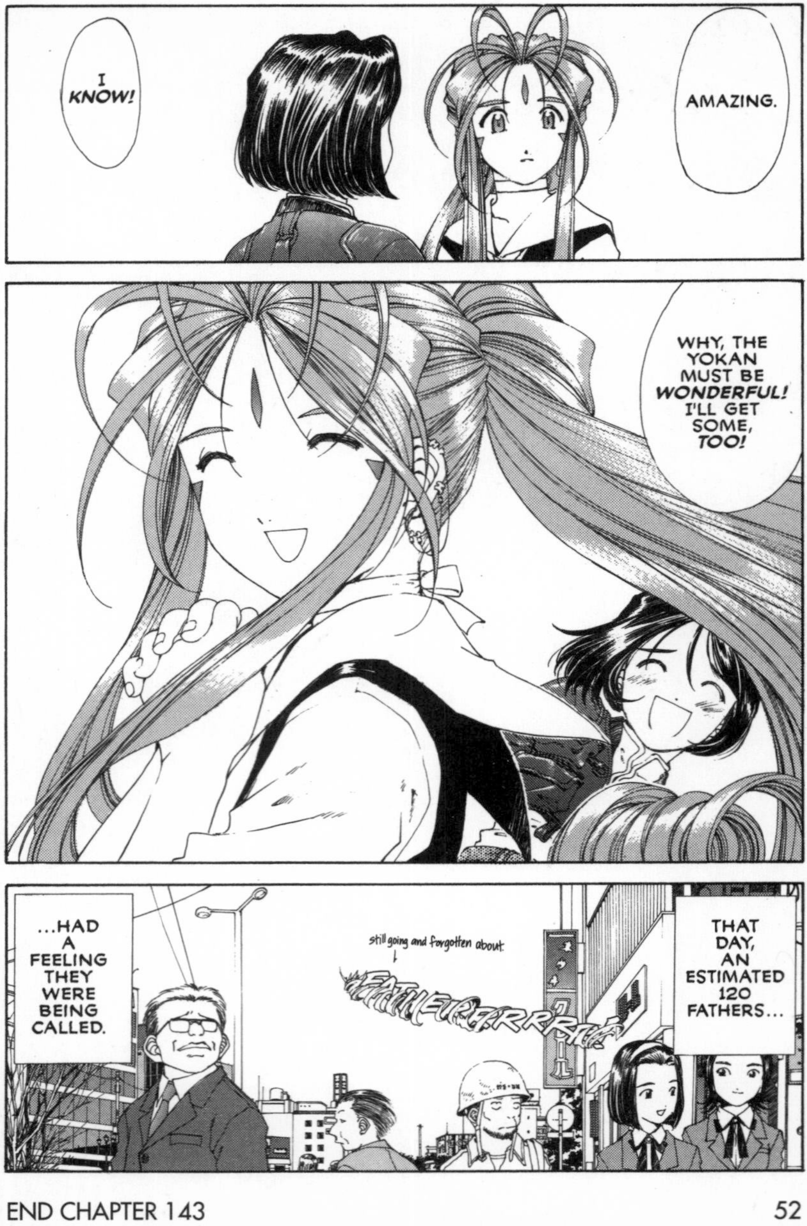
AMAZING.
I KNOW!
WHY, THE YOKAN MUST BE WONDERFUL! I'LL GET SOME, TOO!
THAT DAY, AN ESTIMATED 120 FATHERS...
still going and forgotten about.
...HAD A FEELING THEY WERE BEING CALLED.

END CHAPTER 143

CHAPTER 144

Garden of the Goddesses

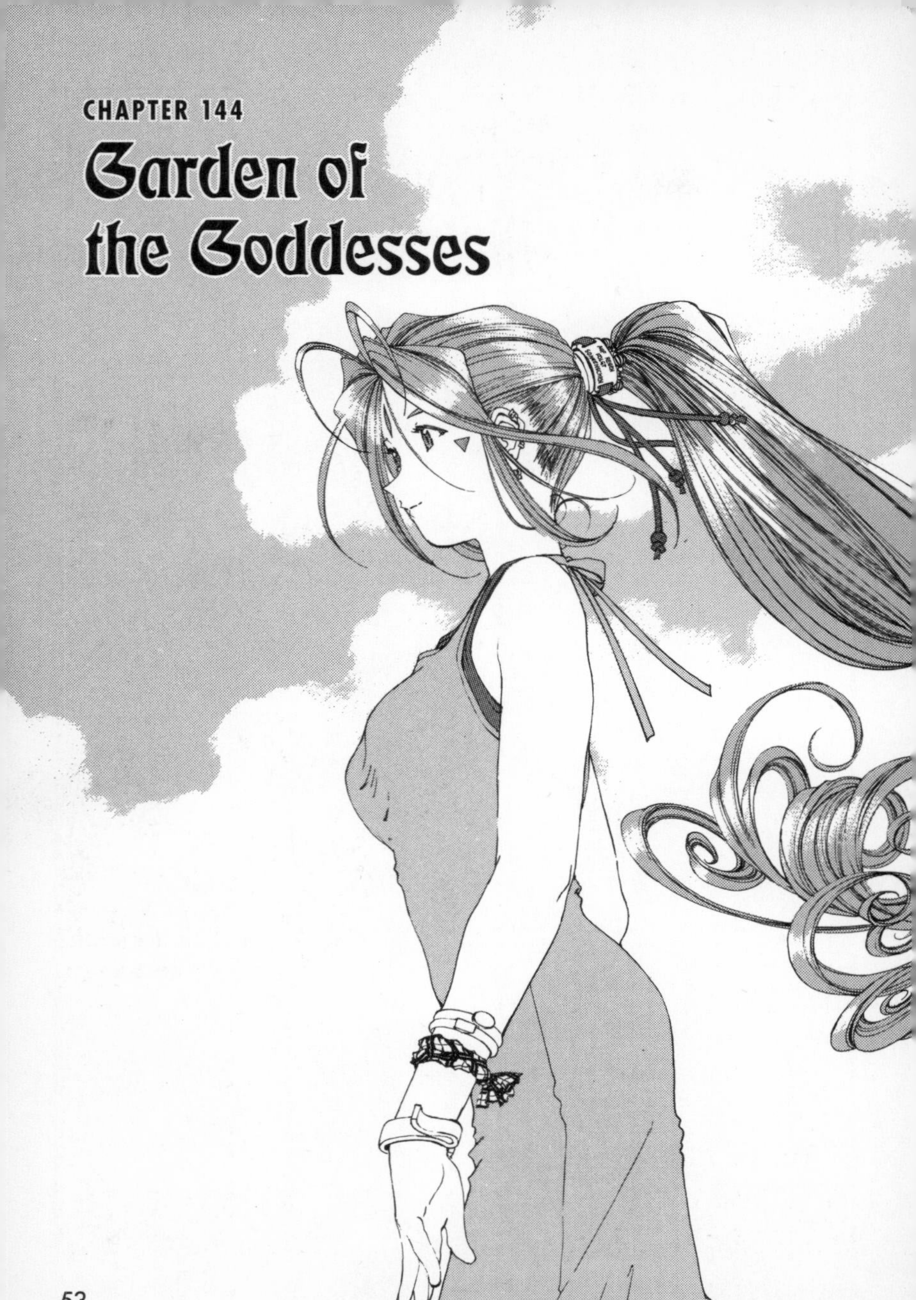

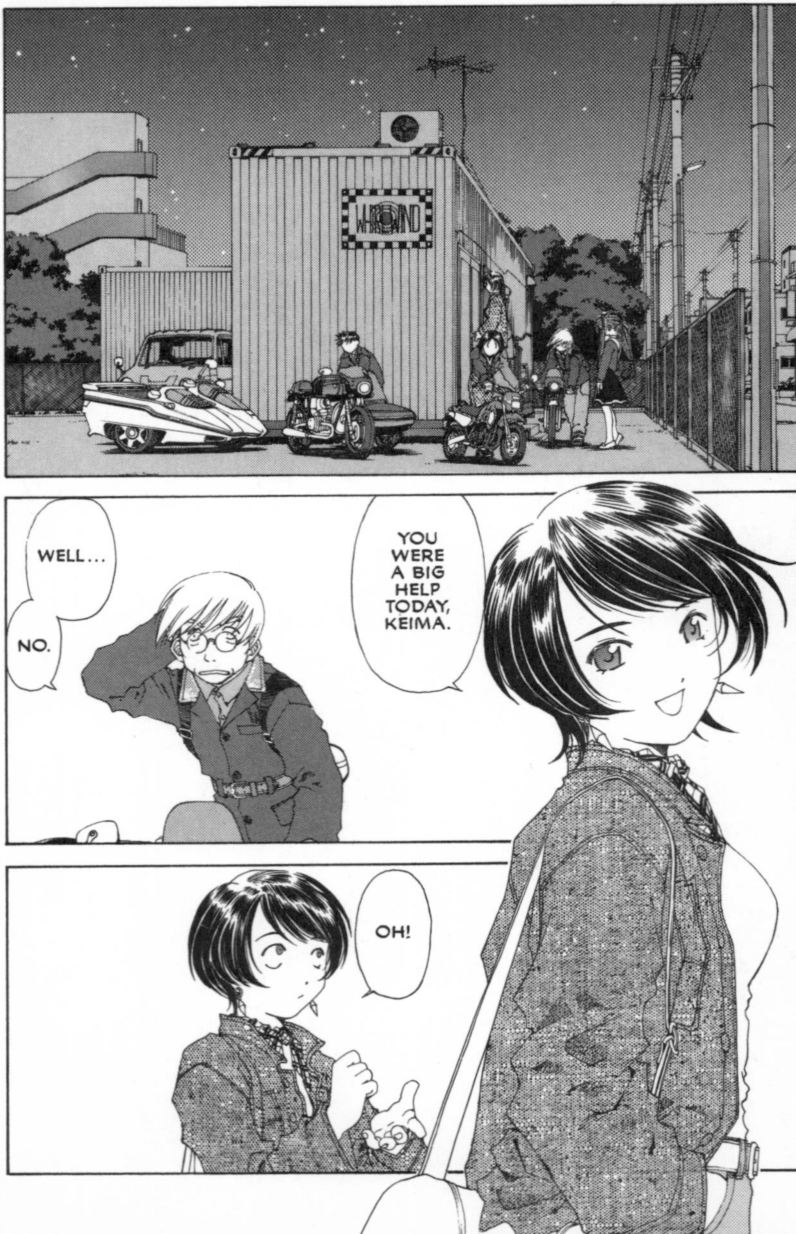
WHIRLWIND
YOU WERE A BIG HELP TODAY, KEIMA.
WELL...
NO.
OH!

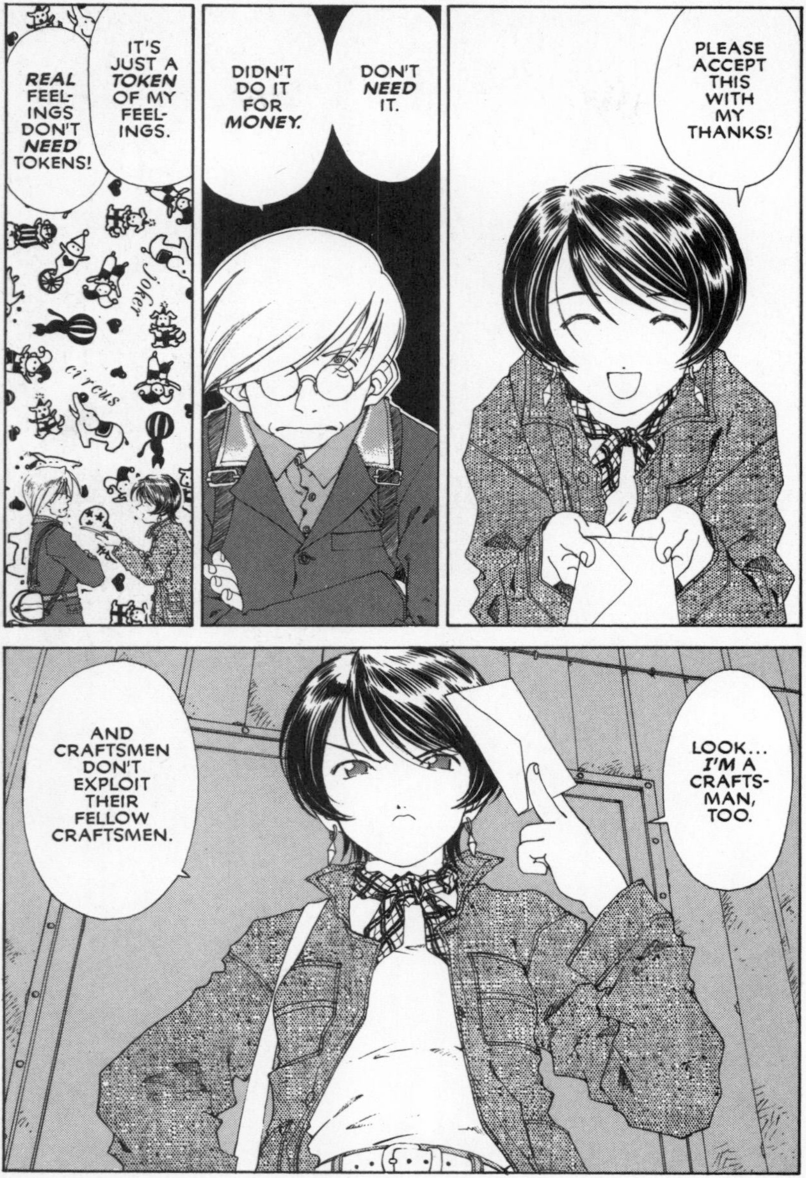

PLEASE ACCEPT THIS WITH MY THANKS!
DON'T *NEED* IT.
DIDN'T DO IT FOR *MONEY.*
IT'S JUST A *TOKEN* OF MY FEELINGS.
REAL FEELINGS DON'T *NEED* TOKENS!
joker
circus
LOOK... *I'M* A CRAFTSMAN, TOO.
AND CRAFTSMEN DON'T EXPLOIT THEIR FELLOW CRAFTSMEN.

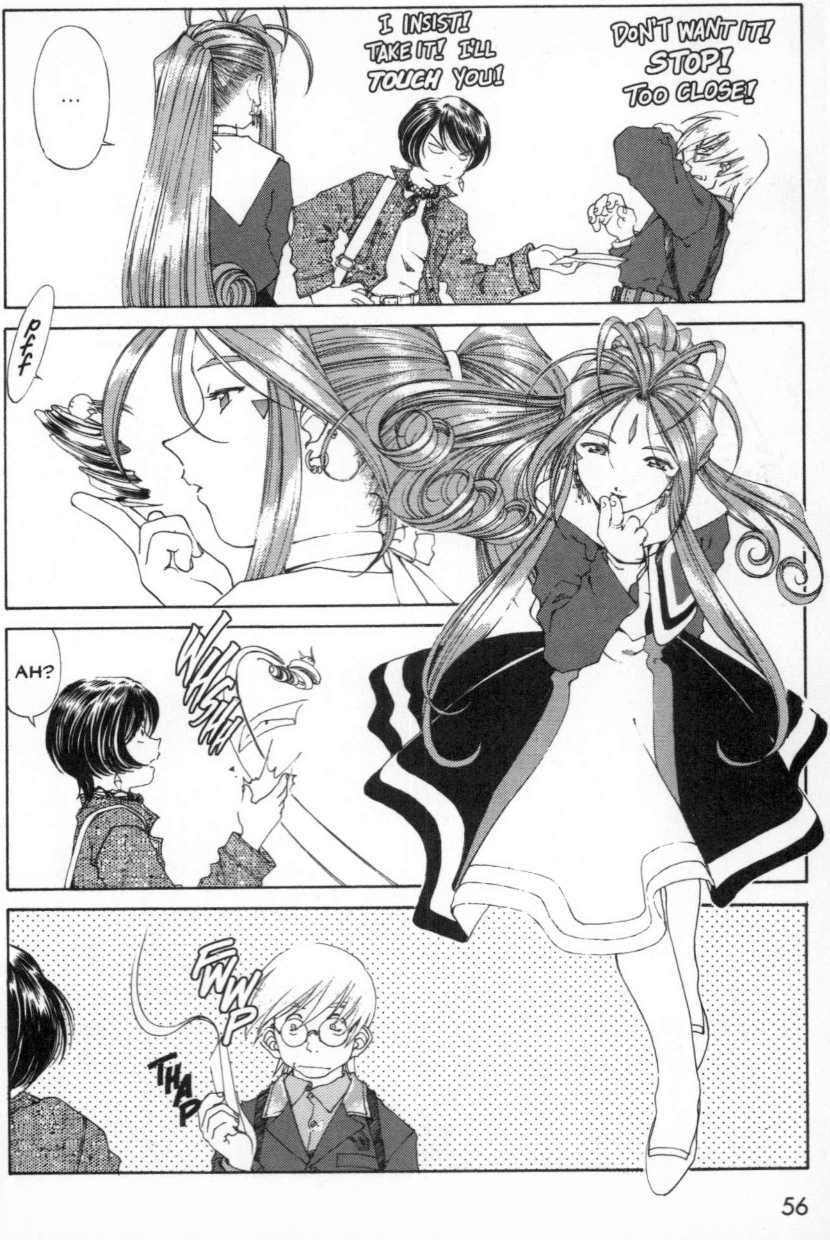
DON'T WANT IT! STOP! TOO CLOSE!
I INSIST! TAKE IT! I'LL TOUCH YOU!
...
pfff
WHSHH
AH?
FWWP
THAP

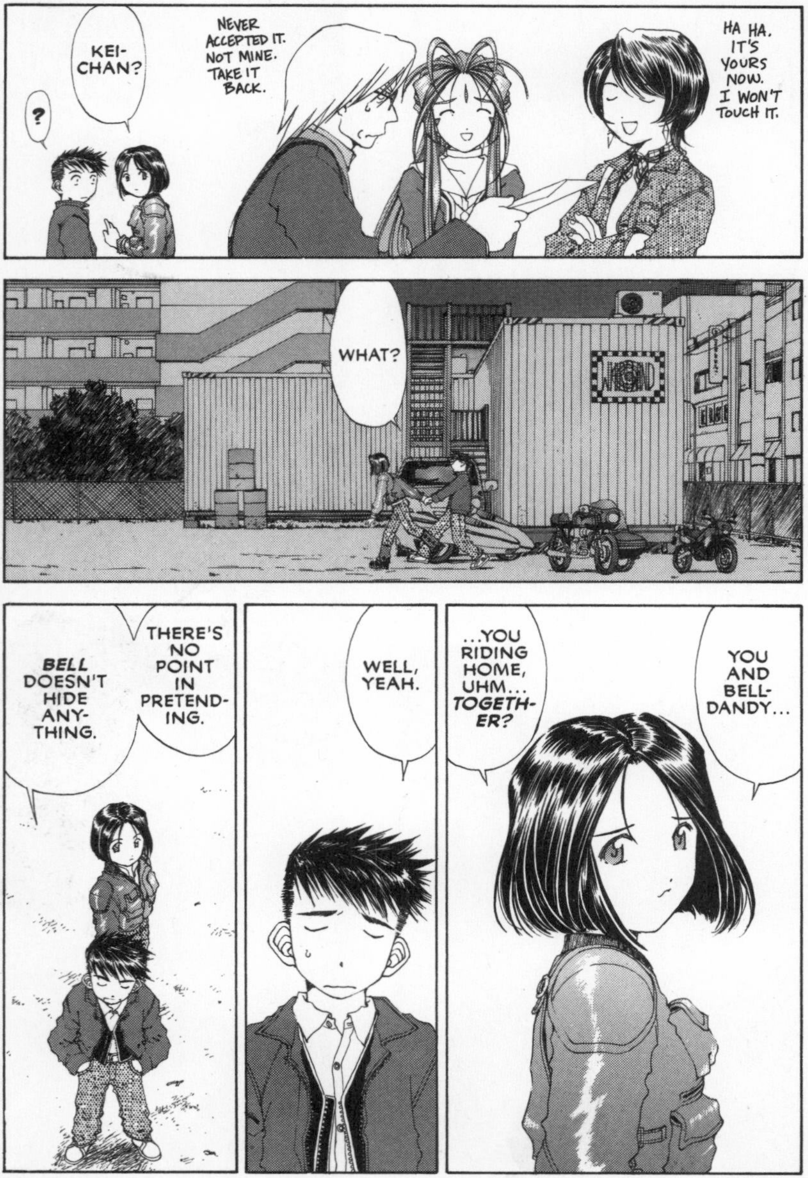
HA HA. IT'S YOURS NOW. I WON'T TOUCH IT.
NEVER ACCEPTED IT. NOT MINE. TAKE IT BACK.
KEI-CHAN?
?
WHAT?
YOU AND BELL-DANDY...
...YOU RIDING HOME, UHM... *TOGETHER?*
WELL, YEAH.
THERE'S NO POINT IN PRETENDING.
BELL DOESN'T HIDE ANYTHING.

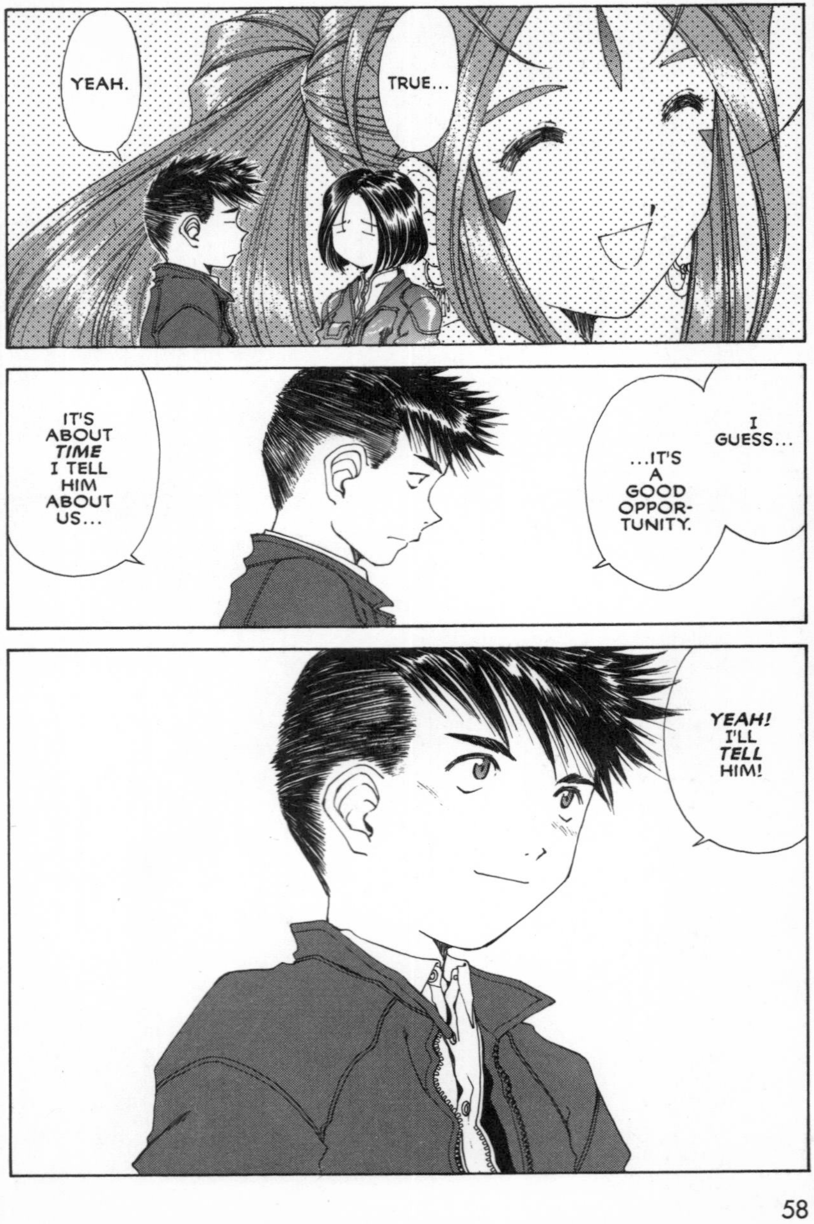
TRUE...
YEAH.
I GUESS... ...IT'S A GOOD OPPORTUNITY.
IT'S ABOUT *TIME* I TELL HIM ABOUT US...
YEAH! I'LL *TELL* HIM!

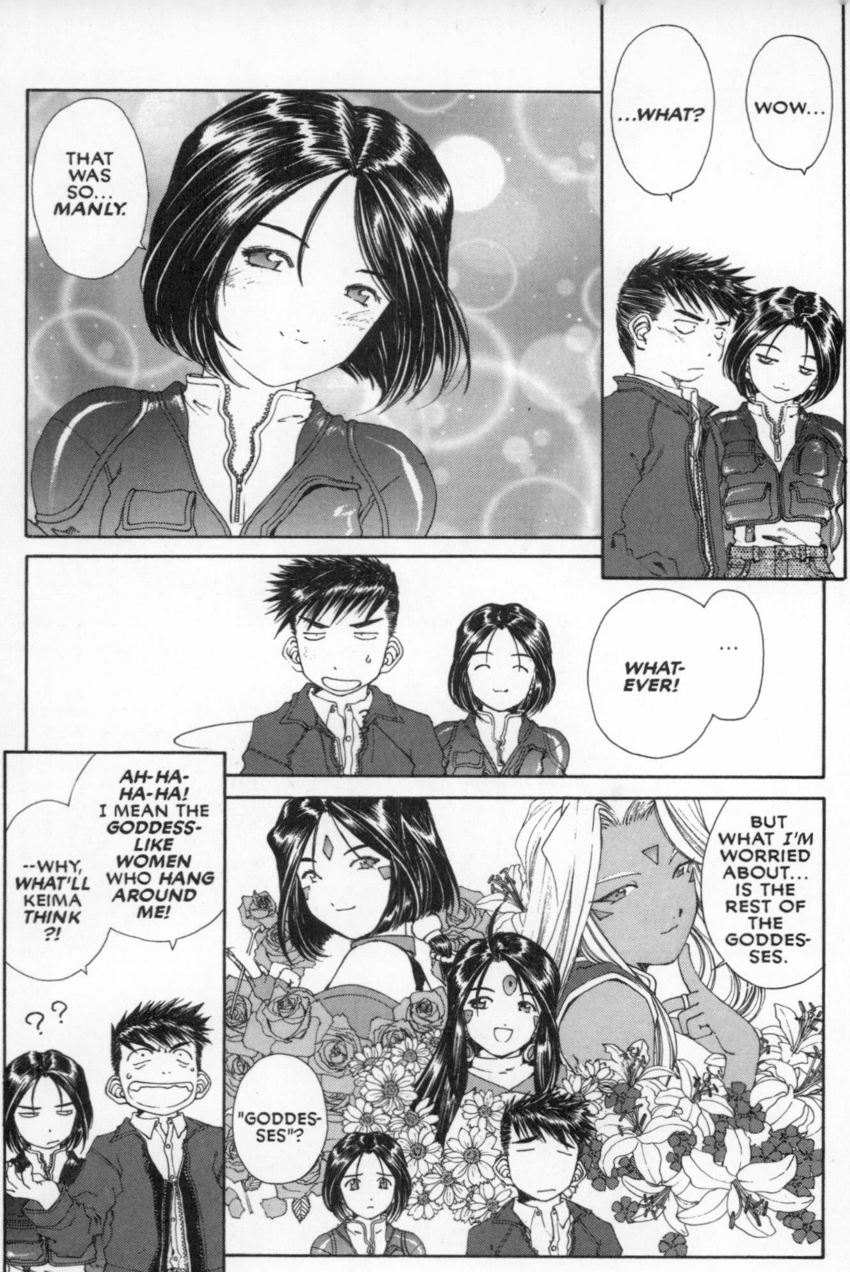
WOW...
...WHAT?
THAT WAS SO... MANLY.
... WHAT-EVER!
BUT WHAT I'M WORRIED ABOUT... IS THE REST OF THE GODDES-SES.
"GODDES-SES"?
AH-HA-HA-HA! I MEAN THE GODDESS-LIKE WOMEN WHO HANG AROUND ME!
--WHY, WHAT'LL KEIMA THINK?!
? ?

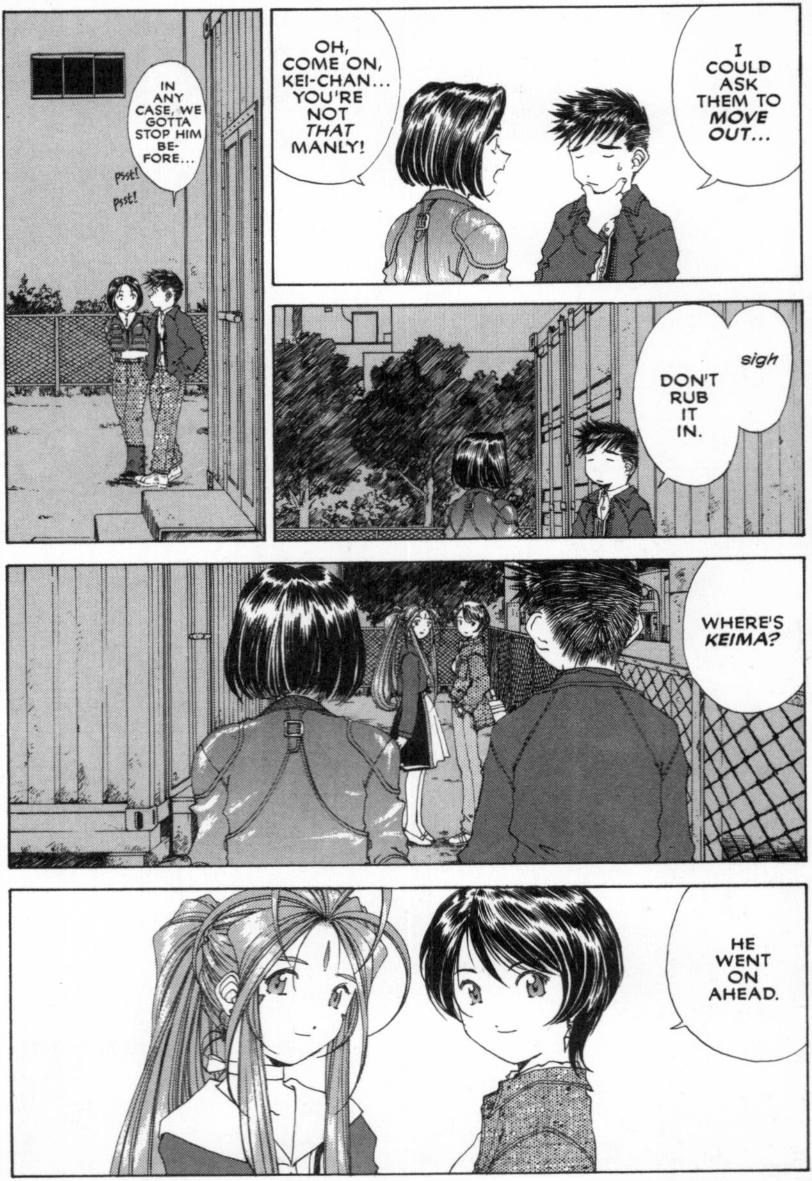
I COULD ASK THEM TO *MOVE OUT...*
OH, COME ON, KEI-CHAN... YOU'RE NOT *THAT* MANLY!
sigh
DON'T RUB IT IN.
IN ANY CASE, WE GOTTA STOP HIM BE-FORE...
psst! psst!
WHERE'S *KEIMA?*
HE WENT ON AHEAD.

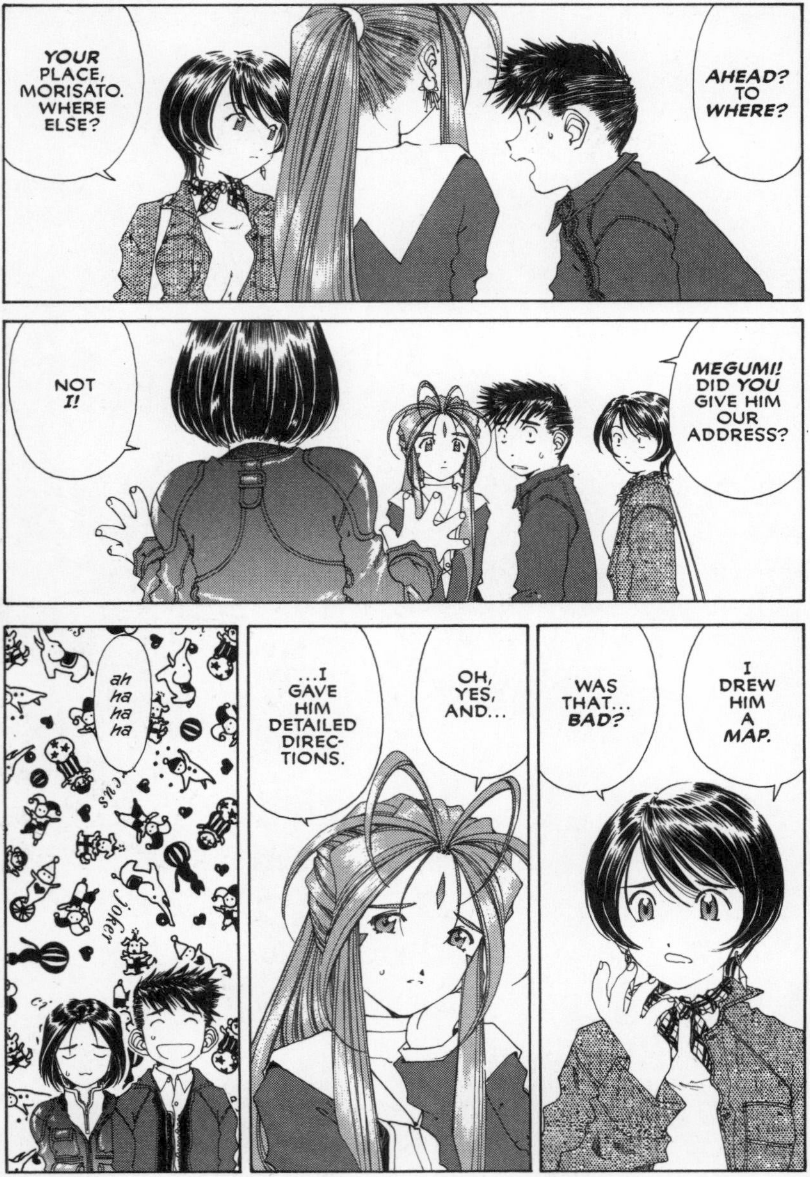
AHEAD? TO WHERE?
YOUR PLACE, MORISATO. WHERE ELSE?
MEGUMI! DID YOU GIVE HIM OUR ADDRESS?
NOT I!
I DREW HIM A MAP.
WAS THAT... BAD?
OH, YES, AND...
...I GAVE HIM DETAILED DIRECTIONS.
ah ha ha ha
Joker

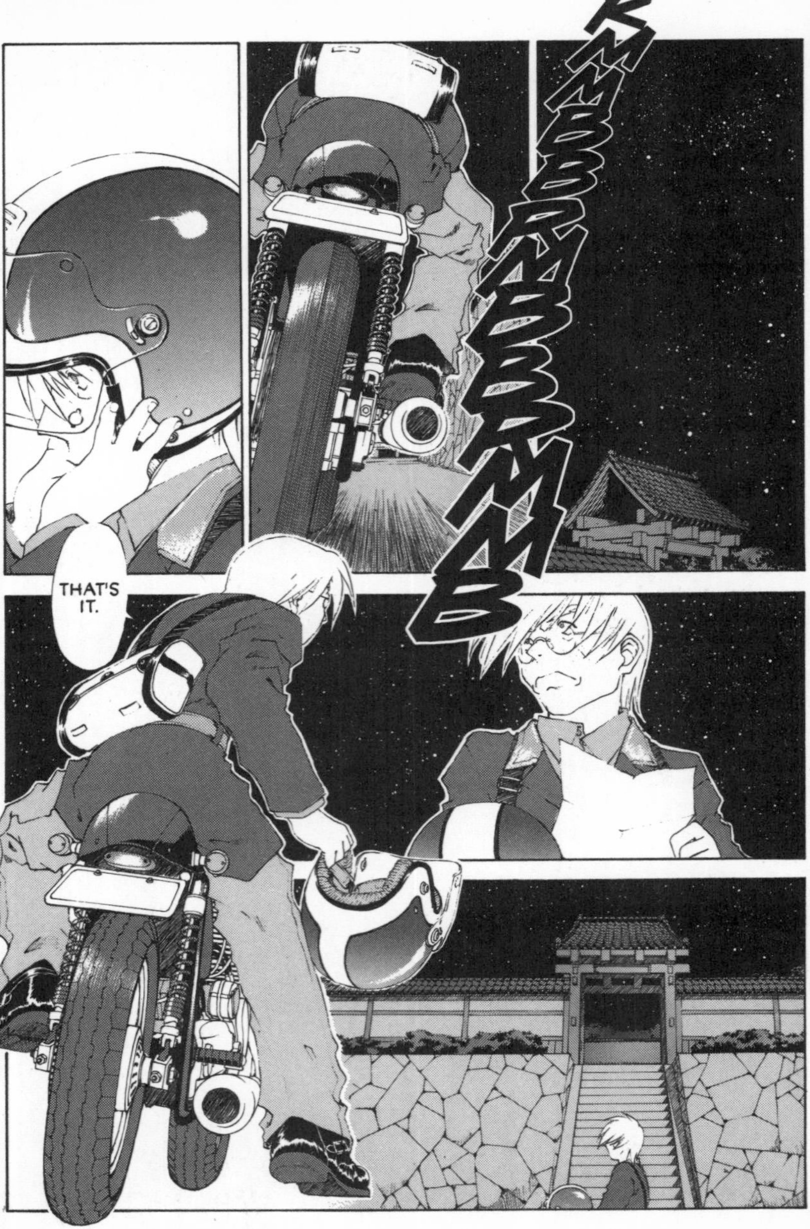
RMMBBRMMBBMMMB
THAT'S IT.

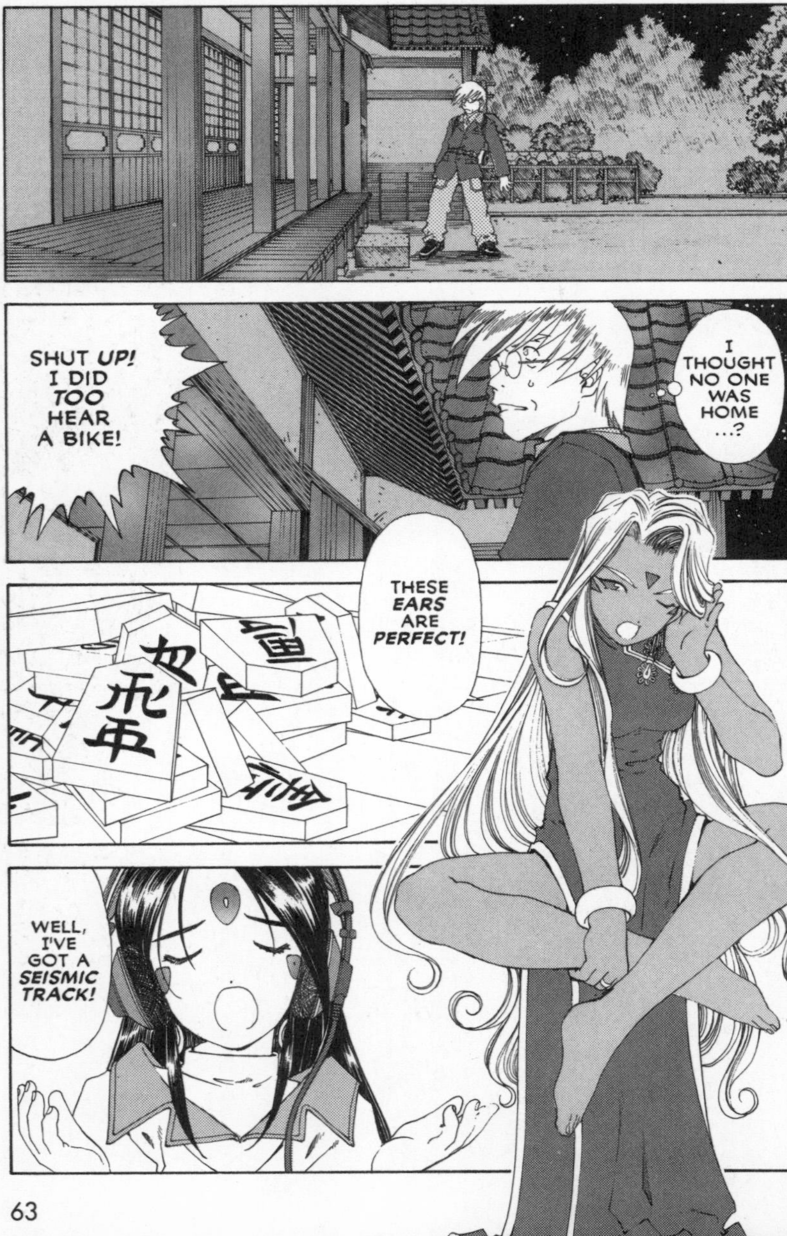
I THOUGHT NO ONE WAS HOME ...?
SHUT UP! I DID TOO HEAR A BIKE!
THESE EARS ARE PERFECT!
WELL, I'VE GOT A SEISMIC TRACK!

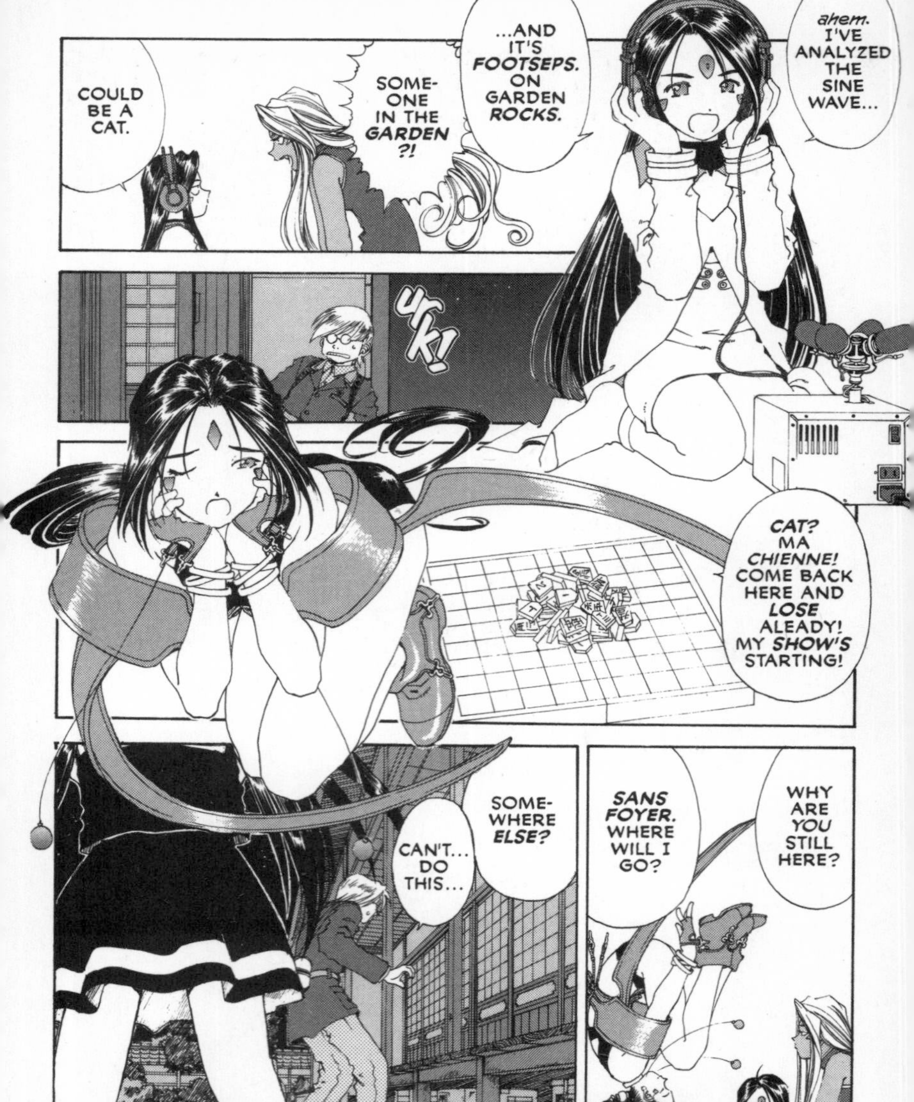
ahem. I'VE ANALYZED THE SINE WAVE...
...AND IT'S FOOTSEPS. ON GARDEN ROCKS.
SOME-ONE IN THE GARDEN ?!
COULD BE A CAT.
URK!
CAT? MA CHIENNE! COME BACK HERE AND LOSE ALEADY! MY SHOW'S STARTING!
WHY ARE YOU STILL HERE?
SANS FOYER. WHERE WILL I GO?
SOME-WHERE ELSE?
CAN'T... DO THIS...

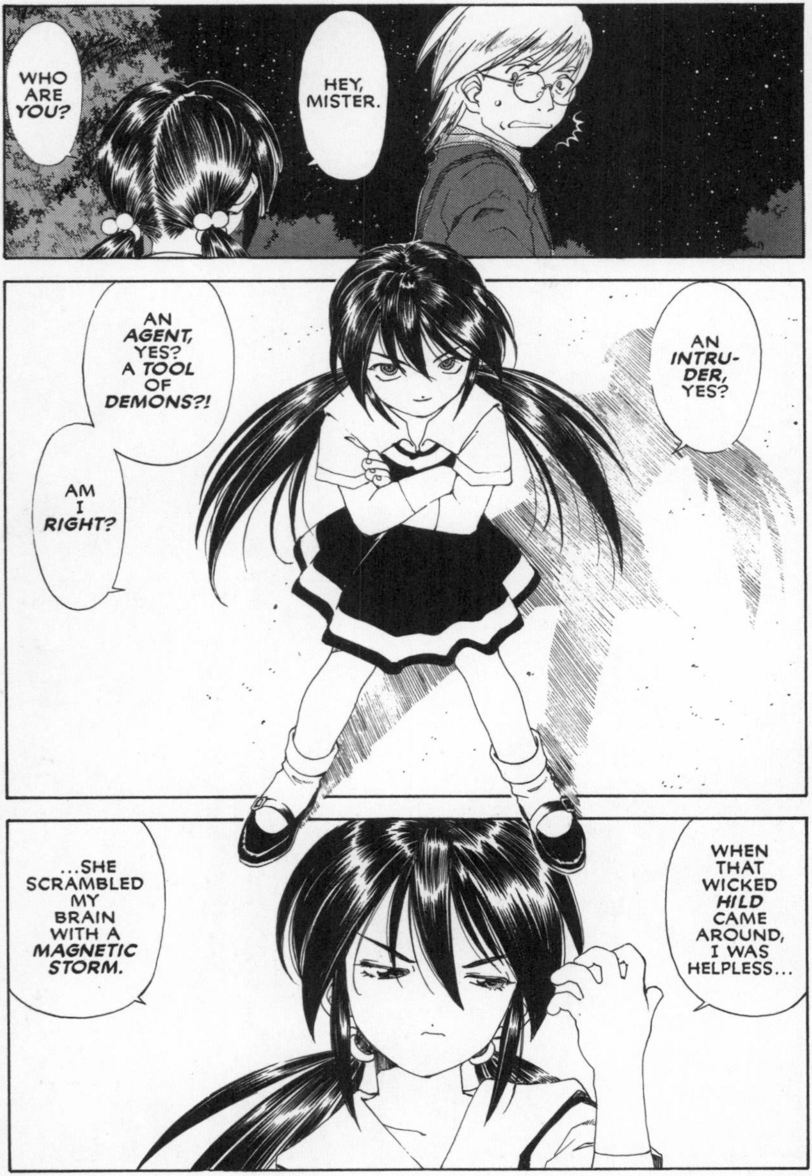
HEY, MISTER.
WHO ARE YOU?
AN INTRUDER, YES?
AN AGENT, YES? A TOOL OF DEMONS?!
AM I RIGHT?
WHEN THAT WICKED HILD CAME AROUND, I WAS HELPLESS...
...SHE SCRAMBLED MY BRAIN WITH A MAGNETIC STORM.

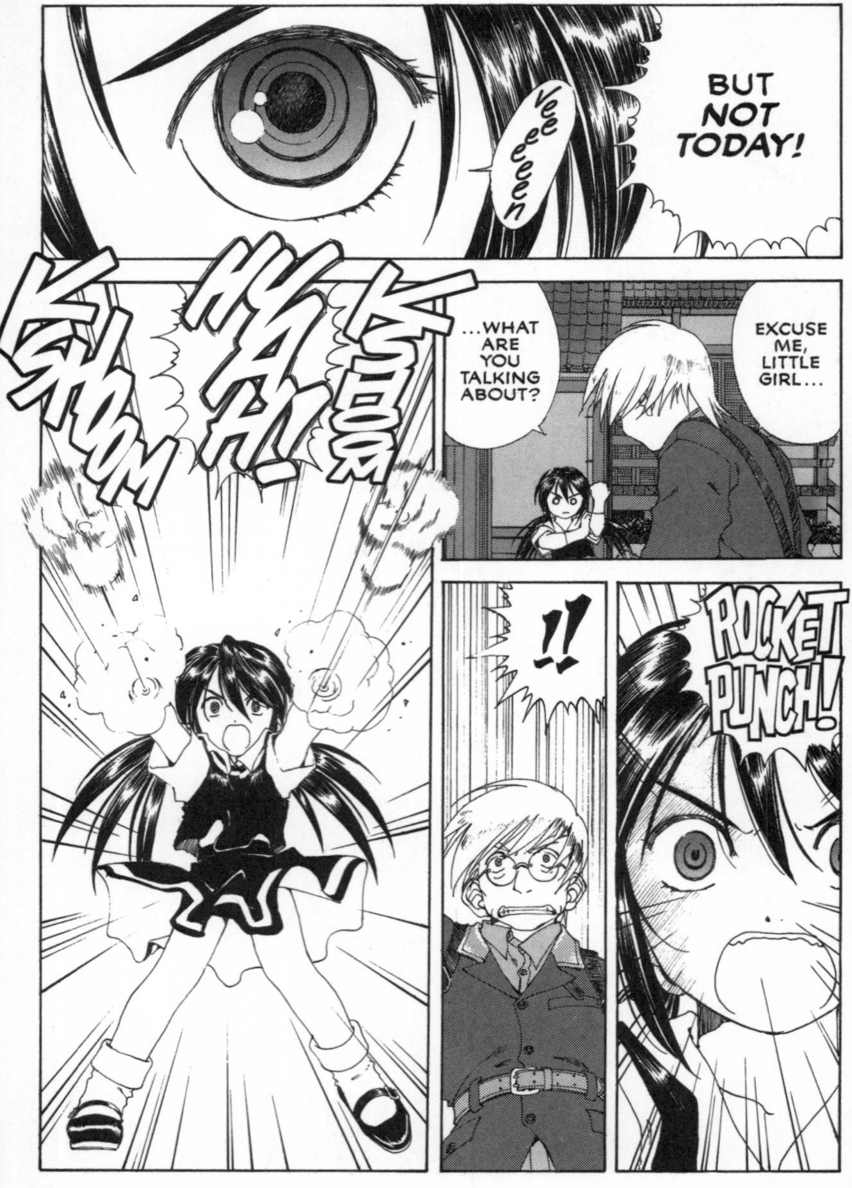
BUT NOT TODAY!
Veeeeeeen
EXCUSE ME, LITTLE GIRL...
...WHAT ARE YOU TALKING ABOUT?
ROCKET PUNCH!
!!
KSBOOM
HYAAH!
KSHOOM

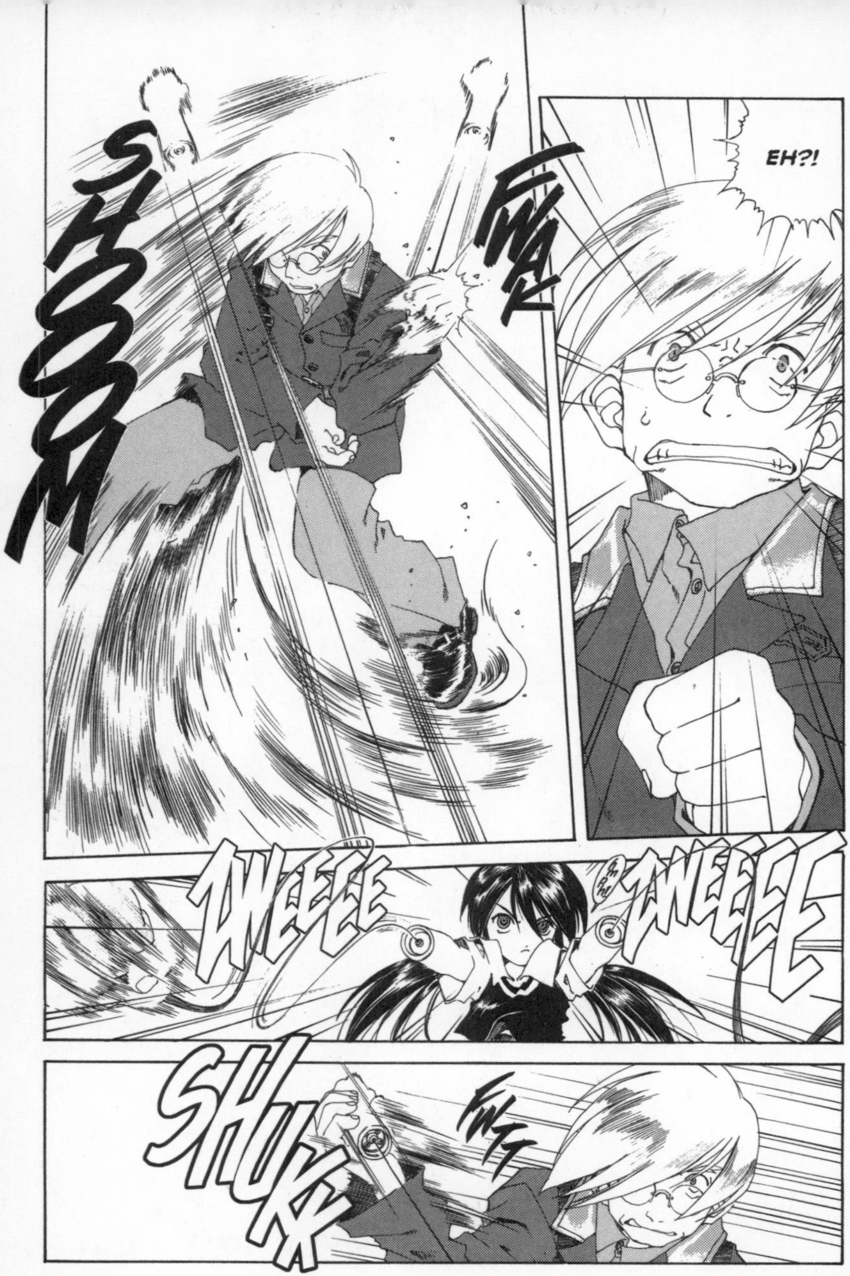
EH?!
FWAK
SHOOOM
ZWEEEE
ZWEEEE
SHUKK
FWTT

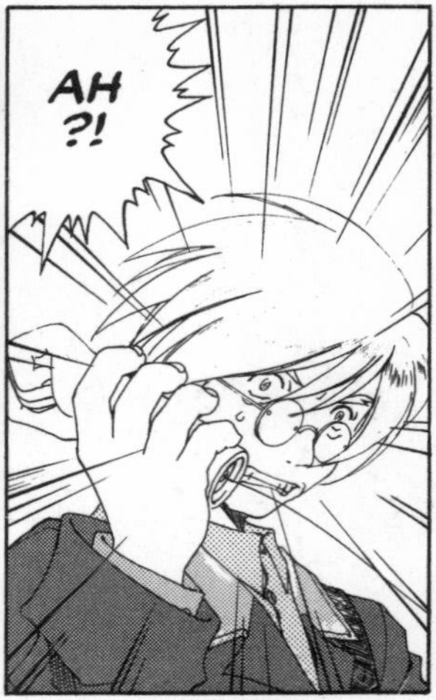
AH ?!
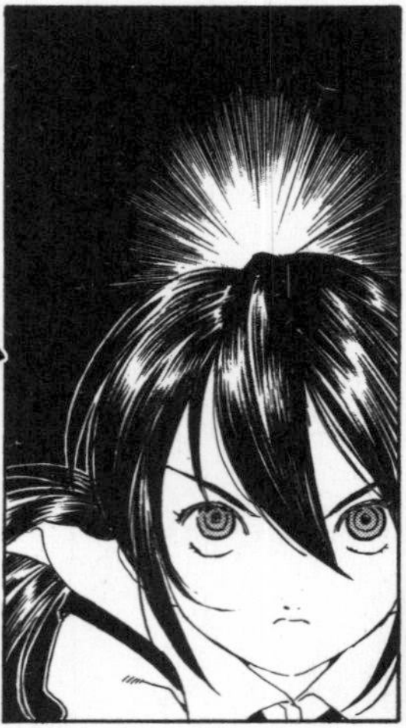
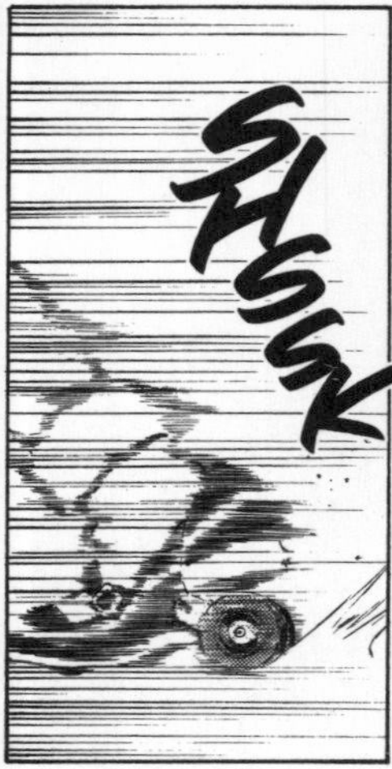
SHSWK
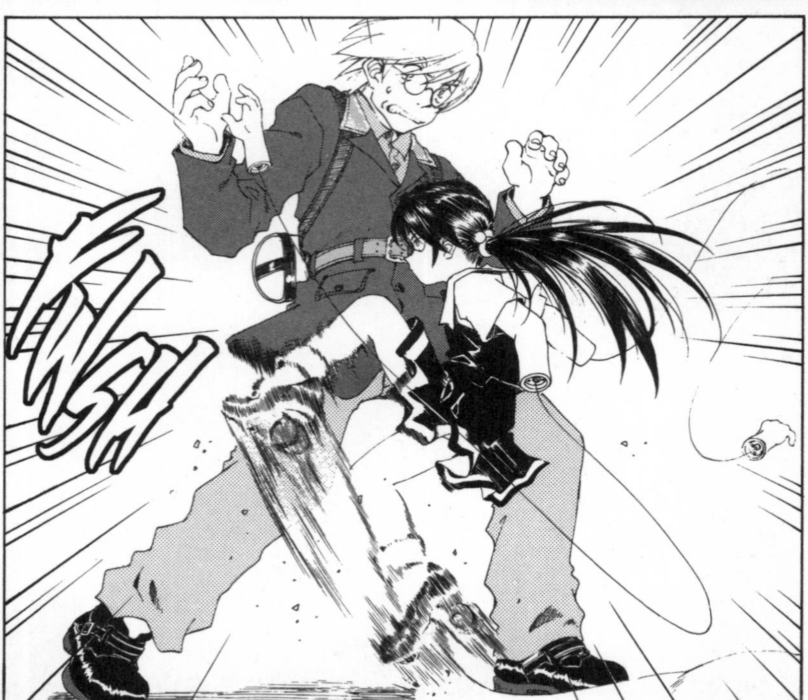
FWSH

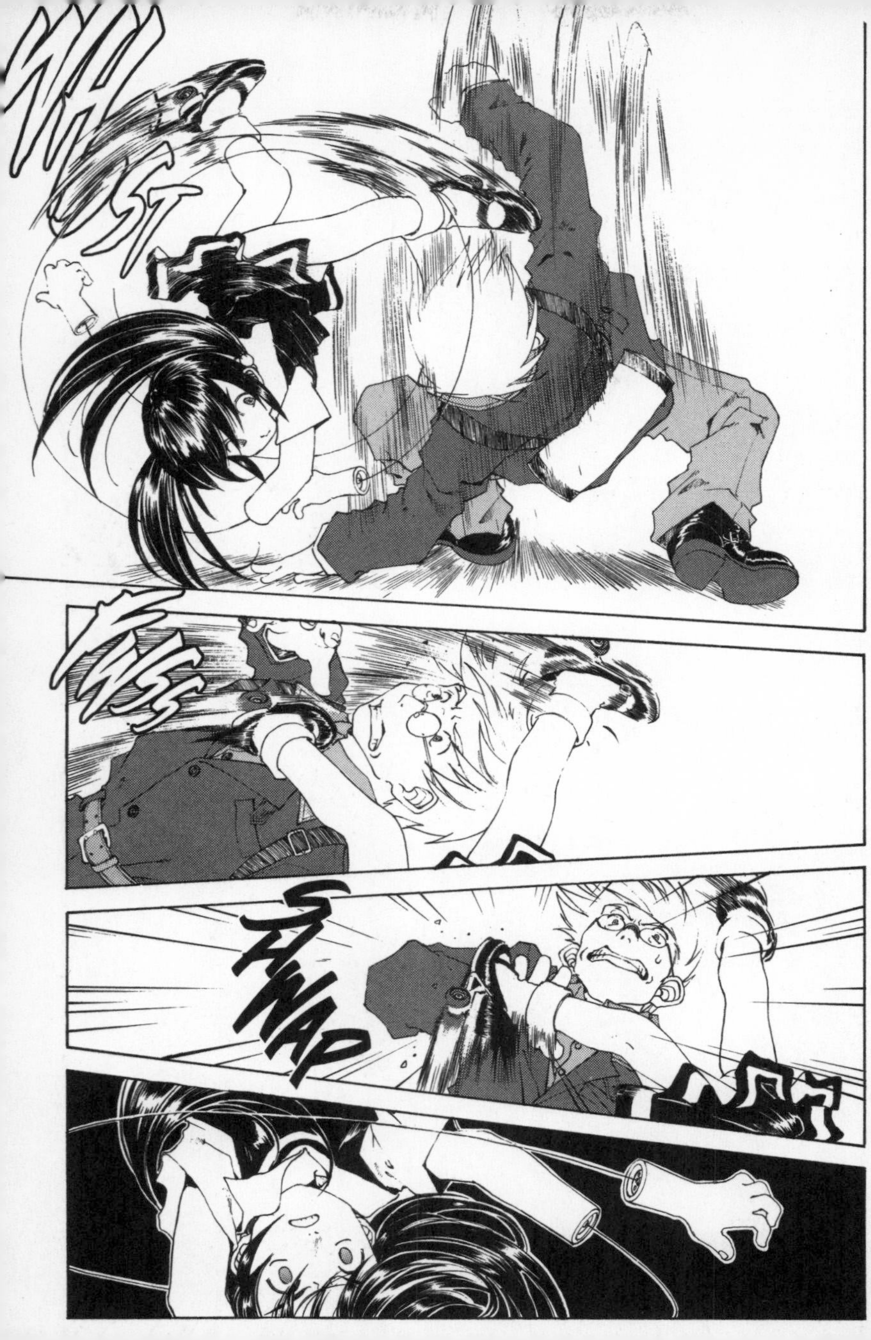
SHWAP

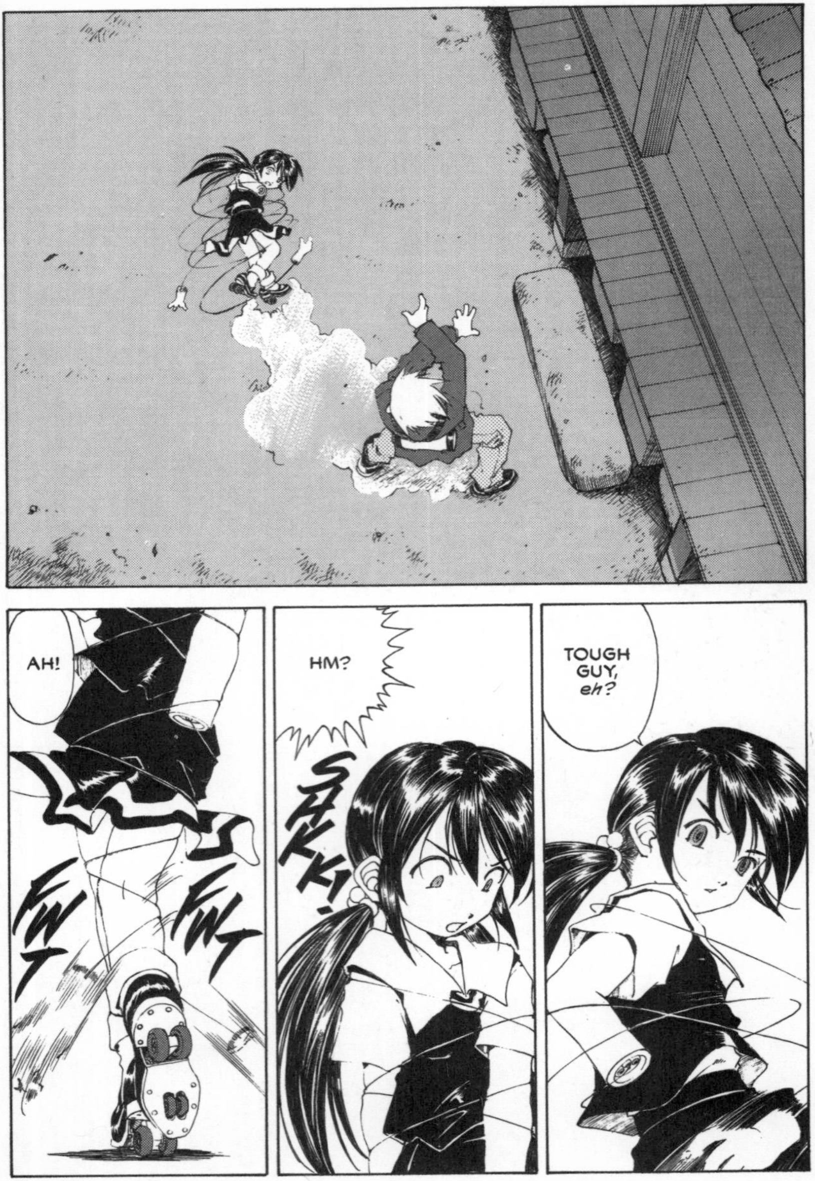
TOUGH GUY, *eh?*
HM?
AH!

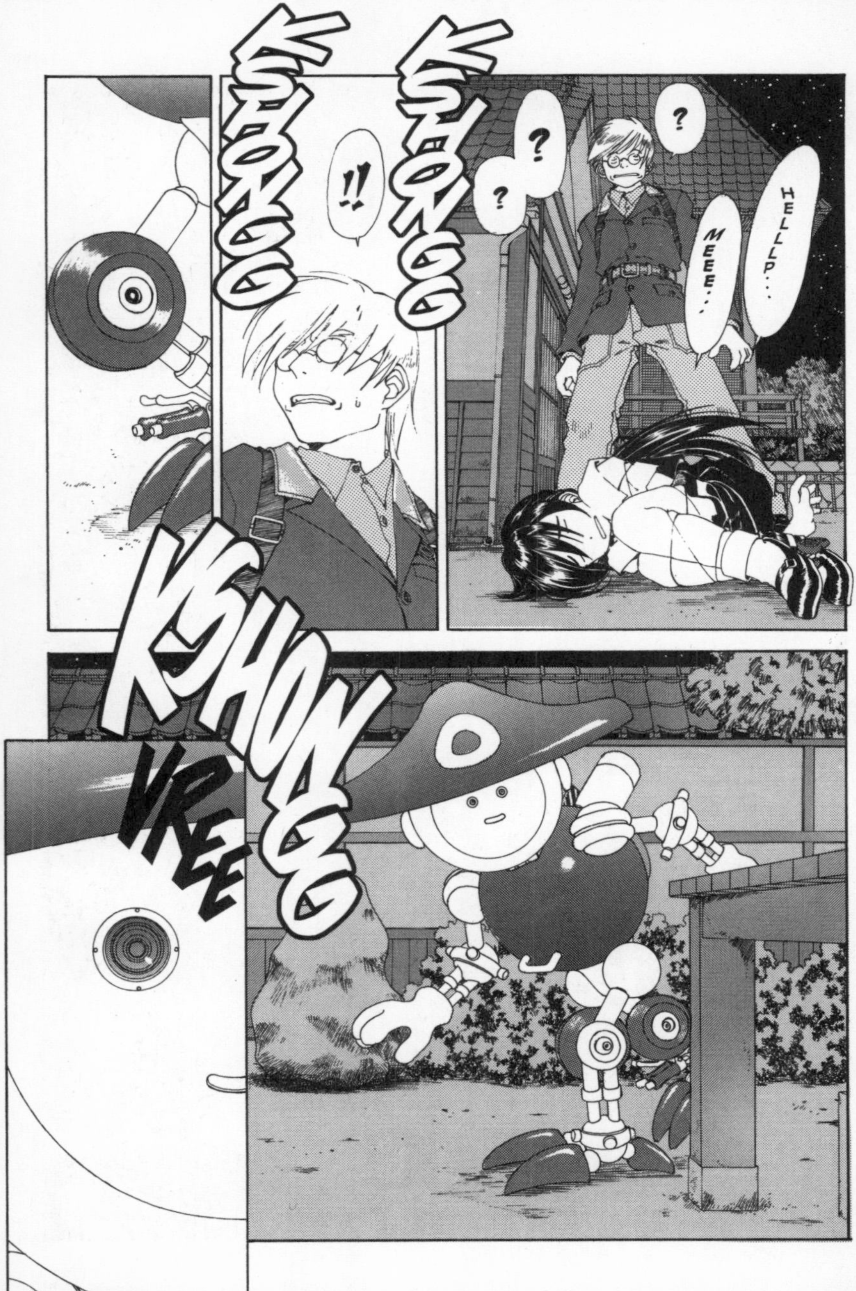
KSHONGG
?
HELLLP...
MEEE...
?
?
KSHONGG
!!
KSHONGG
VREE

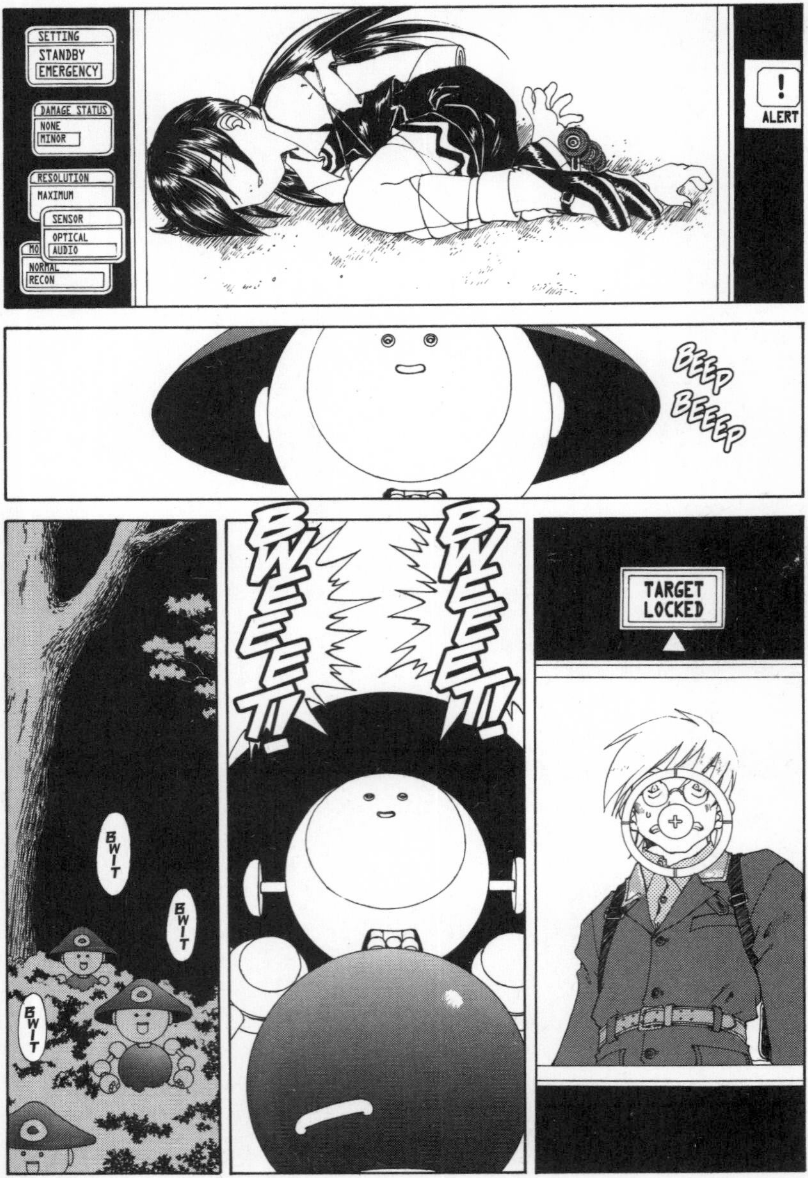
!
ALERT
SETTING
STANDBY
EMERGENCY
DAMAGE STATUS
NONE
MINOR
RESOLUTION
MAXIMUM
SENSOR
OPTICAL
AUDIO
NORMAL
RECON
BEEP
BEEEP
TARGET
LOCKED
BWEEET!!
BWEEET!!
BWIT
BWIT
BWIT

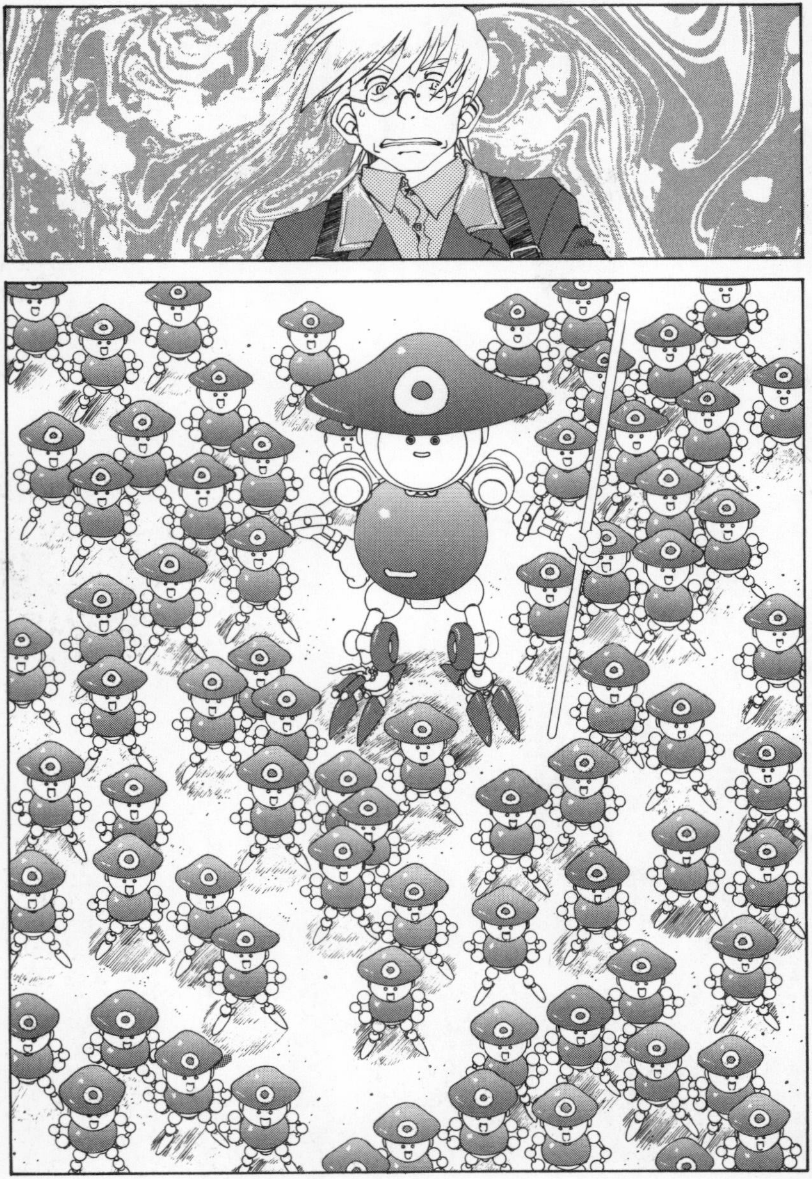

OH MY GODDESS!
M E G U M I

CHAPTER 145

Dad in Hell

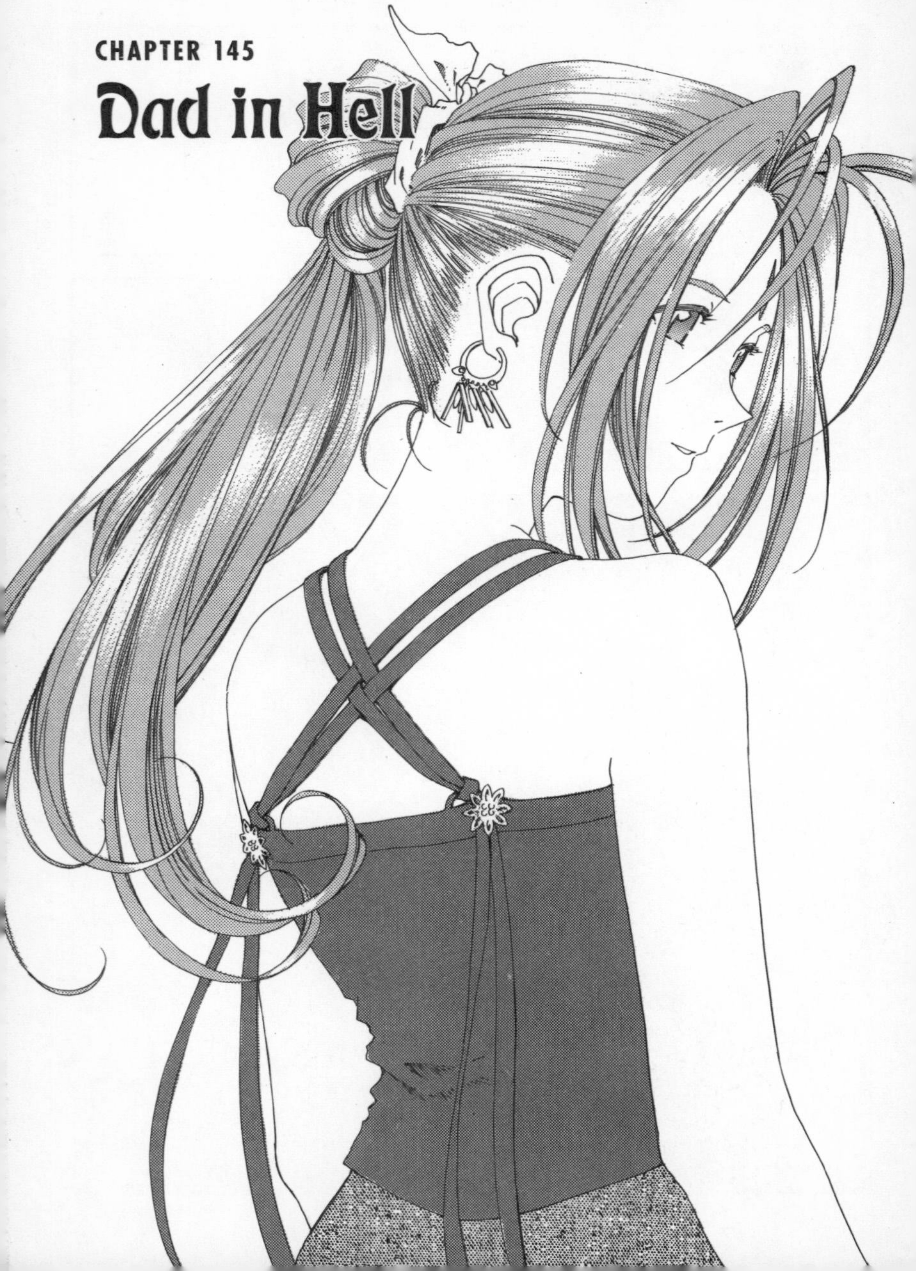

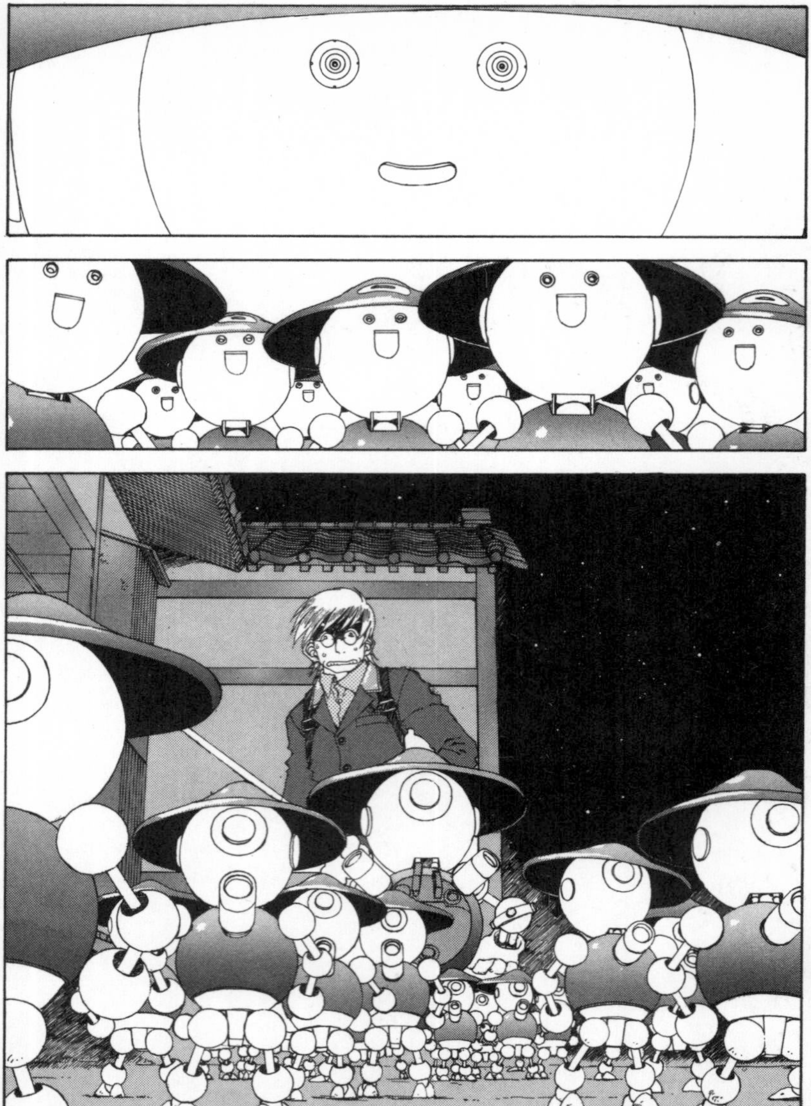

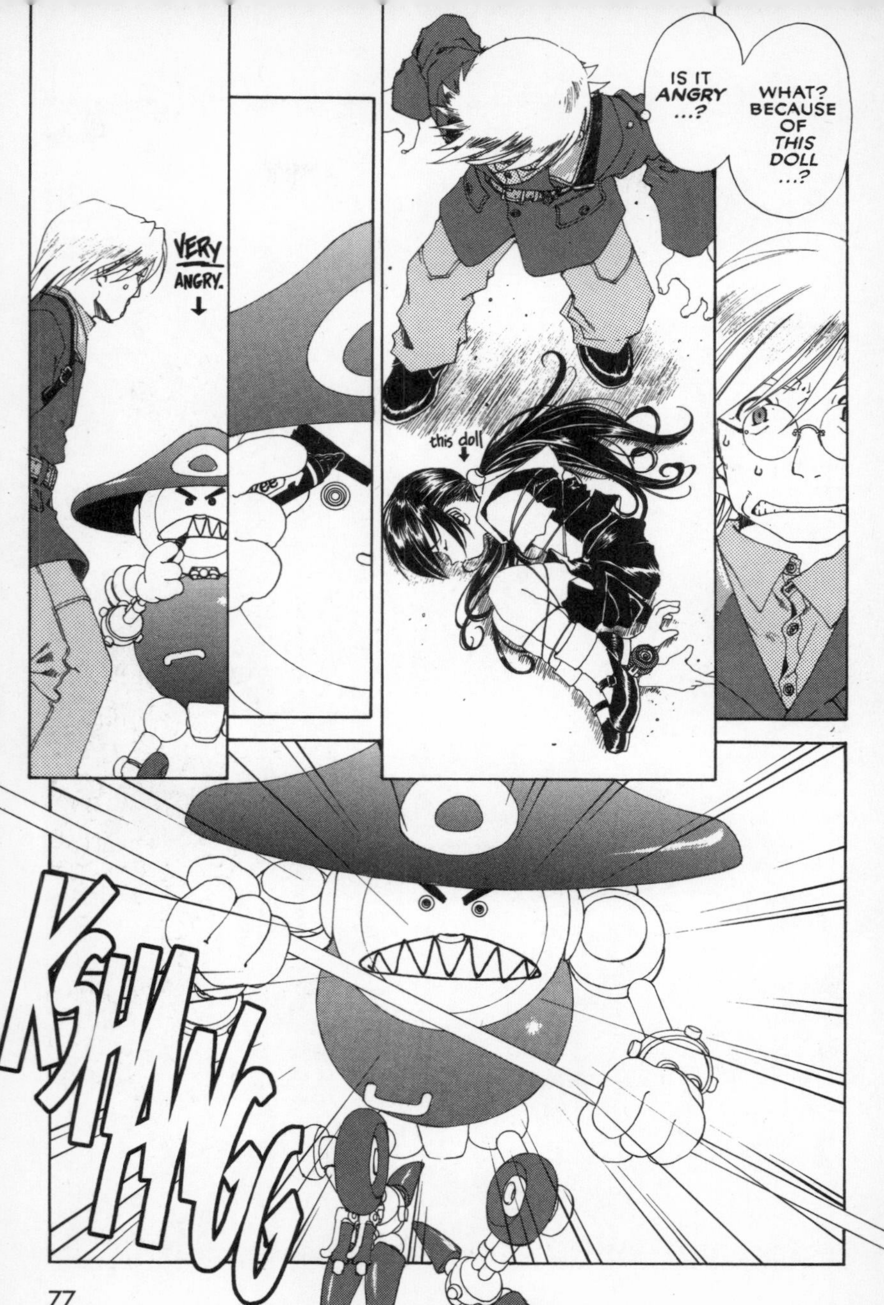
IS IT ANGRY ...?
WHAT? BECAUSE OF THIS DOLL ...?
this doll
VERY ANGRY.
KSHANGG

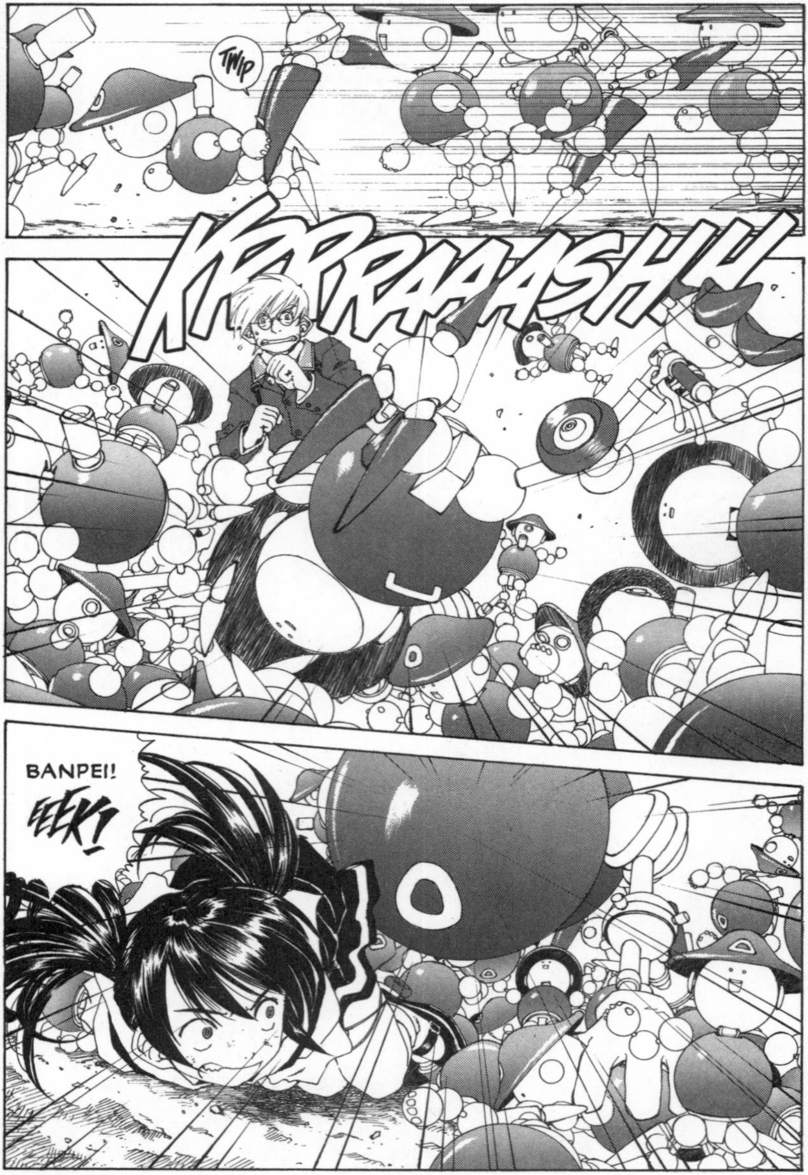
TWIP
KRRRAAASHH
BANPEI!
EEEK!

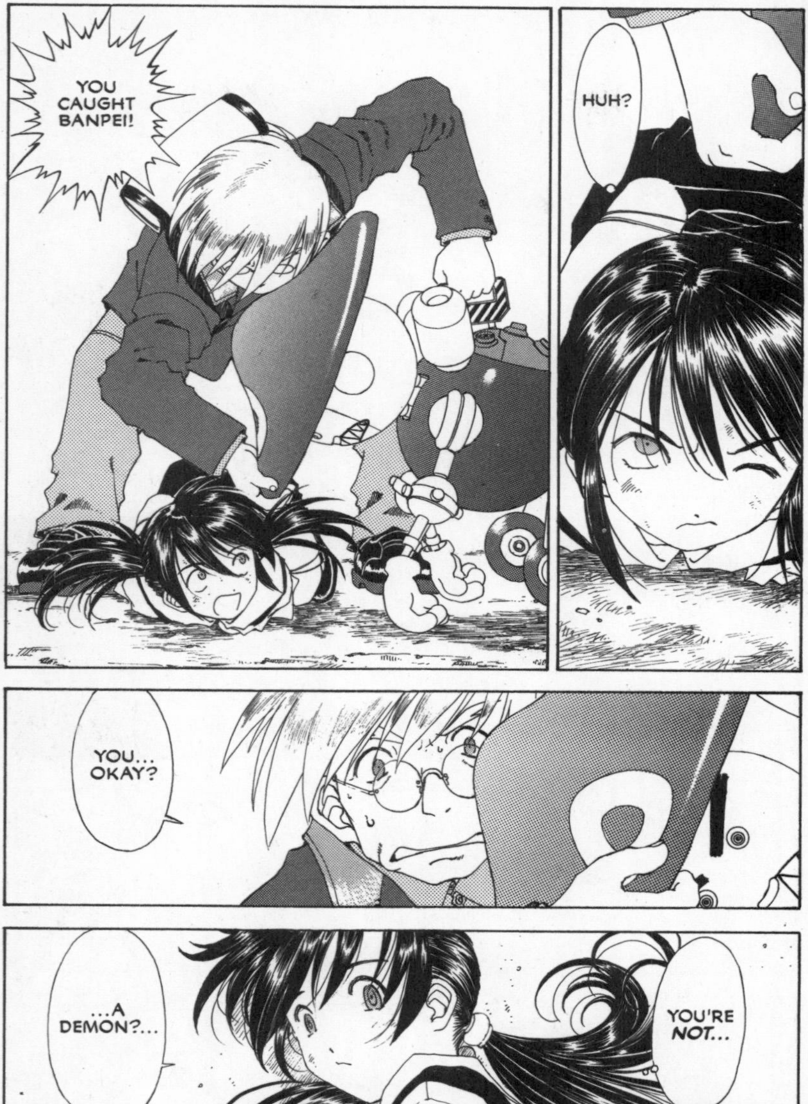
HUH?
YOU CAUGHT BANPEI!
YOU... OKAY?
YOU'RE *NOT*...
...A DEMON?...

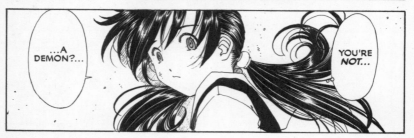

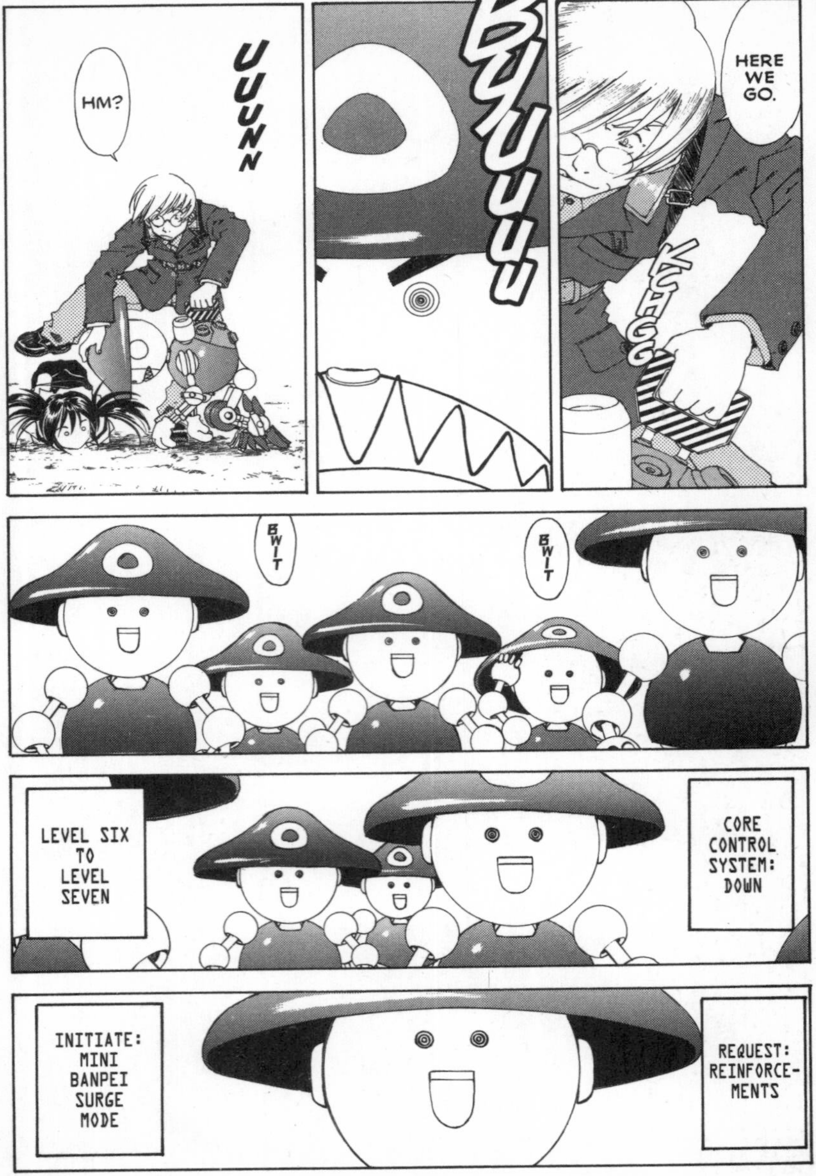
HERE WE GO.
KCHGG
BYUUUUUU
UUUUNN
HM?
BWIT
BWIT
CORE CONTROL SYSTEM: DOWN
LEVEL SIX TO LEVEL SEVEN
REQUEST: REINFORCE-MENTS
INITIATE: MINI BANPEI SURGE MODE

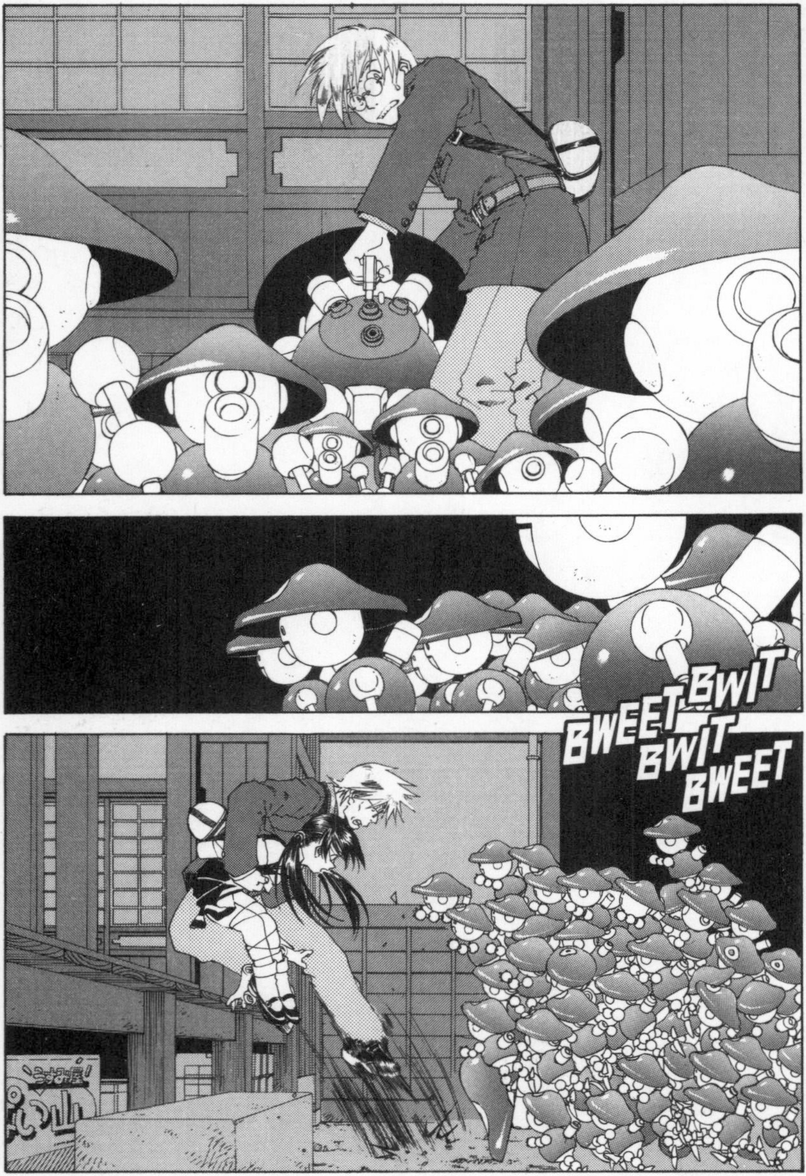
BWEET BWIT
BWIT
BWEET

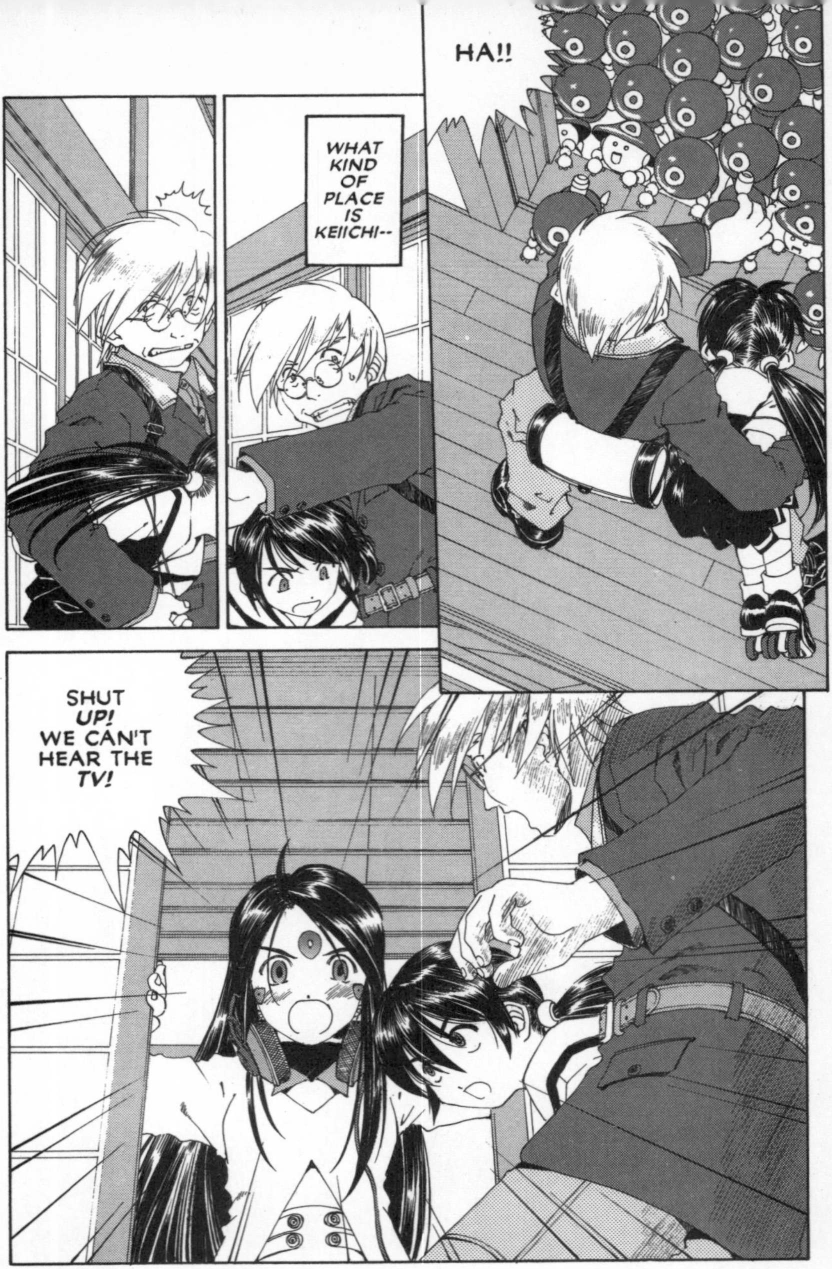
HA!!
WHAT KIND OF PLACE IS KEIICHI--
SHUT *UP!* WE CAN'T HEAR THE *TV!*

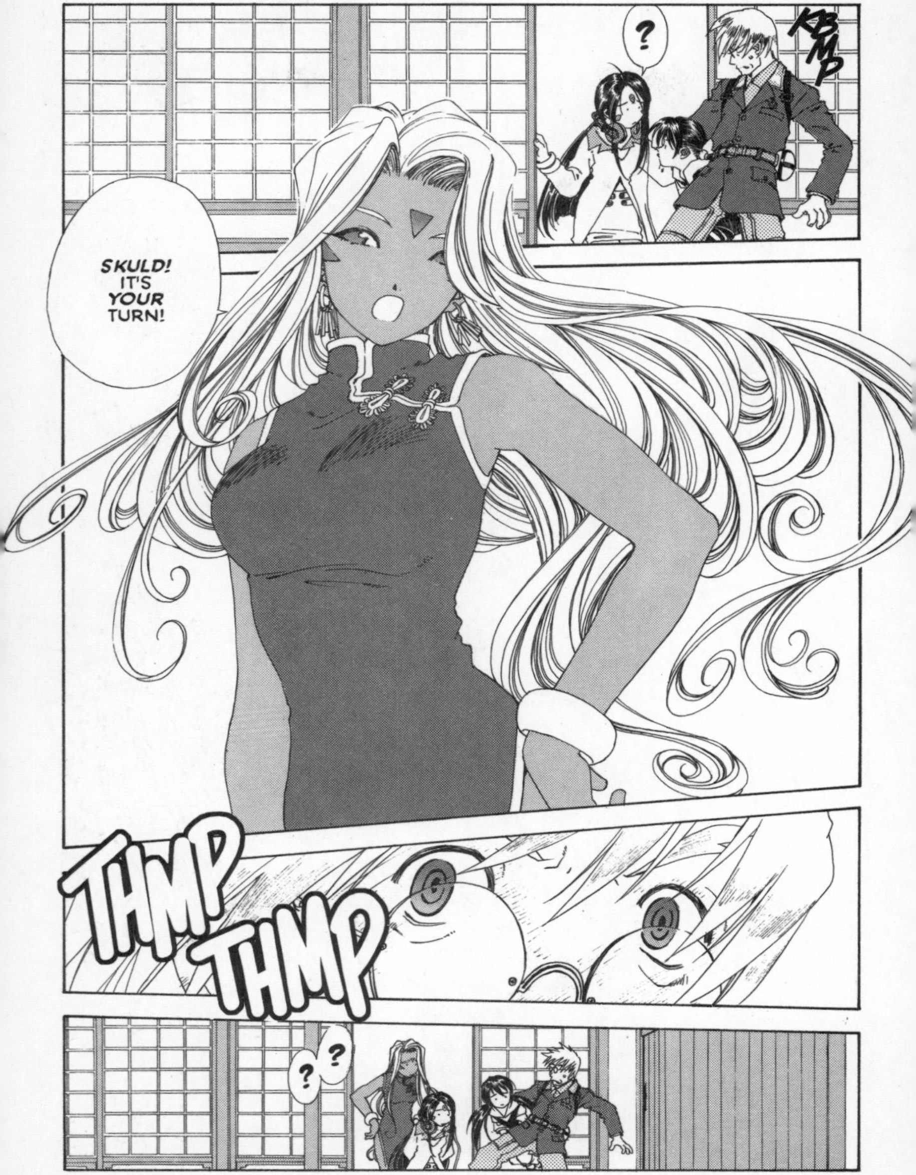
KBMP
?
SKULD! IT'S YOUR TURN!
THMP THMP
? ?

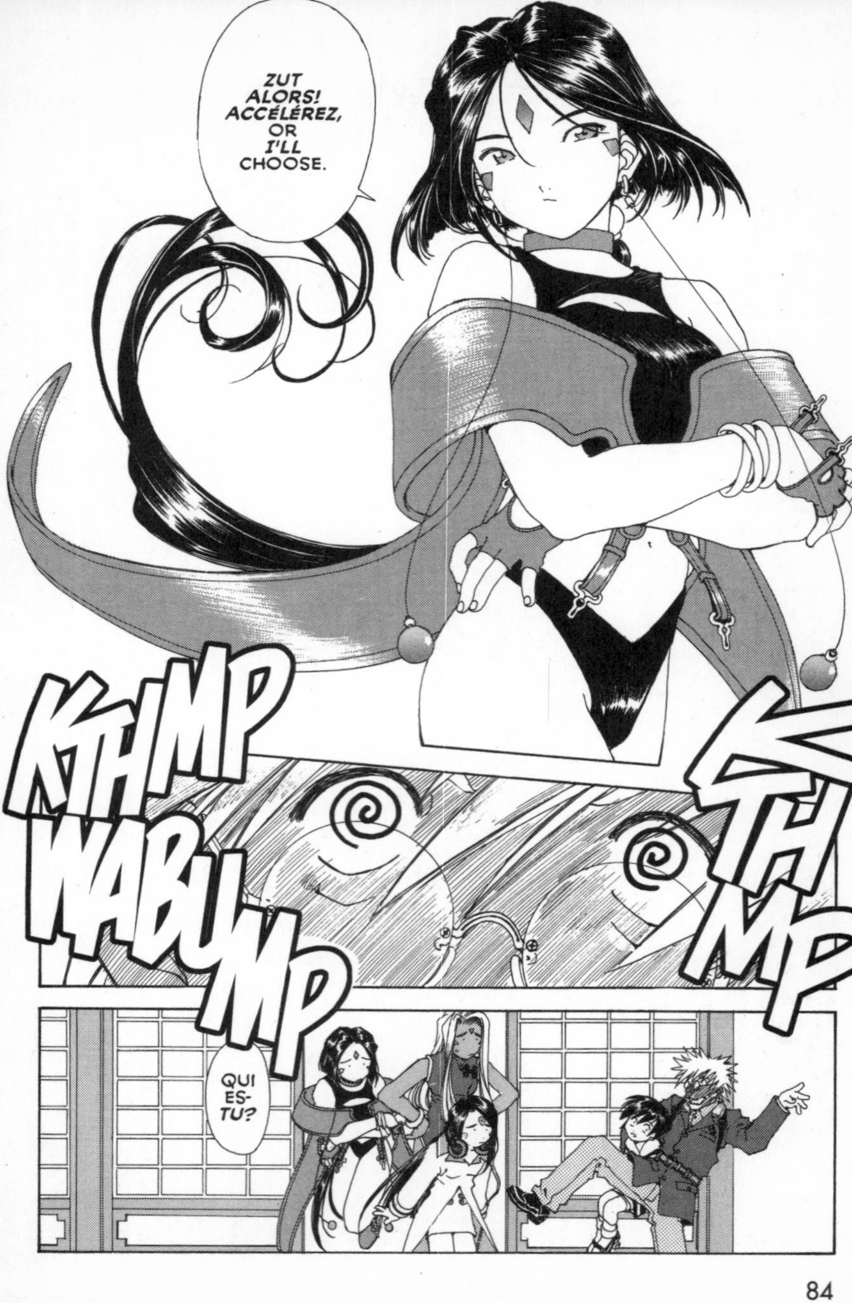
ZUT ALORS! ACCÉLÉREZ, OR I'LL CHOOSE.
KTHMP
KTHIMP
WABUMP
QUI ES-TU?

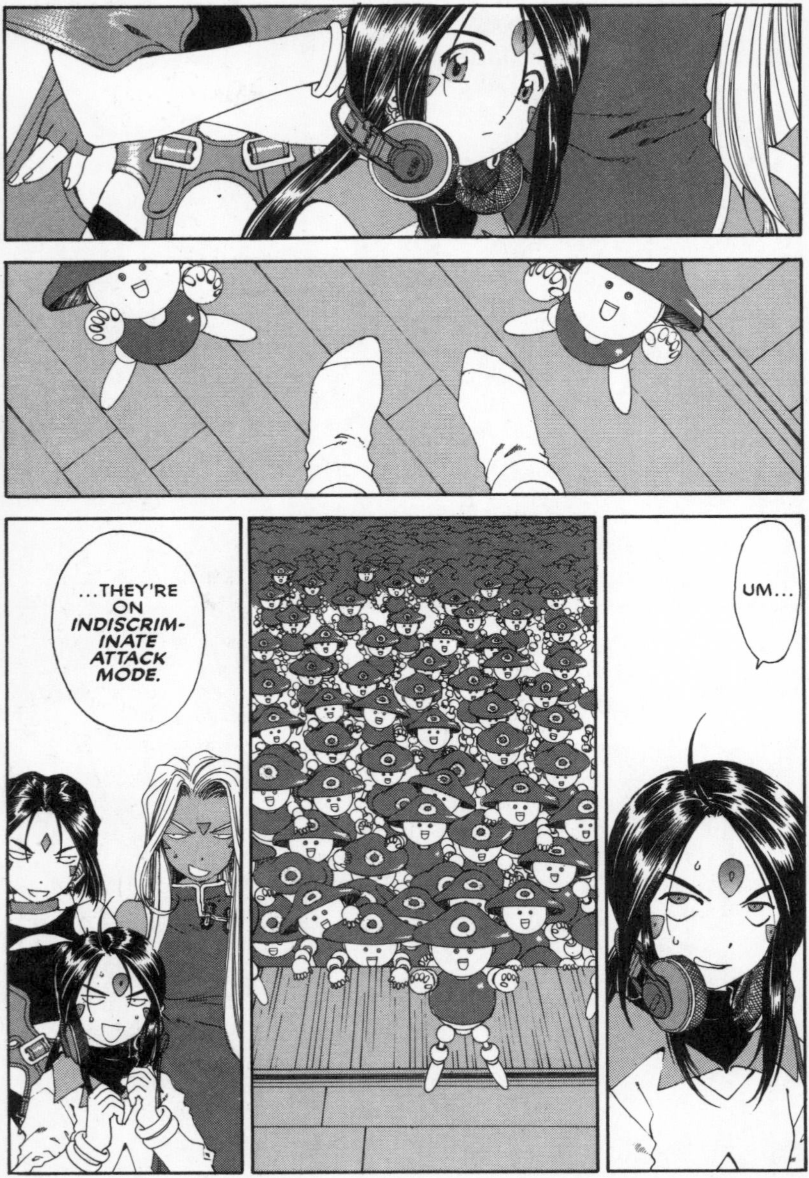
UM...
...THEY'RE ON INDISCRIMINATE ATTACK MODE.

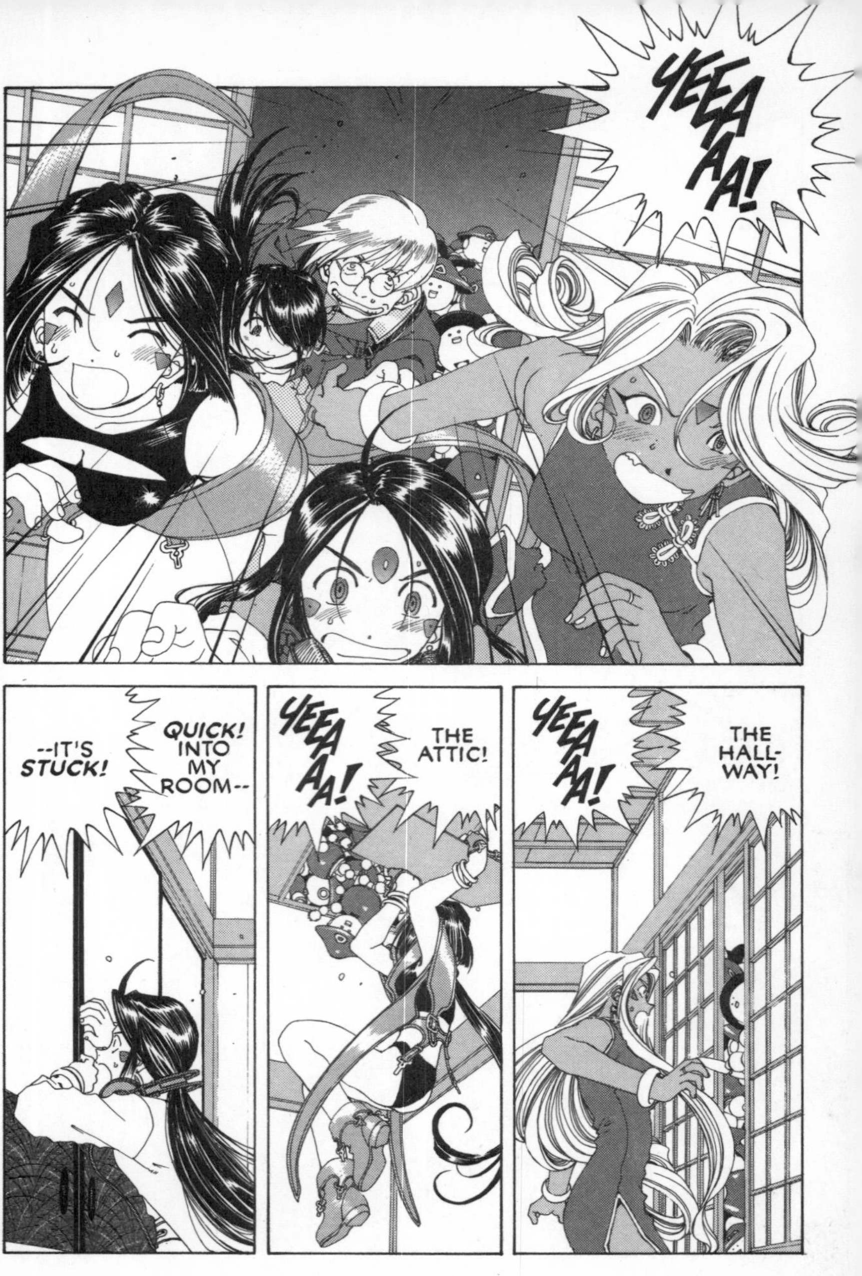

YEEEAAA!
YEEEAAA!
THE HALL-WAY!
YEEEAAA!
THE ATTIC!
QUICK! INTO MY ROOM--
--IT'S STUCK!

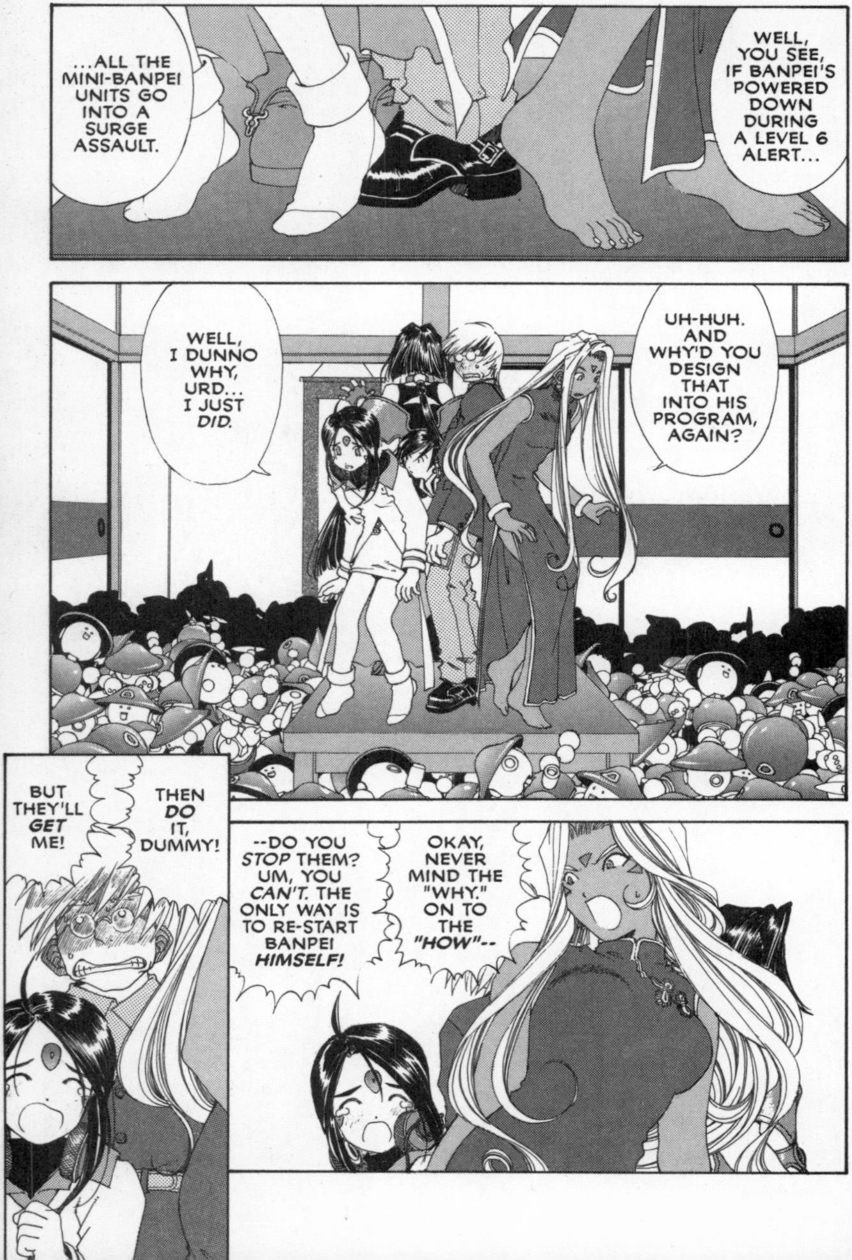
WELL, YOU SEE, IF BANPEI'S POWERED DOWN DURING A LEVEL 6 ALERT...
...ALL THE MINI-BANPEI UNITS GO INTO A SURGE ASSAULT.
UH-HUH. AND WHY'D YOU DESIGN THAT INTO HIS PROGRAM, AGAIN?
WELL, I DUNNO WHY, URD... I JUST *DID.*
OKAY, NEVER MIND THE "WHY." ON TO THE ***"HOW"***--
--DO YOU *STOP* THEM? UM, YOU *CAN'T.* THE ONLY WAY IS TO RE-START BANPEI ***HIMSELF!***
THEN *DO* IT, DUMMY!
BUT THEY'LL *GET* ME!

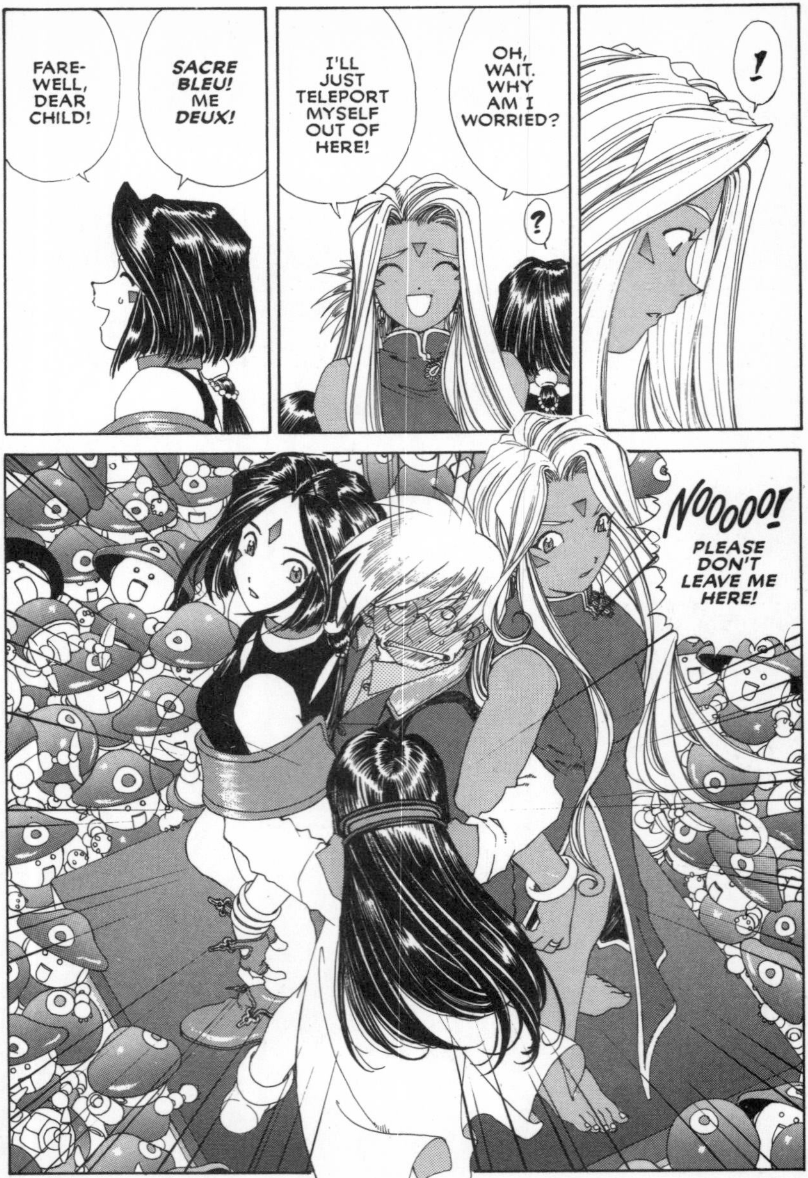
!
OH, WAIT. WHY AM I WORRIED?
I'LL JUST TELEPORT MYSELF OUT OF HERE!
?
SACRE BLEU! ME DEUX!
FARE-WELL, DEAR CHILD!
NOOOOO! PLEASE DON'T LEAVE ME HERE!

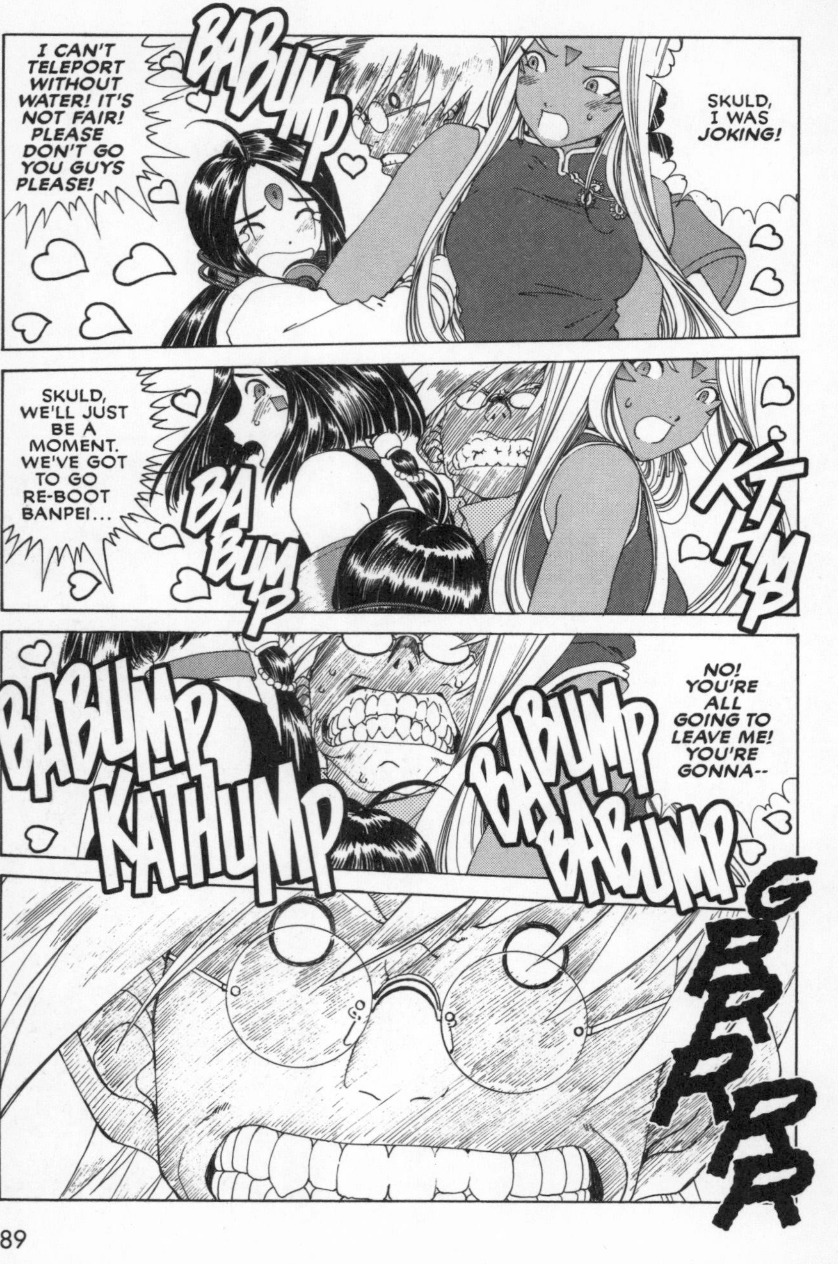
BABUMP
I CAN'T TELEPORT WITHOUT WATER! IT'S NOT FAIR! PLEASE DON'T GO YOU GUYS PLEASE!
SKULD, I WAS JOKING!
SKULD, WE'LL JUST BE A MOMENT. WE'VE GOT TO GO RE-BOOT BANPEI...
BABUMP
KTHMP
BABUMP KATHUMP
BABUMP BABUMP BABUMP
NO! YOU'RE ALL GOING TO LEAVE ME! YOU'RE GONNA--
GRRRRRR

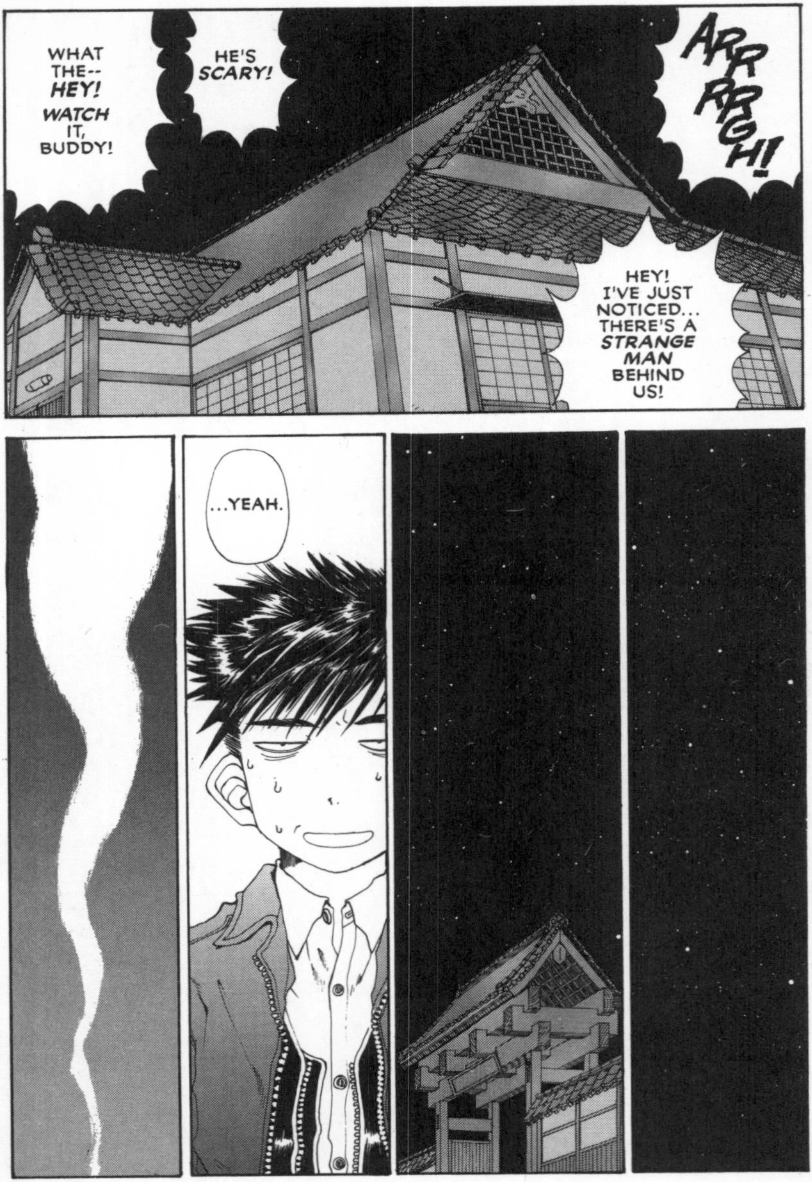
ARRRRGH!
HEY! I'VE JUST NOTICED... THERE'S A STRANGE MAN BEHIND US!
HE'S SCARY!
WHAT THE-- HEY! WATCH IT, BUDDY!
...YEAH.

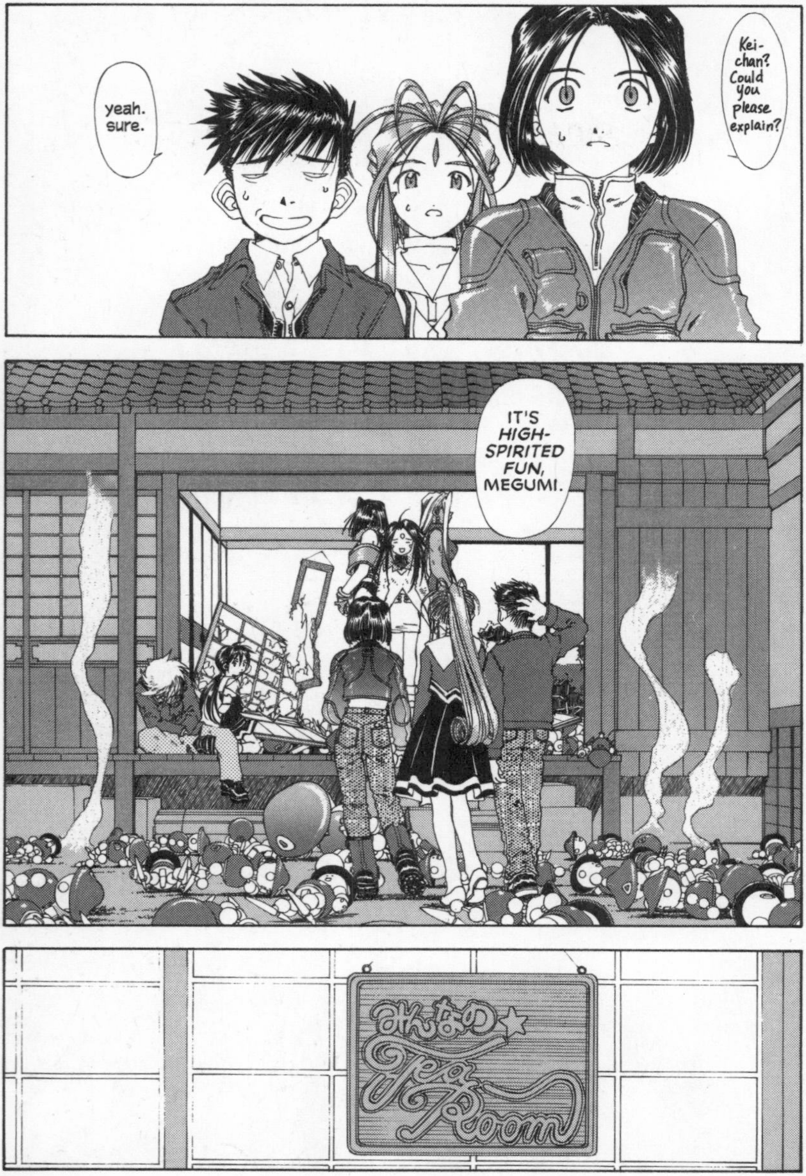
Kei-chan? Could you please explain?
yeah. sure.
IT'S HIGH-SPIRITED FUN, MEGUMI.
みんなの★
Tea Room

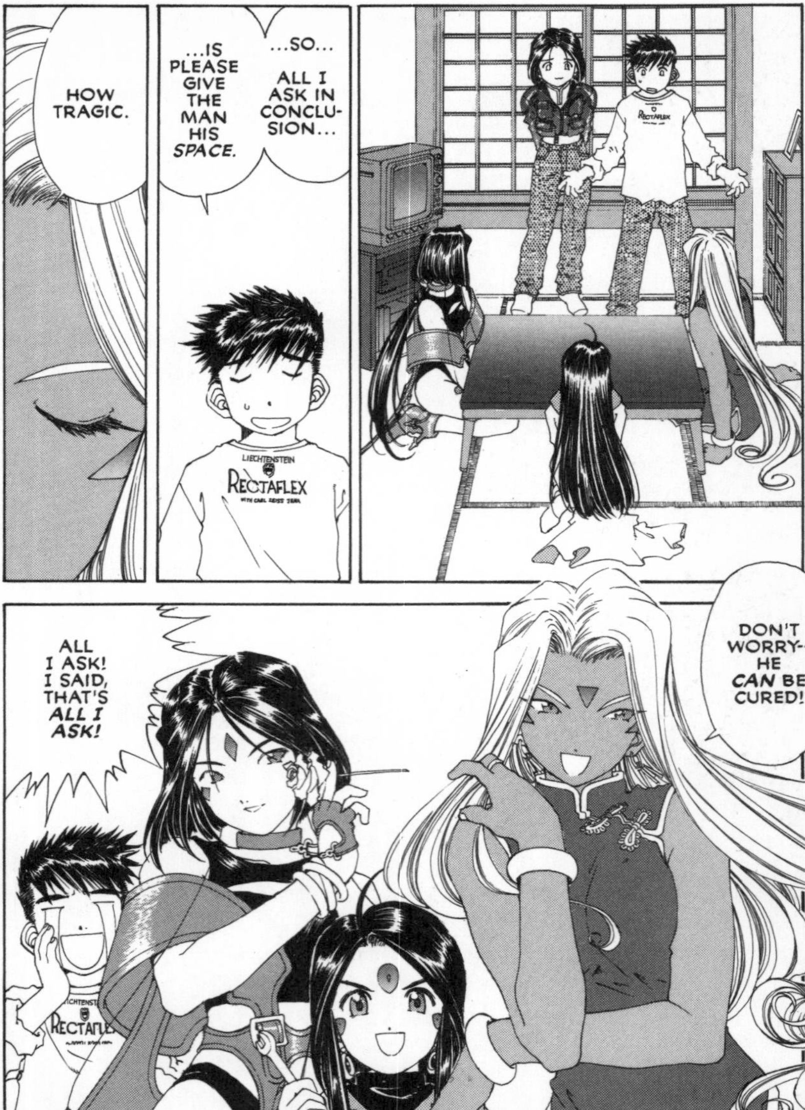
...SO... ALL I ASK IN CONCLUSION...
...IS PLEASE GIVE THE MAN HIS *SPACE.*
HOW TRAGIC.
DON'T WORRY-- HE *CAN* BE CURED!
ALL I ASK! I SAID, THAT'S ***ALL I ASK!***

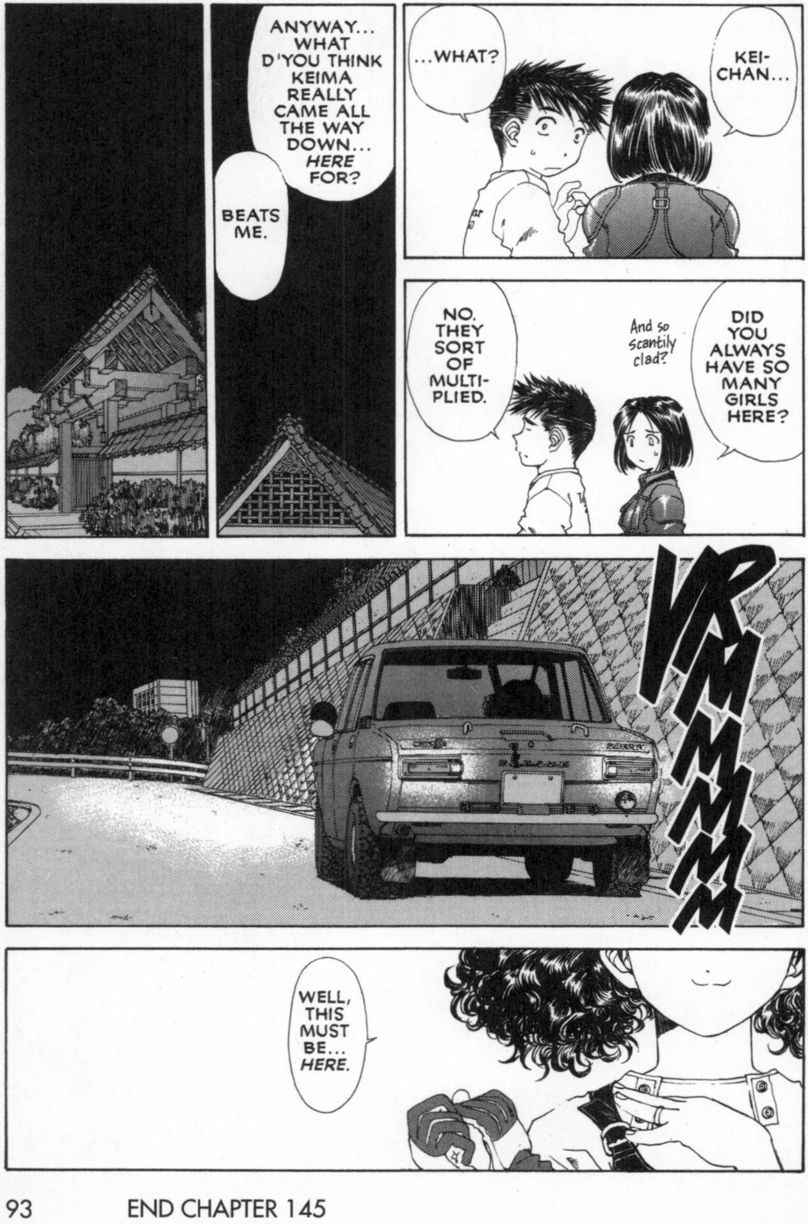
KEI-CHAN...
...WHAT?
DID YOU ALWAYS HAVE SO MANY GIRLS HERE?
And so scantily clad?
NO. THEY SORT OF MULTI-PLIED.
ANYWAY... WHAT D'YOU THINK KEIMA REALLY CAME ALL THE WAY DOWN... *HERE* FOR?
BEATS ME.
VRMMMMMM
WELL, THIS MUST BE... *HERE.*

END CHAPTER 145

OH MY GODDESS!

TAKANO

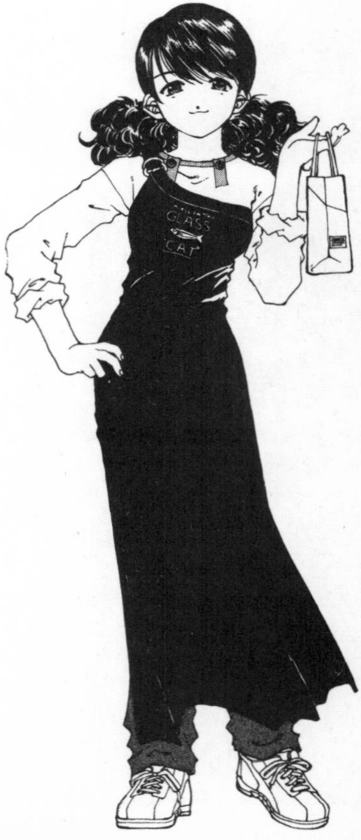
GLASS
CAT

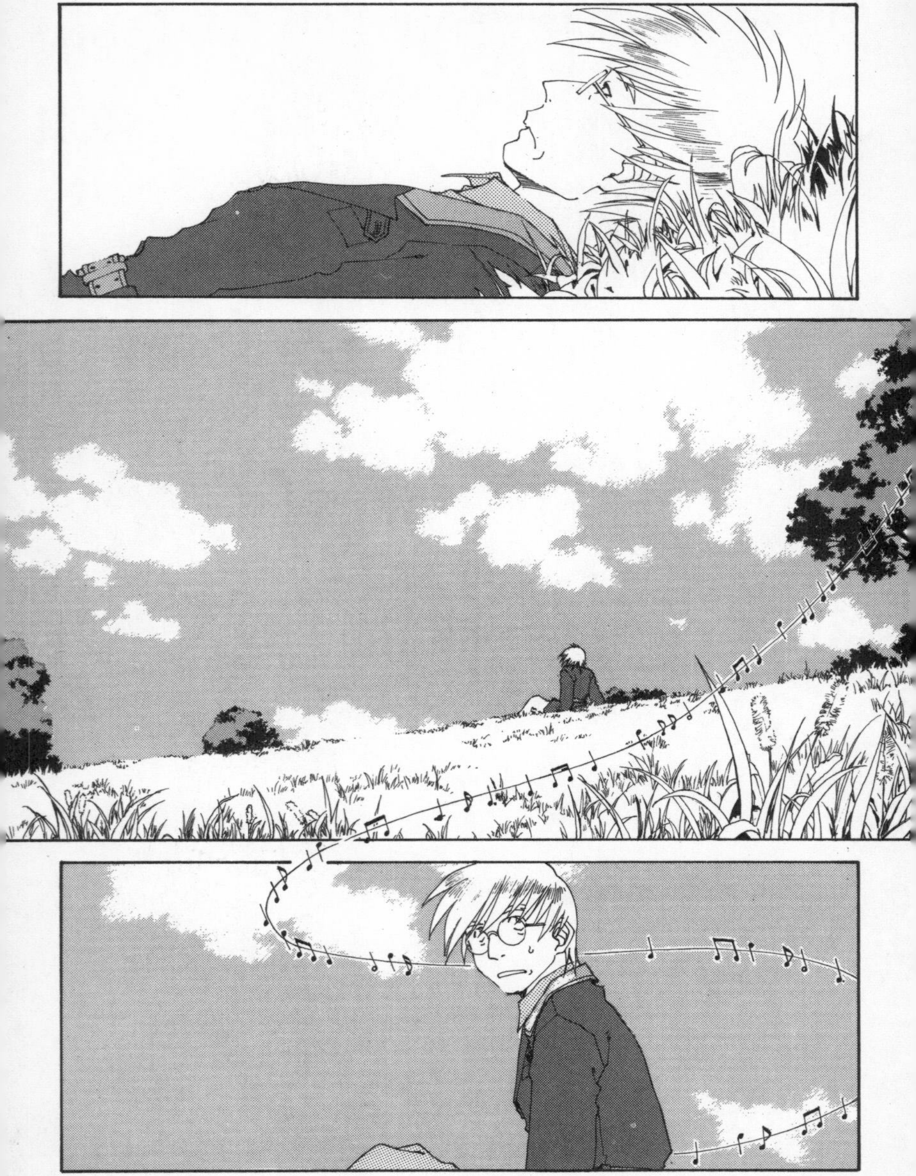

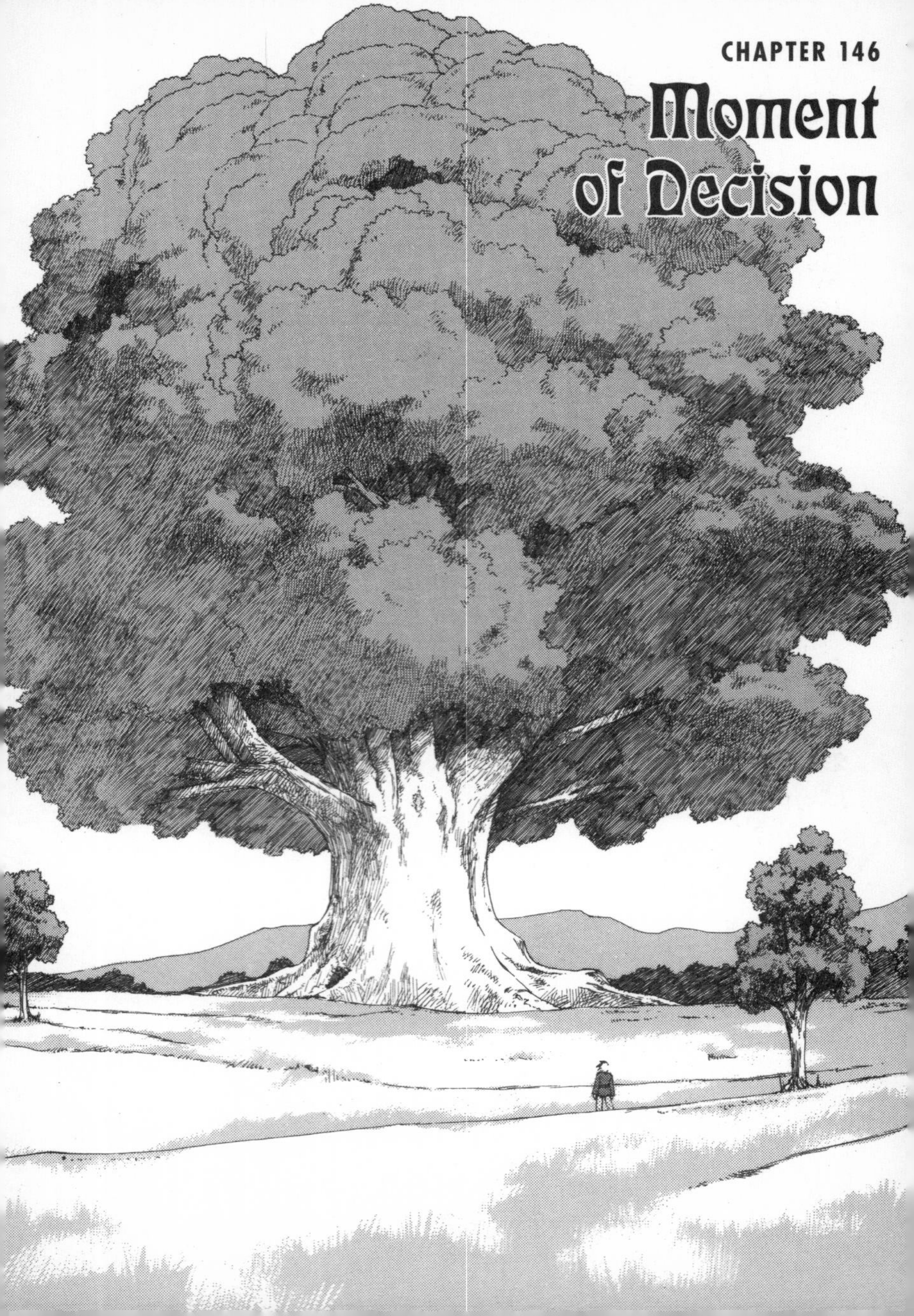
CHAPTER 146
Moment
of Decision

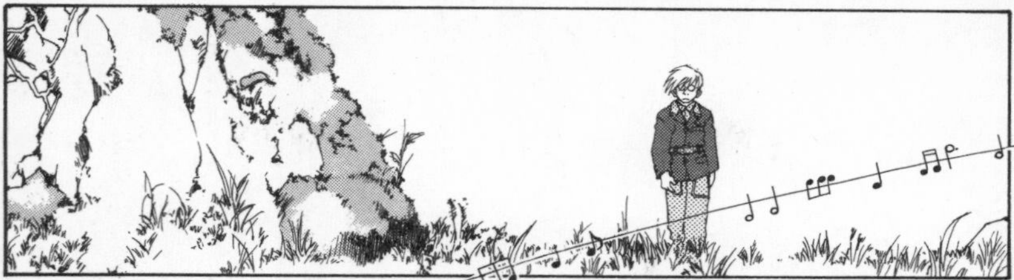
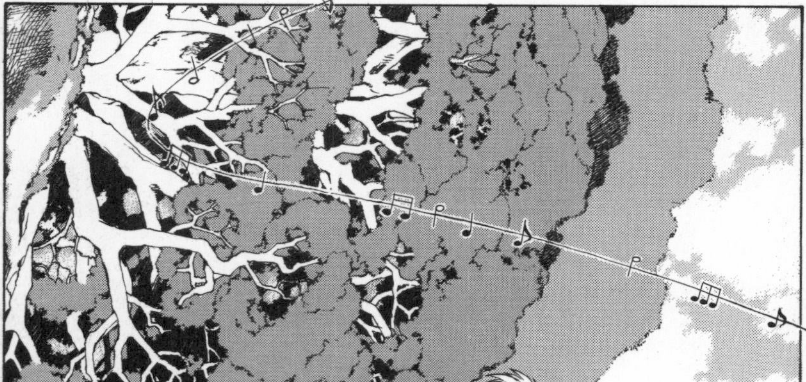
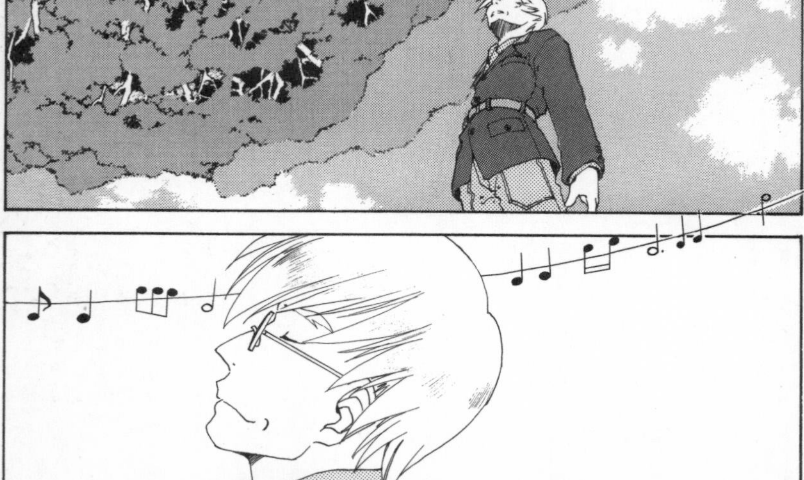

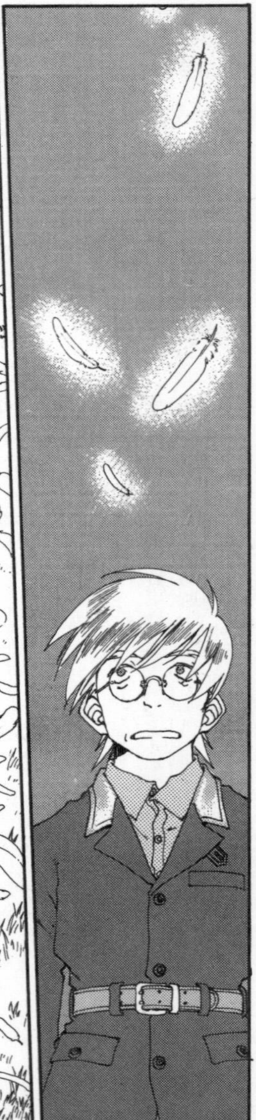

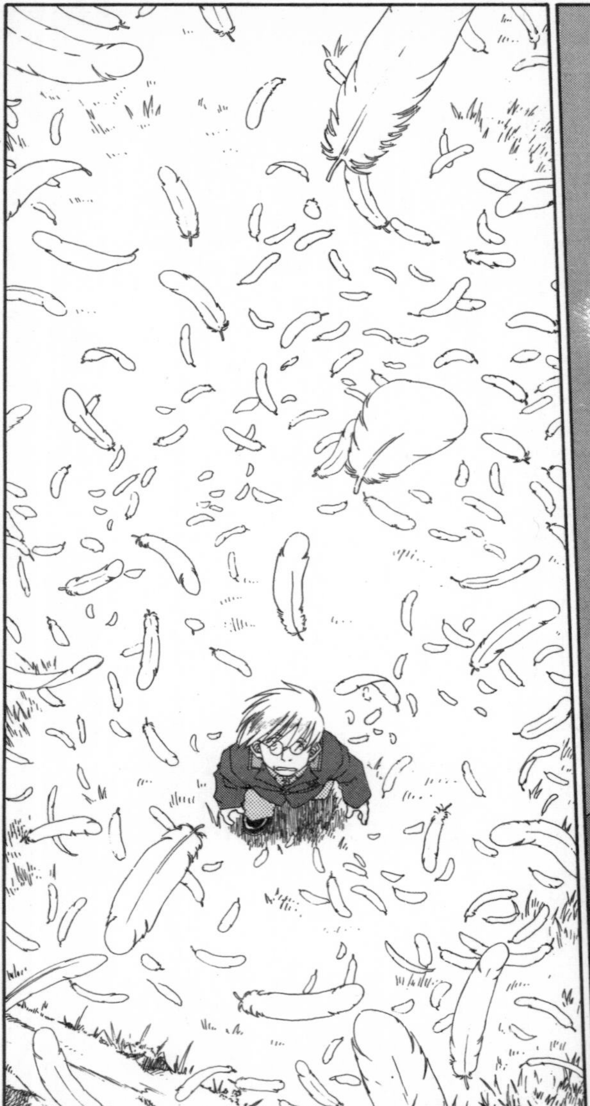

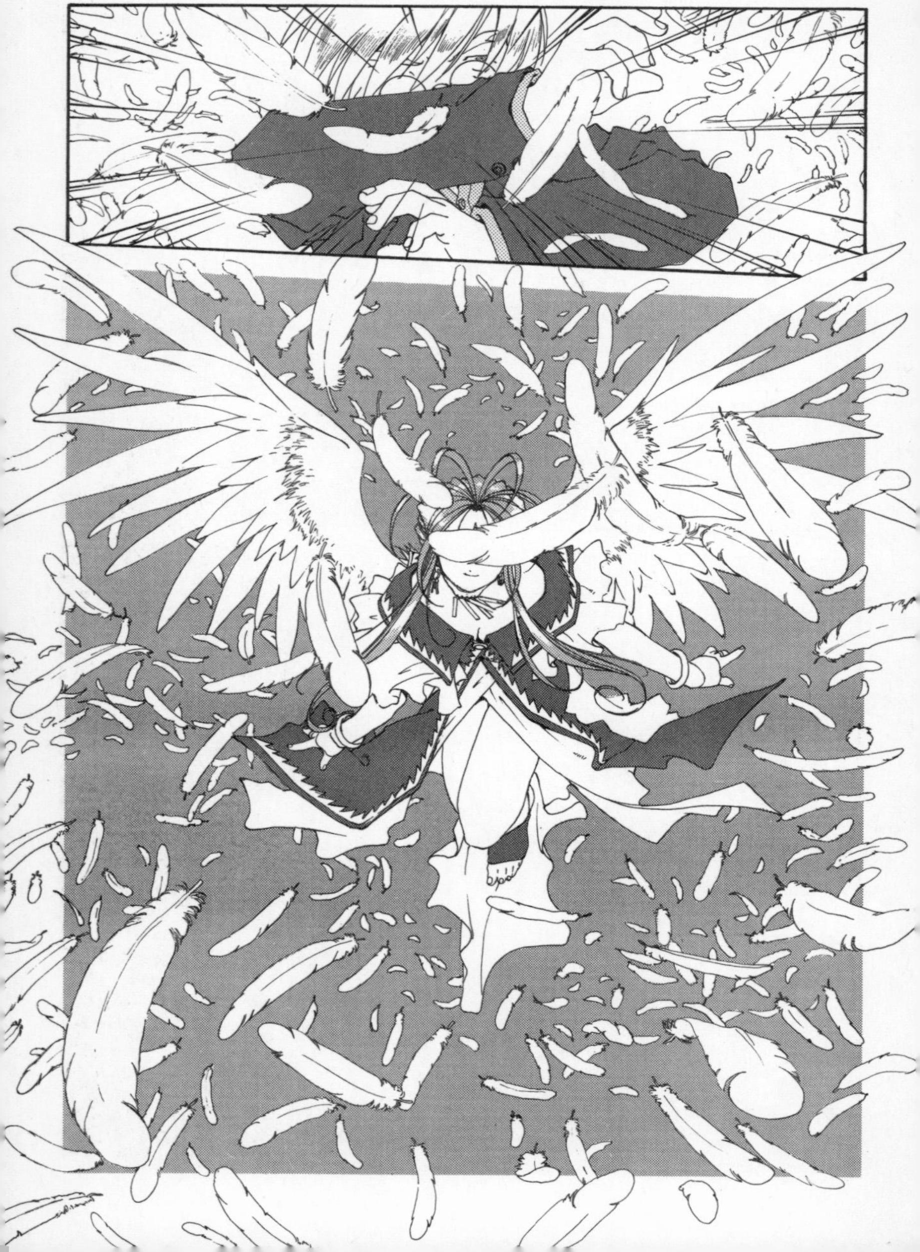

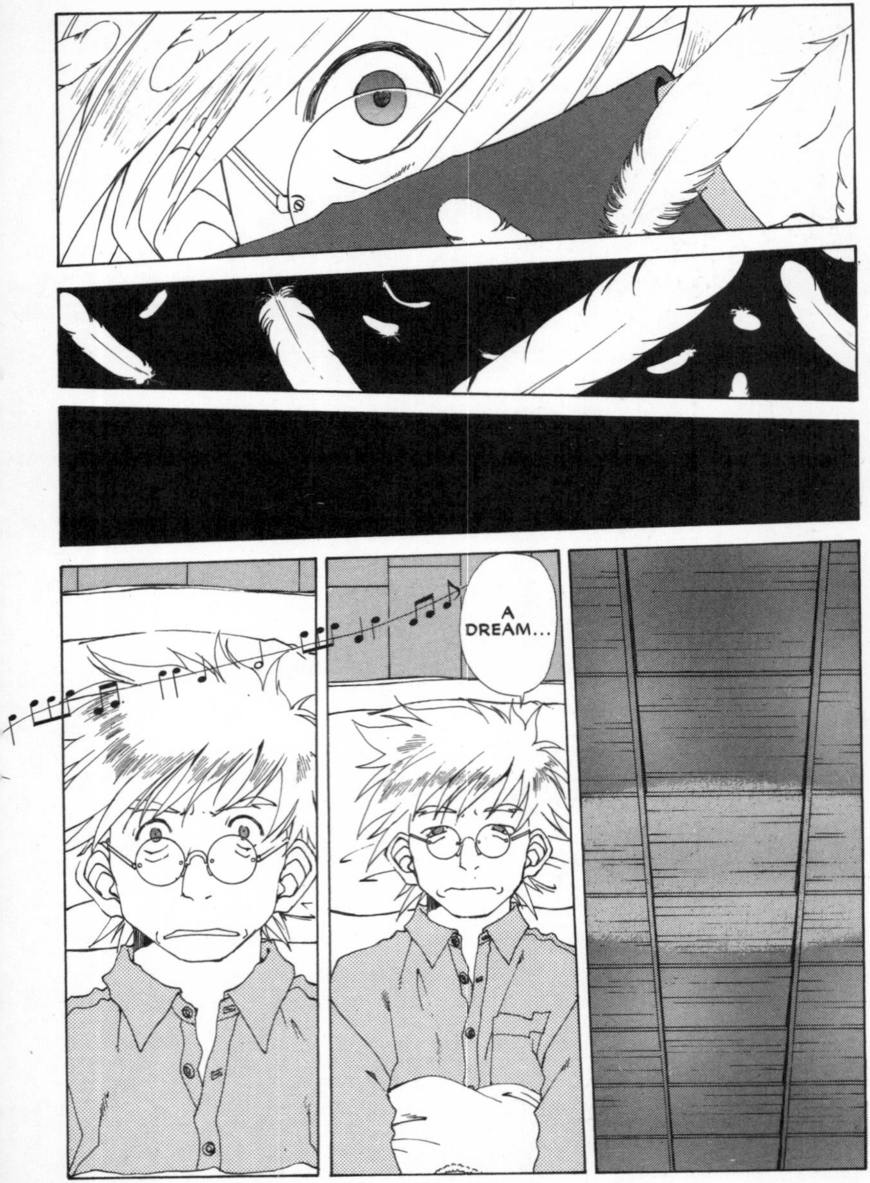
A DREAM...

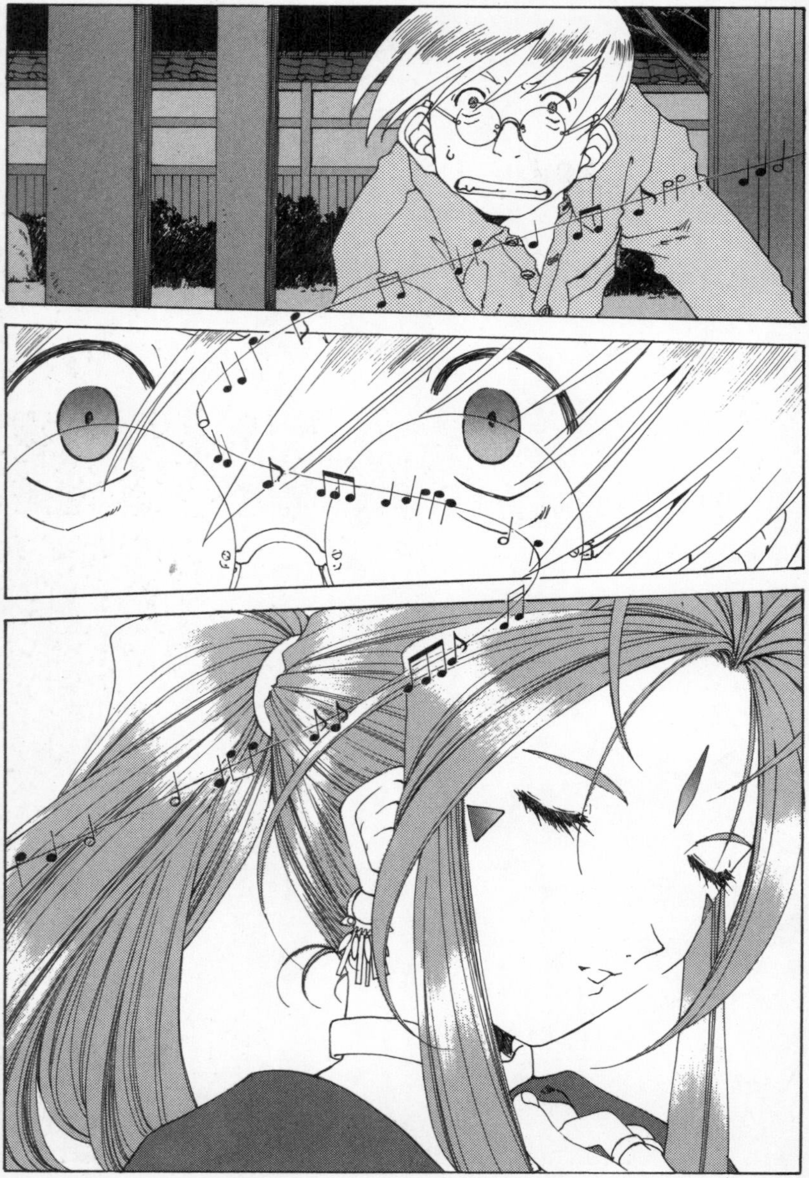

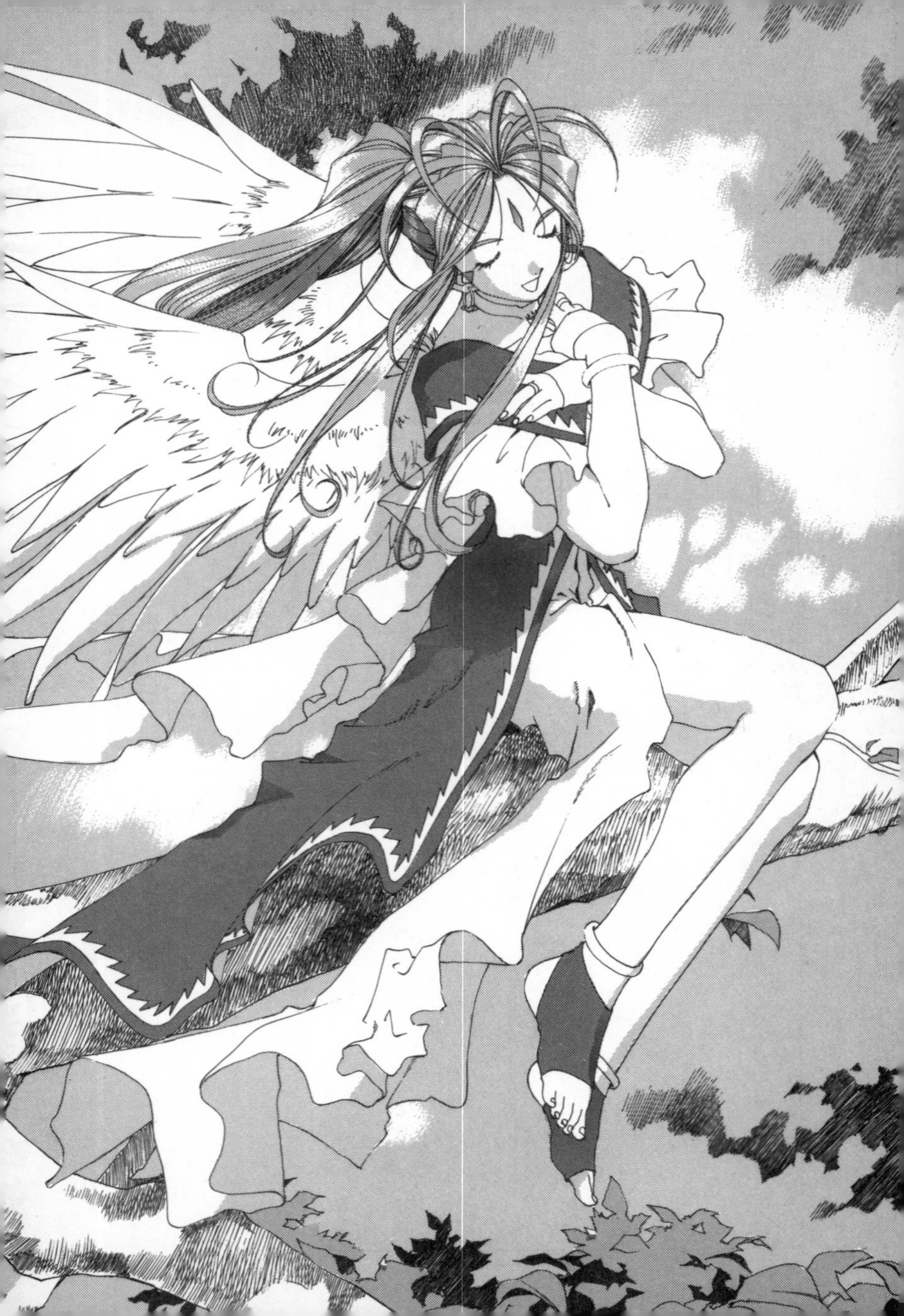

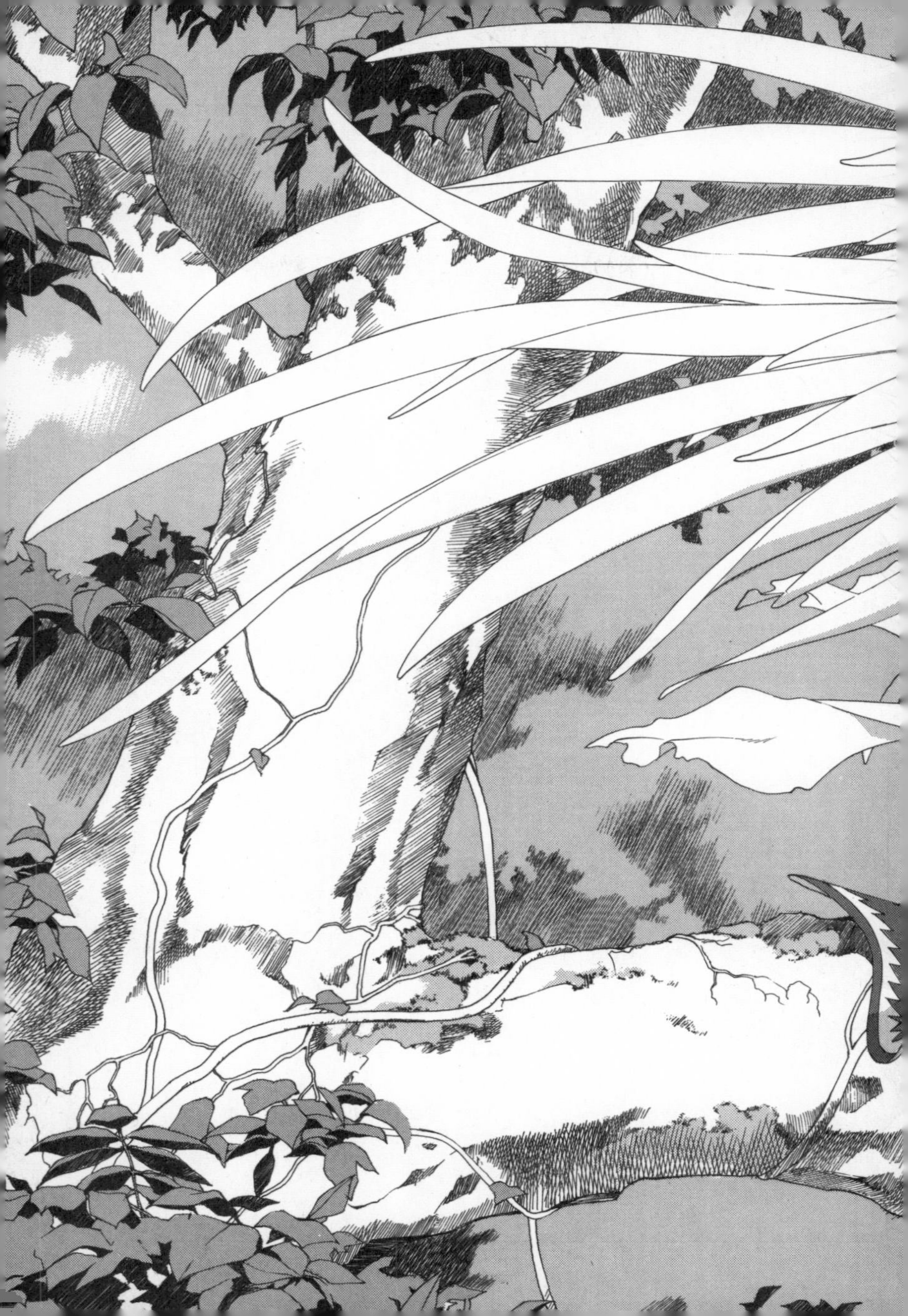

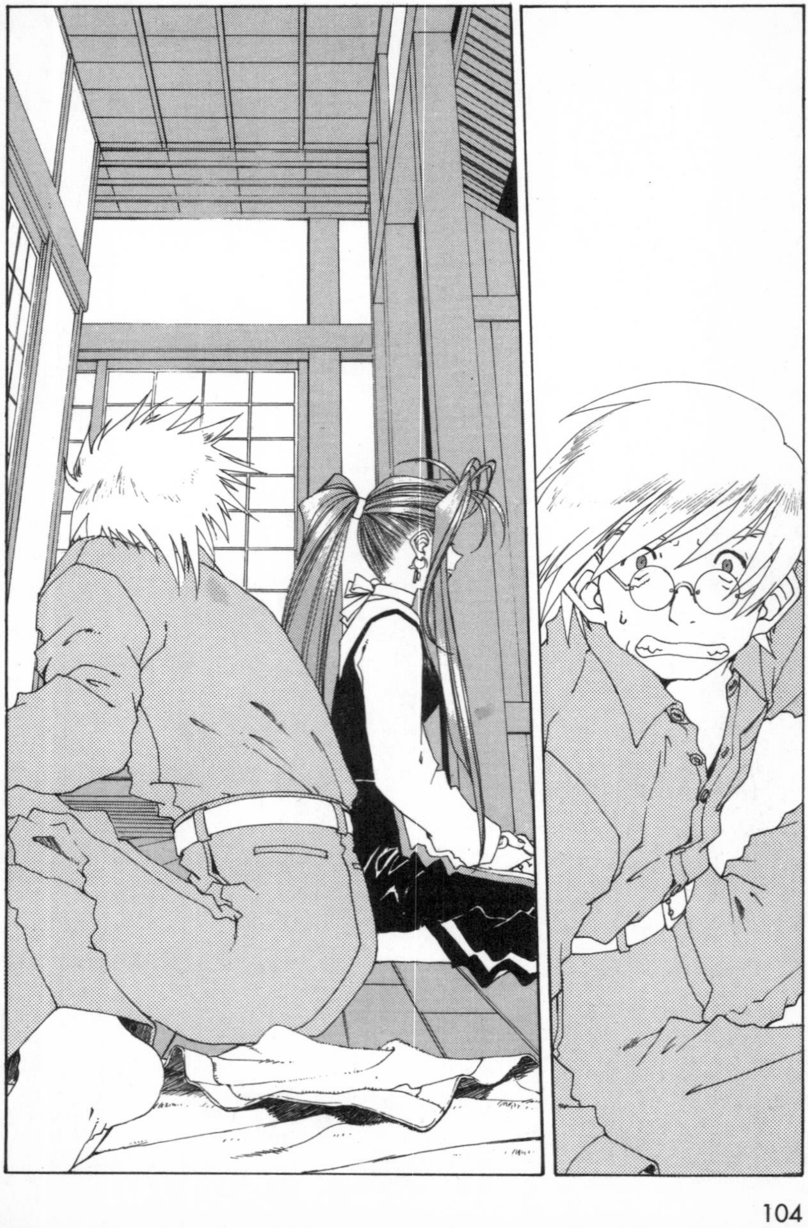

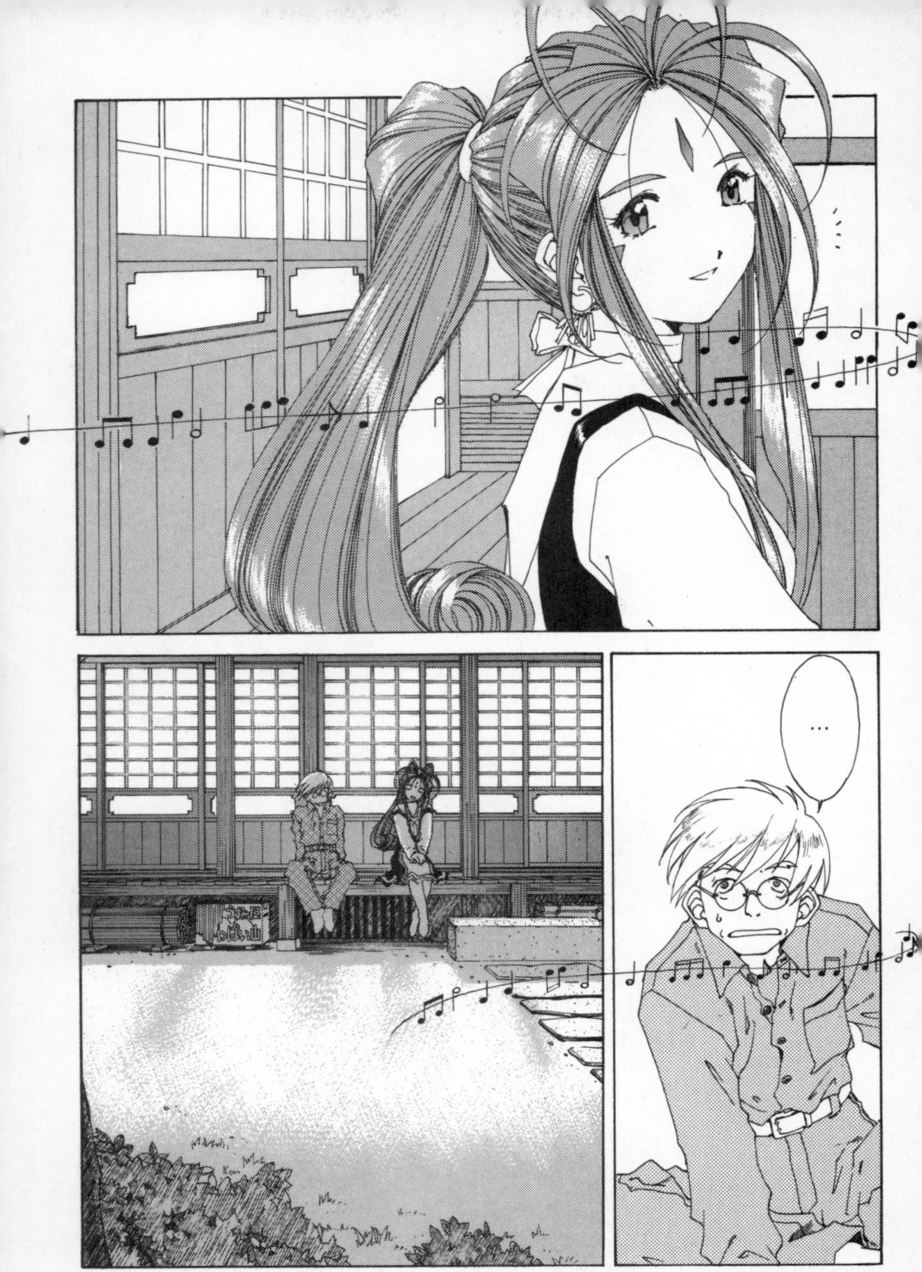
...

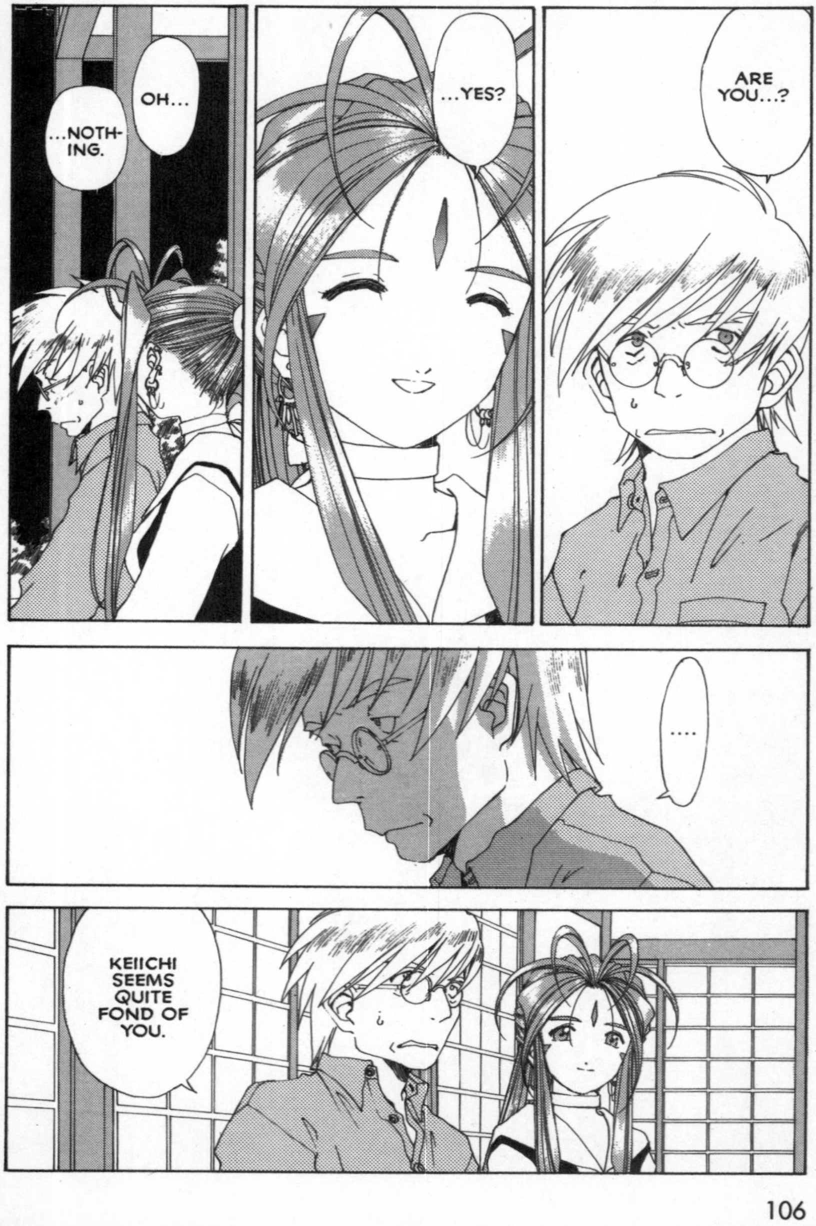
ARE YOU...?
...YES?
OH...
...NOTH-ING.
....
KEIICHI SEEMS QUITE FOND OF YOU.

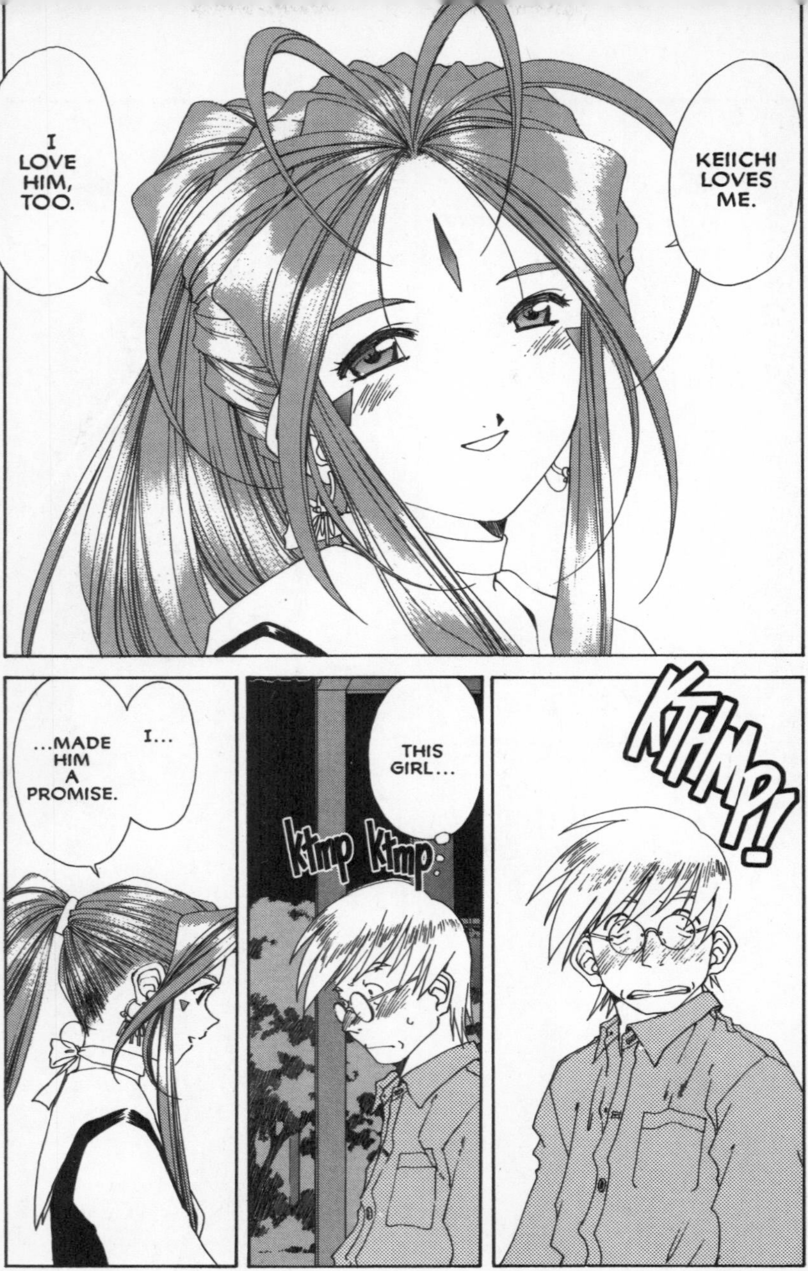
KEIICHI LOVES ME.
I LOVE HIM, TOO.
KTHMP!
ktmp ktmp
THIS GIRL...
I...
...MADE HIM A PROMISE.

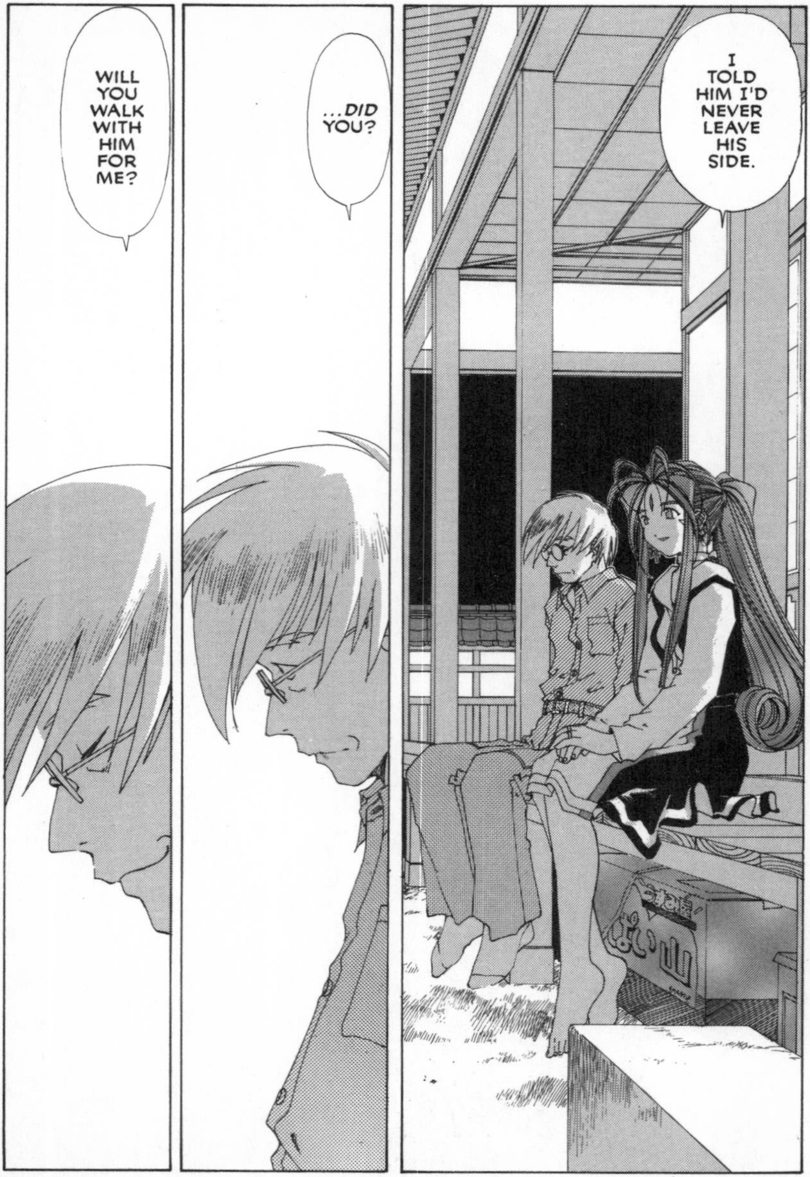
I TOLD HIM I'D NEVER LEAVE HIS SIDE.
...DID YOU?
WILL YOU WALK WITH HIM FOR ME?

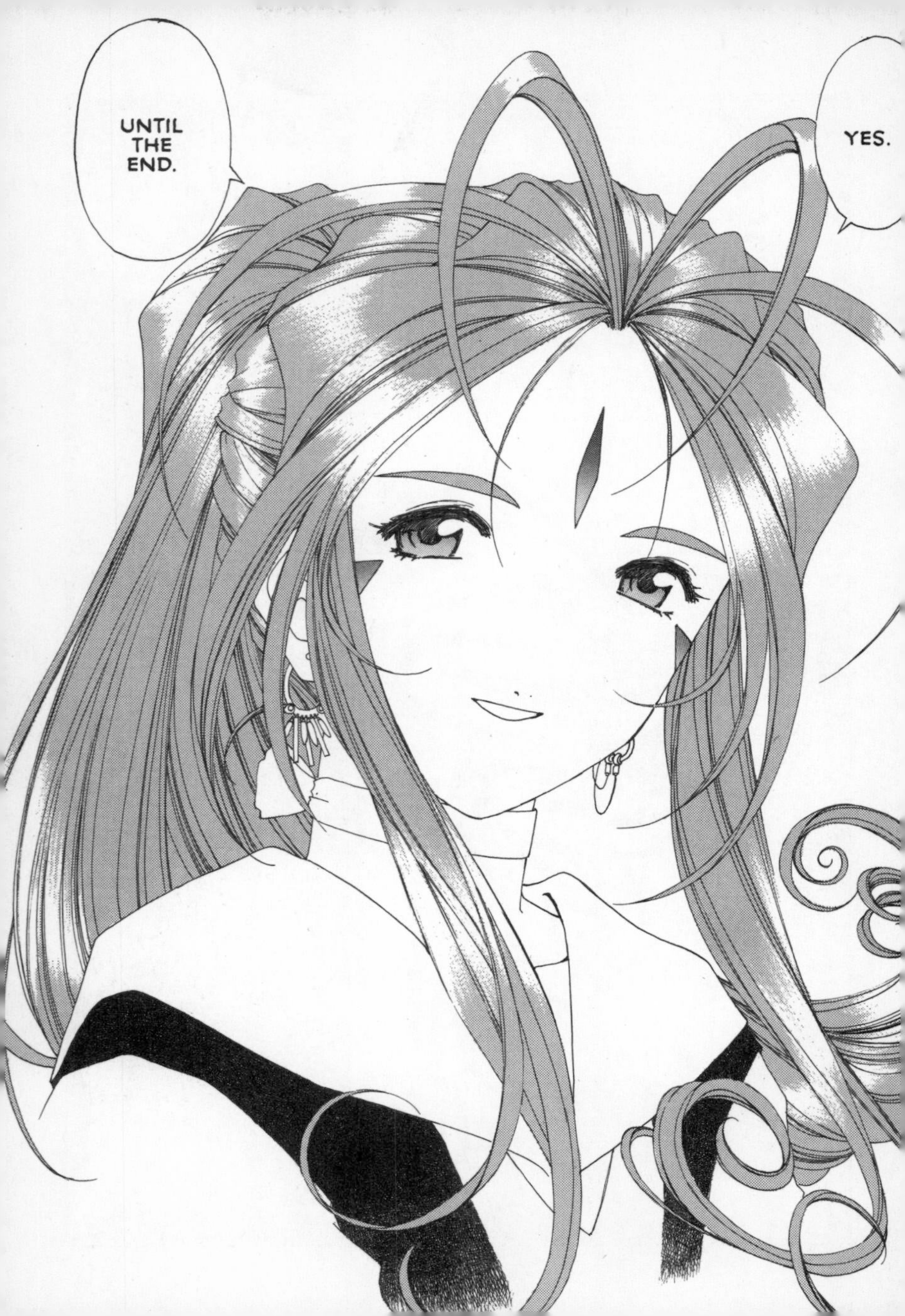
YES.
UNTIL THE END.

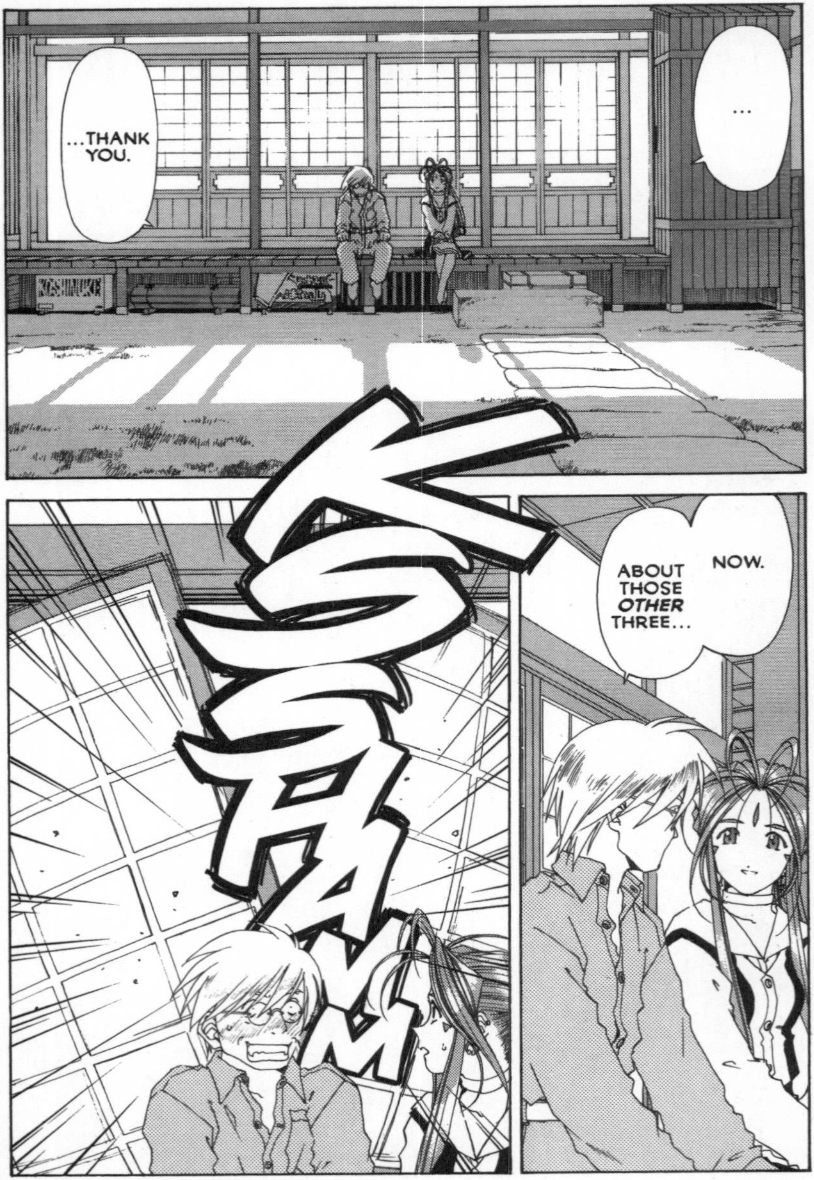
...
...THANK YOU.
NOW.
ABOUT THOSE *OTHER* THREE...

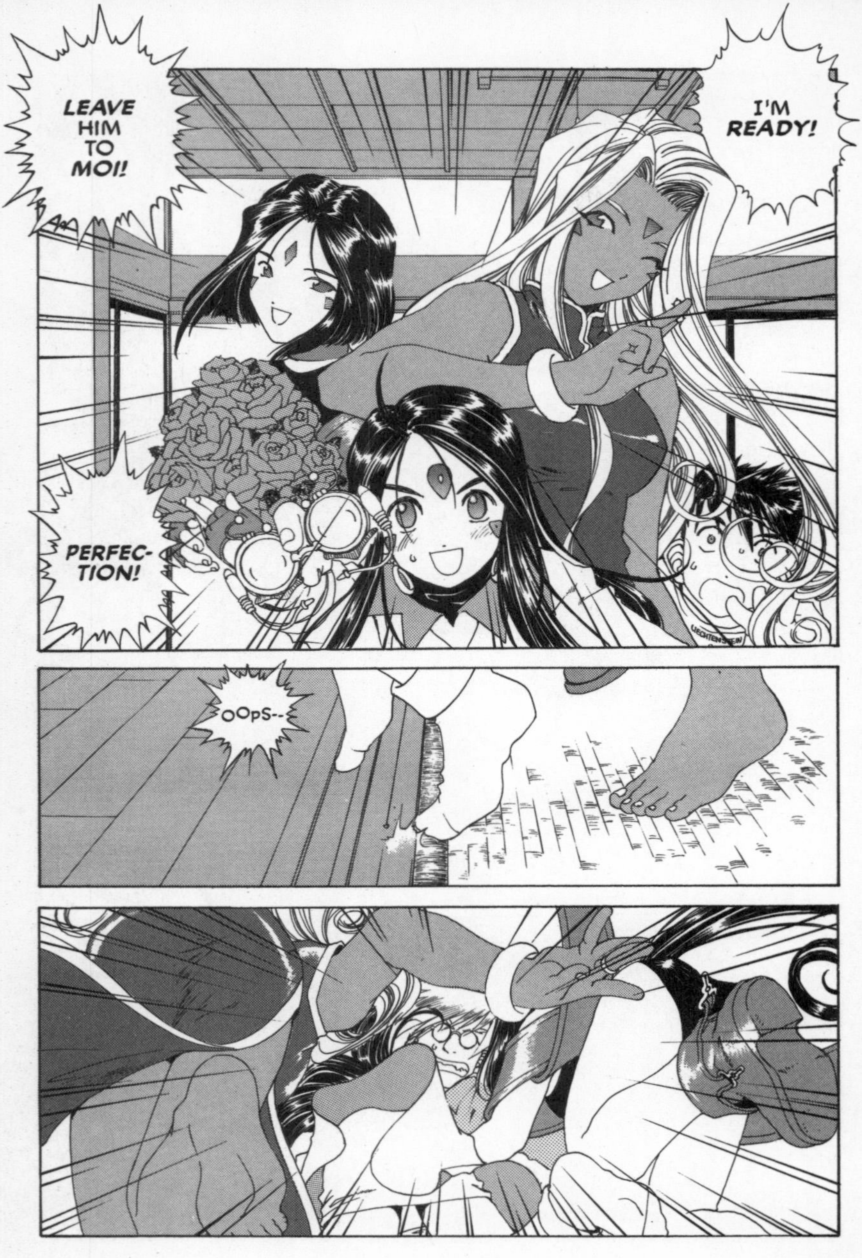
I'M READY!
LEAVE HIM TO MOI!
PERFECTION!
OOPS--

GRRR

GONK

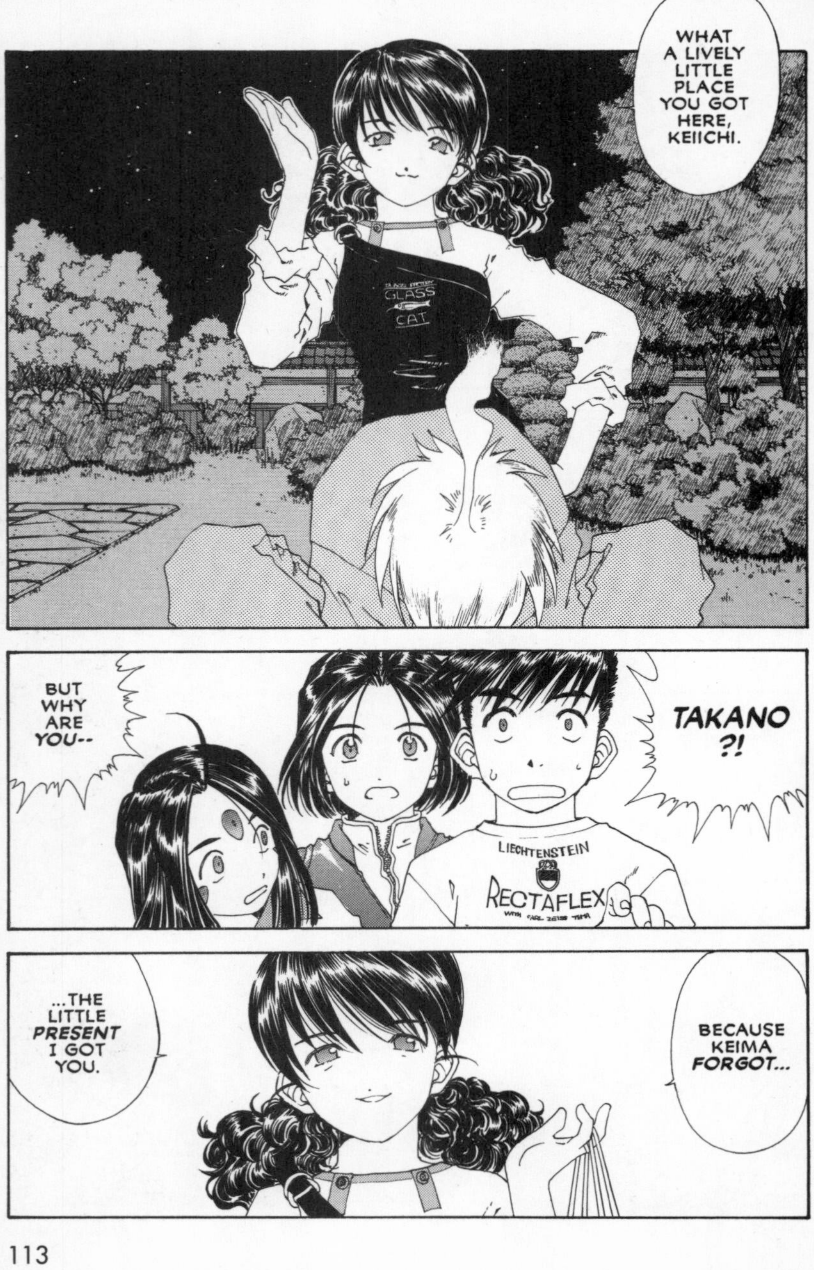
WHAT A LIVELY LITTLE PLACE YOU GOT HERE, KEIICHI.
GLASS CAT
TAKANO ?!
BUT WHY ARE *YOU*--
LIECHTENSTEIN
RECTAFLEX
BECAUSE KEIMA *FORGOT...*
...THE LITTLE *PRESENT* I GOT YOU.

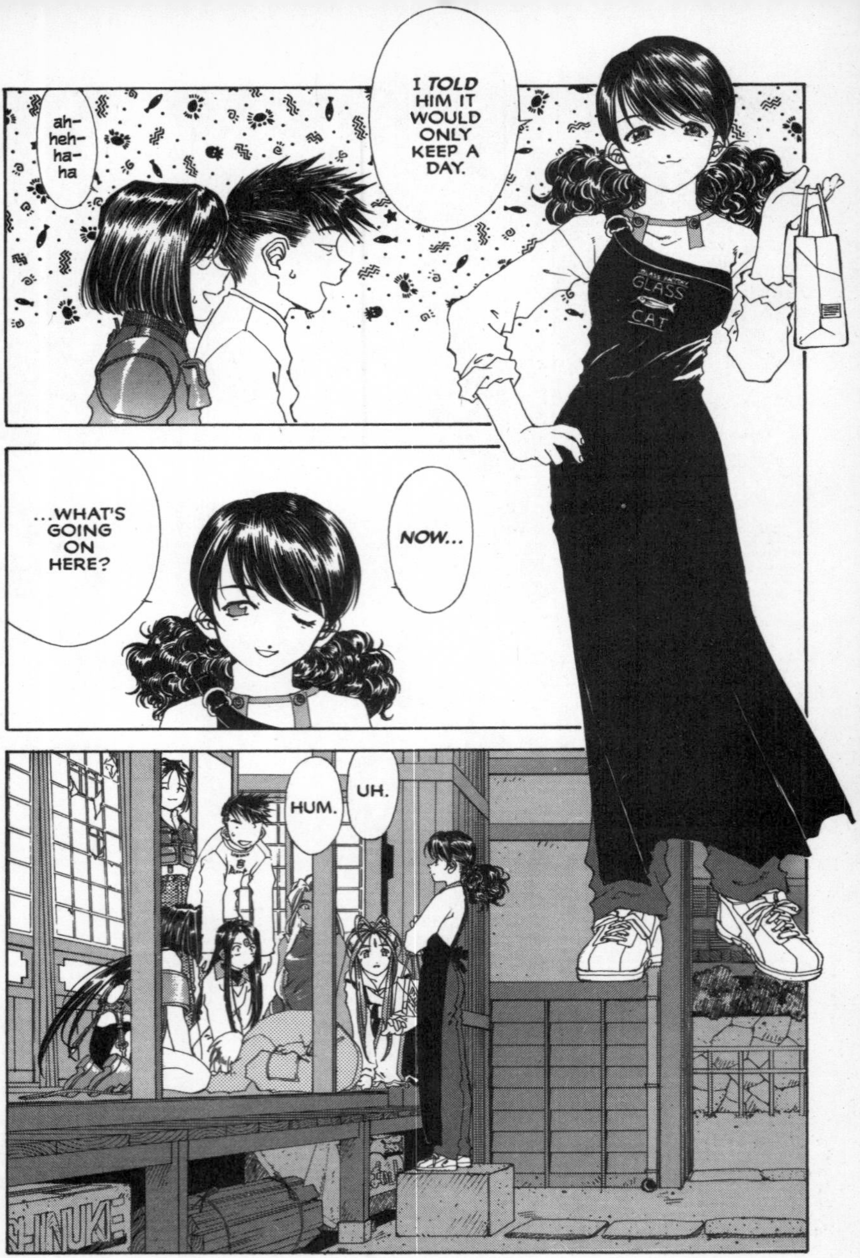
I TOLD HIM IT WOULD ONLY KEEP A DAY.
GLASS CAT
ah-heh-ha-ha
NOW...
...WHAT'S GOING ON HERE?
UH.
HUM.

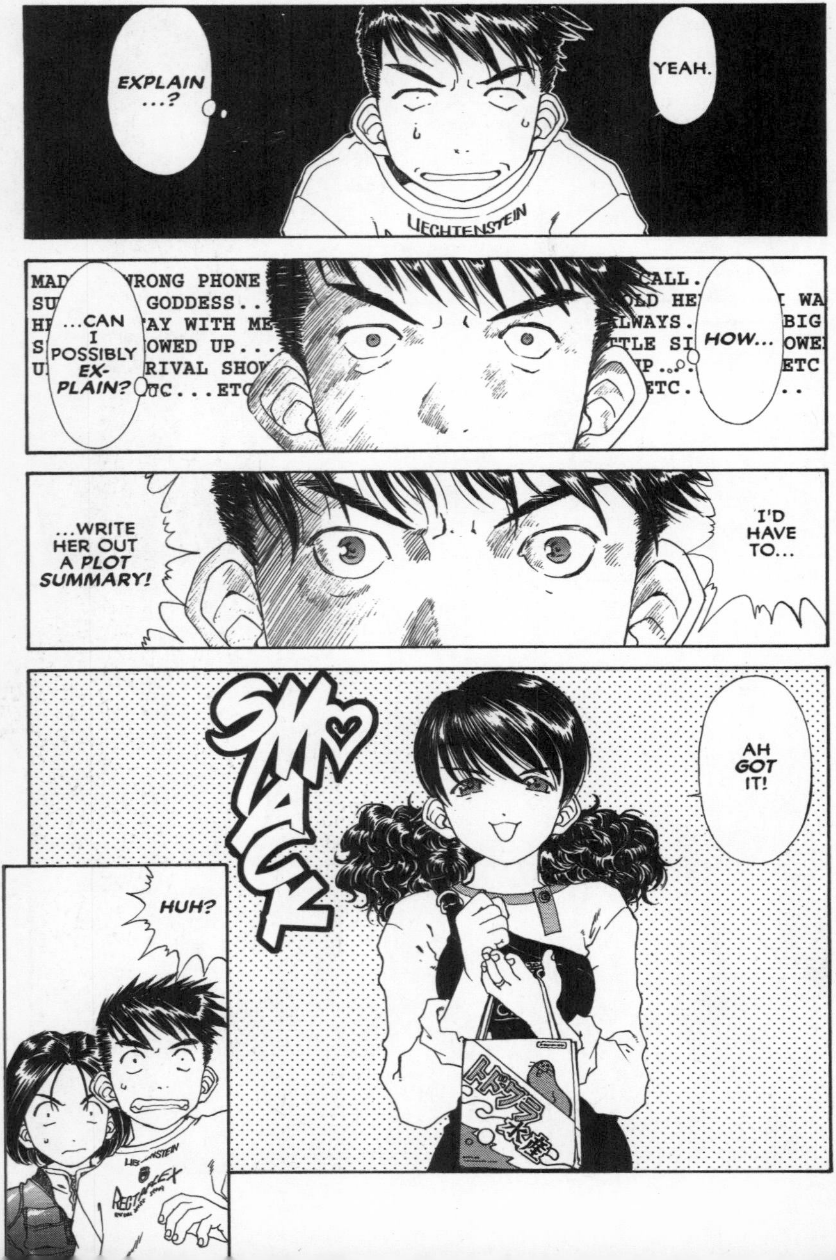
YEAH.
EXPLAIN ...?
HOW...
...CAN I POSSIBLY EX-PLAIN?
I'D HAVE TO...
...WRITE HER OUT A PLOT SUMMARY!
AH GOT IT!
SMACK
HUH?

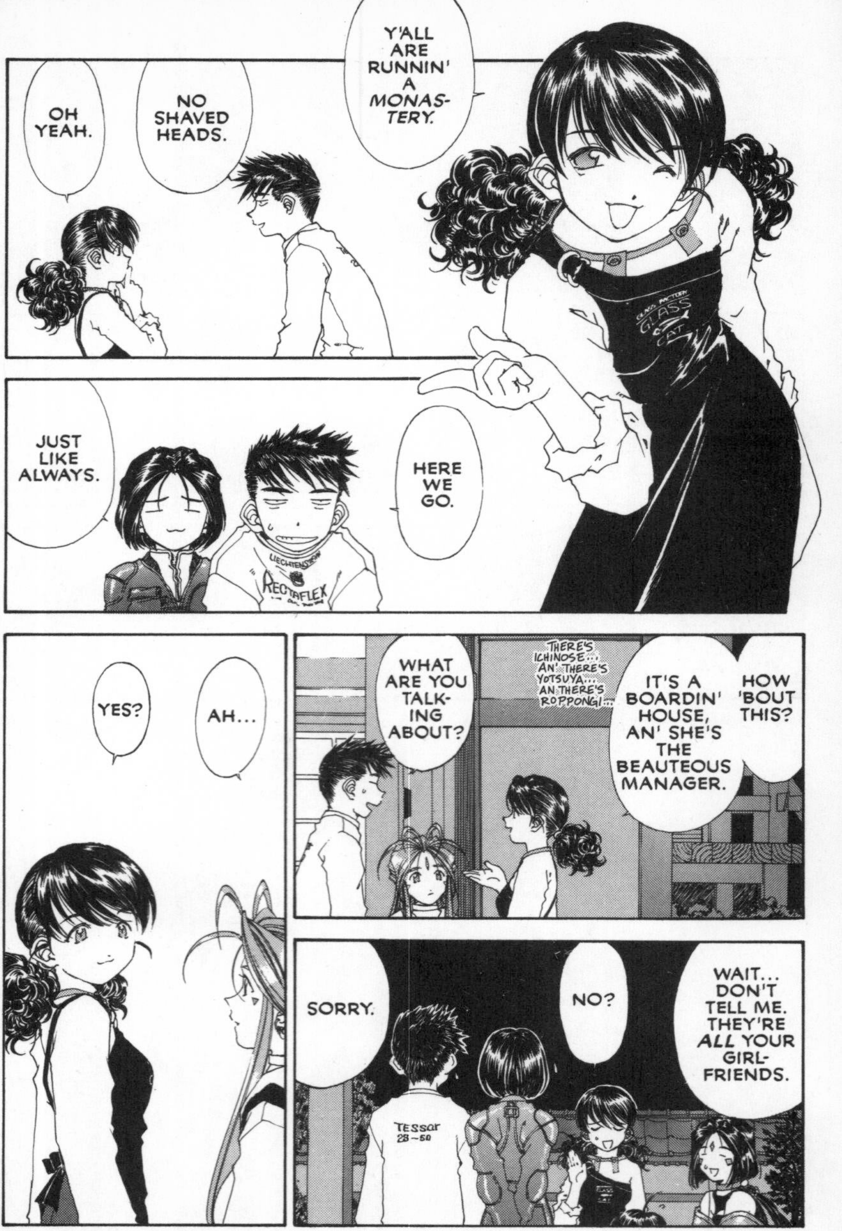
Y'ALL ARE RUNNIN' A *MONASTERY.*
NO SHAVED HEADS.
OH YEAH.
HERE WE GO.
JUST LIKE ALWAYS.
HOW 'BOUT THIS?
IT'S A BOARDIN' HOUSE, AN' SHE'S THE BEAUTEOUS MANAGER.
THERE'S ICHINOSE... AN' THERE'S YOTSUYA... AN' THERE'S ROPPONGI...
WHAT ARE YOU TALK-ING ABOUT?
WAIT... DON'T TELL ME. THEY'RE *ALL* YOUR GIRL-FRIENDS.
NO?
SORRY.
AH...
YES?

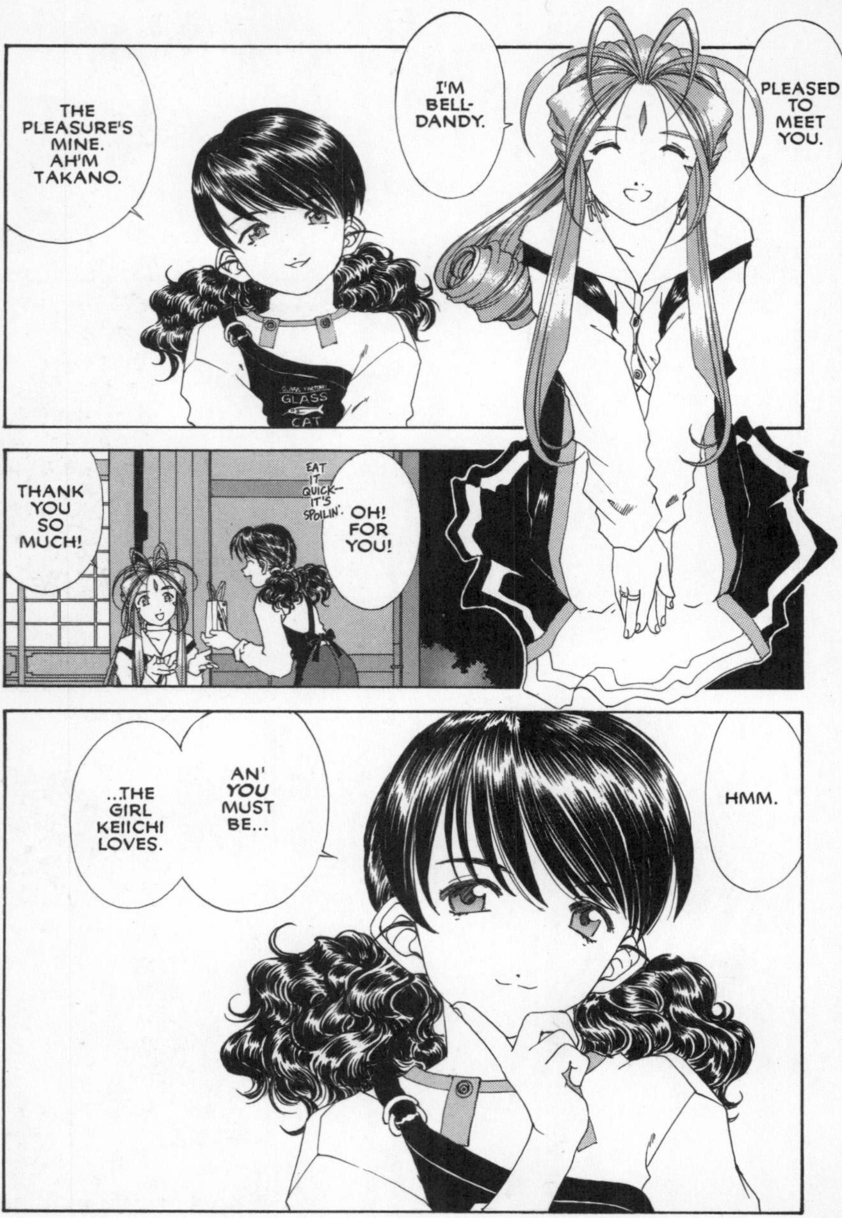
PLEASED TO MEET YOU.
I'M BELL-DANDY.
THE PLEASURE'S MINE. AH'M TAKANO.
GLASS CAT
OH! FOR YOU!
EAT IT QUICK--IT'S SPOILIN'.
THANK YOU SO MUCH!
HMM.
AN' *YOU* MUST BE...
...THE GIRL KEIICHI LOVES.

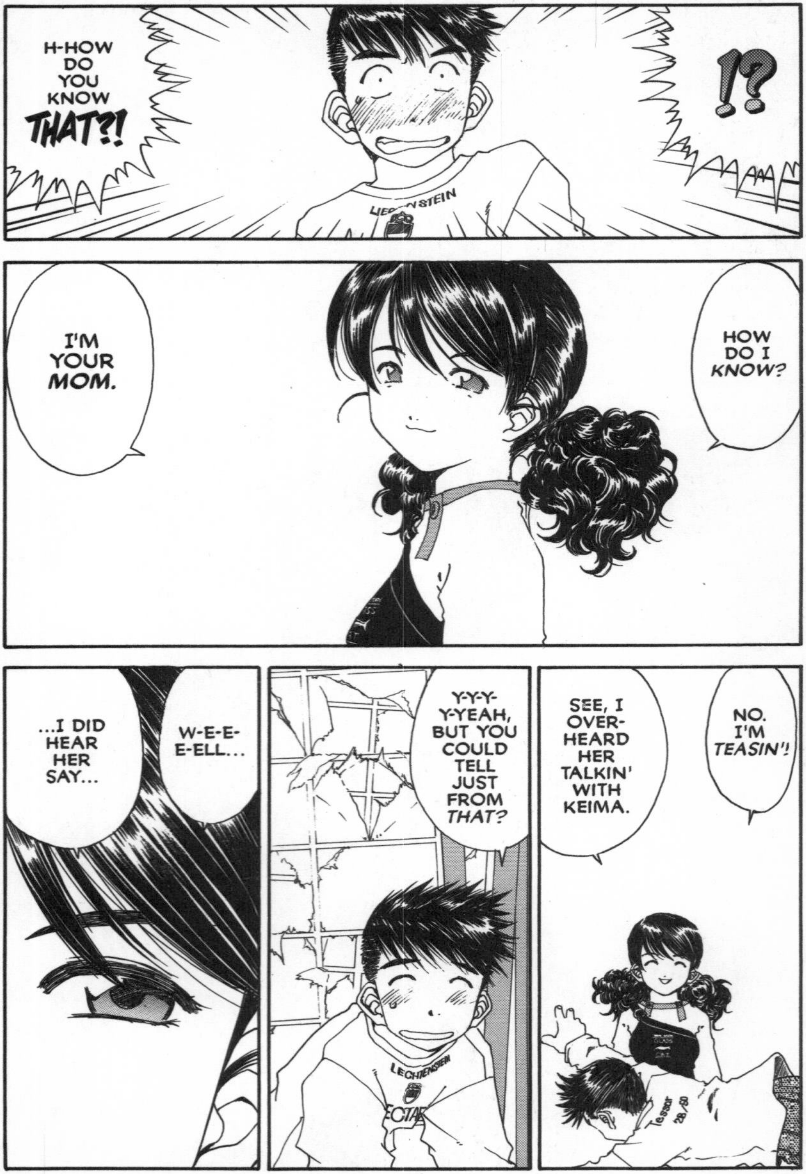
!?
H-HOW DO YOU KNOW THAT?!
HOW DO I KNOW?
I'M YOUR MOM.
NO. I'M TEASIN'!
SEE, I OVER-HEARD HER TALKIN' WITH KEIMA.
Y-Y-Y-Y-YEAH, BUT YOU COULD TELL JUST FROM THAT?
W-E-E-E-ELL...
...I DID HEAR HER SAY...

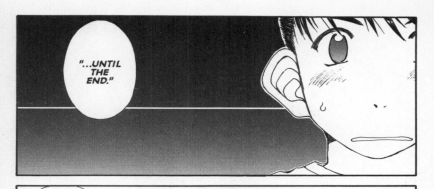

"...UNTIL THE END."

KEIICHI. WOULD YOU PROTECT THIS GIRL WITH *YOUR* LIFE?

AN' SO.

GLASS FACTORY
GLASS
CAT

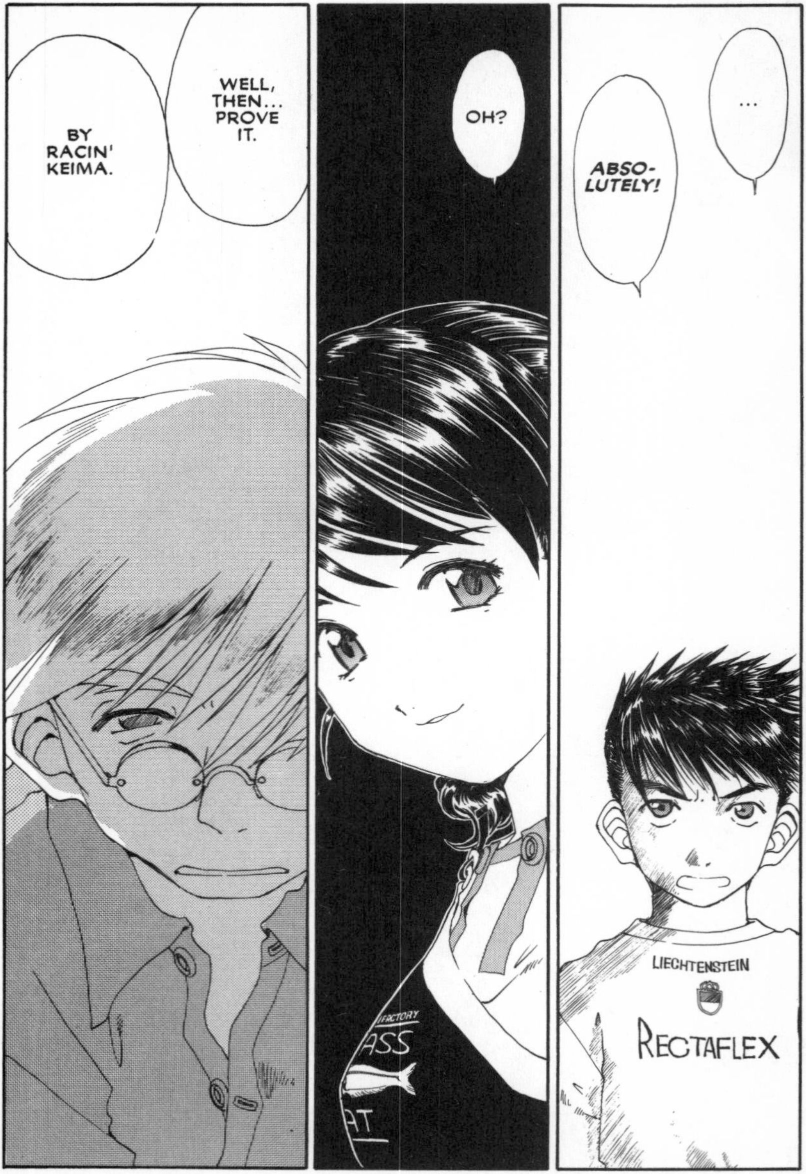
...
ABSO-LUTELY!
LIECHTENSTEIN
RECTAFLEX
OH?
WELL, THEN... PROVE IT.
BY RACIN' KEIMA.

END CHAPTER 146

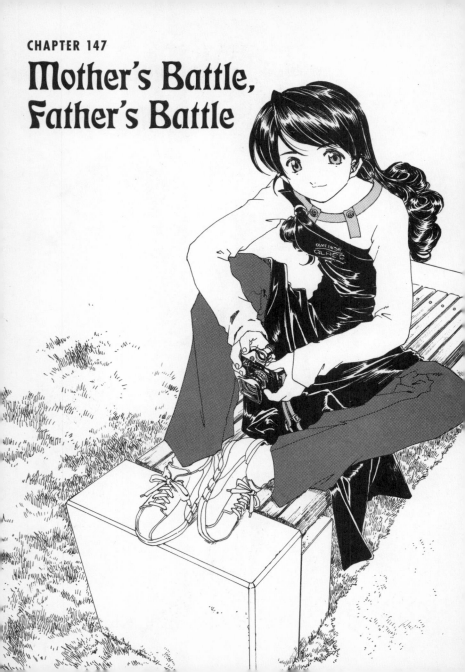

CHAPTER 147
Mother's Battle, Father's Battle

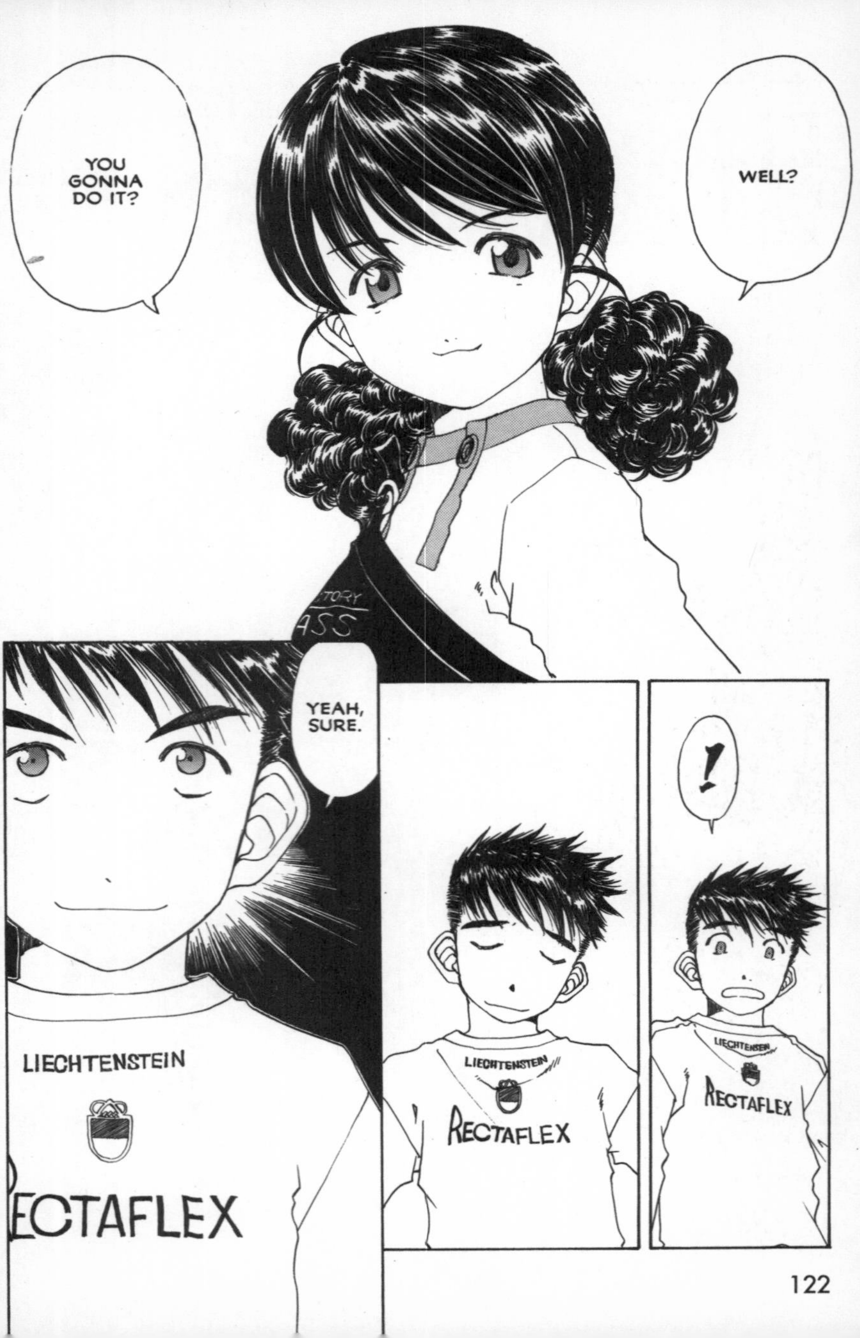
WELL?
YOU GONNA DO IT?
!
LIECHTENSEIN
RECTAFLEX
LIECHTENSTEIN
RECTAFLEX
YEAH, SURE.
LIECHTENSTEIN
ECTAFLEX

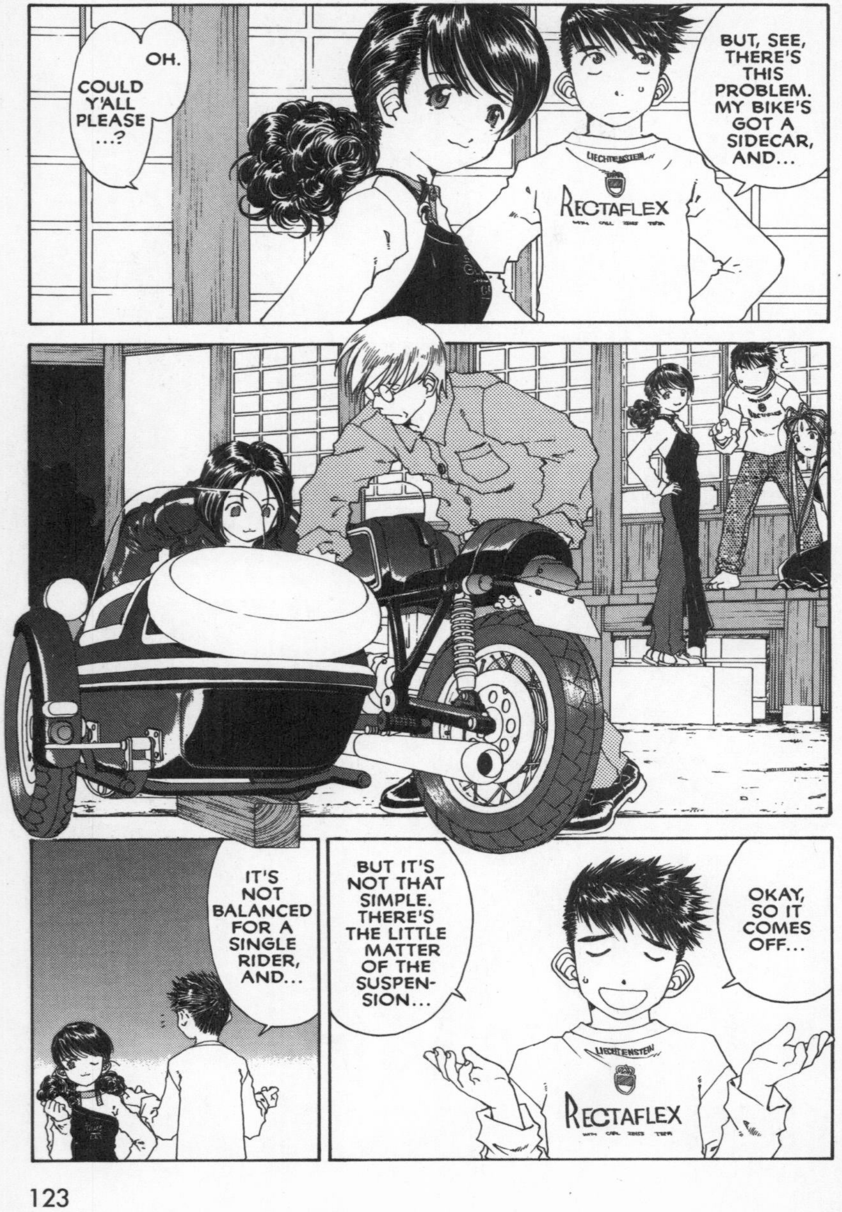
BUT, SEE, THERE'S THIS PROBLEM. MY BIKE'S GOT A SIDECAR, AND...
LIECHTENSTEIN
RECTAFLEX
OH.
COULD Y'ALL PLEASE ...?
OKAY, SO IT COMES OFF...
LIECHTENSTEIN
RECTAFLEX
BUT IT'S NOT THAT SIMPLE. THERE'S THE LITTLE MATTER OF THE SUSPEN-SION...
IT'S NOT BALANCED FOR A SINGLE RIDER, AND...

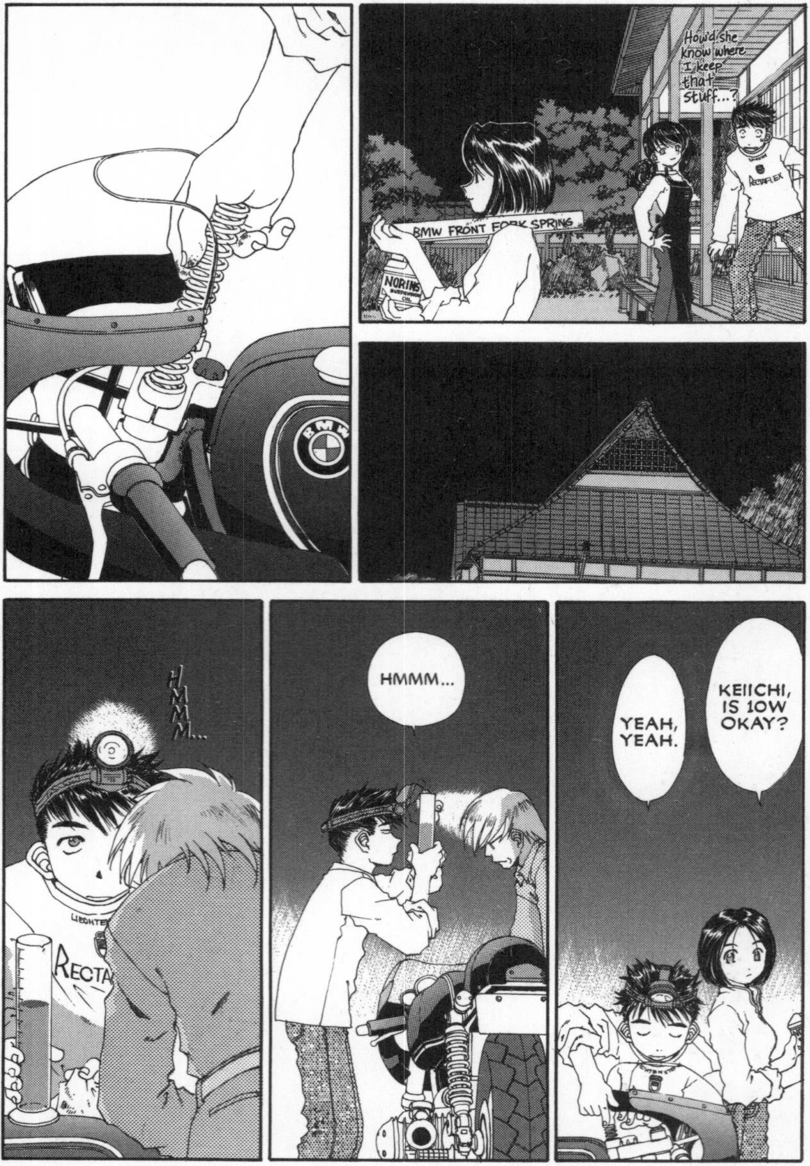
BMW FRONT FORK SPRING
NORINS
How'd she know where I keep that stuff...?
KEIICHI, IS 10W OKAY?
YEAH, YEAH.
HMMM...
HMMM...

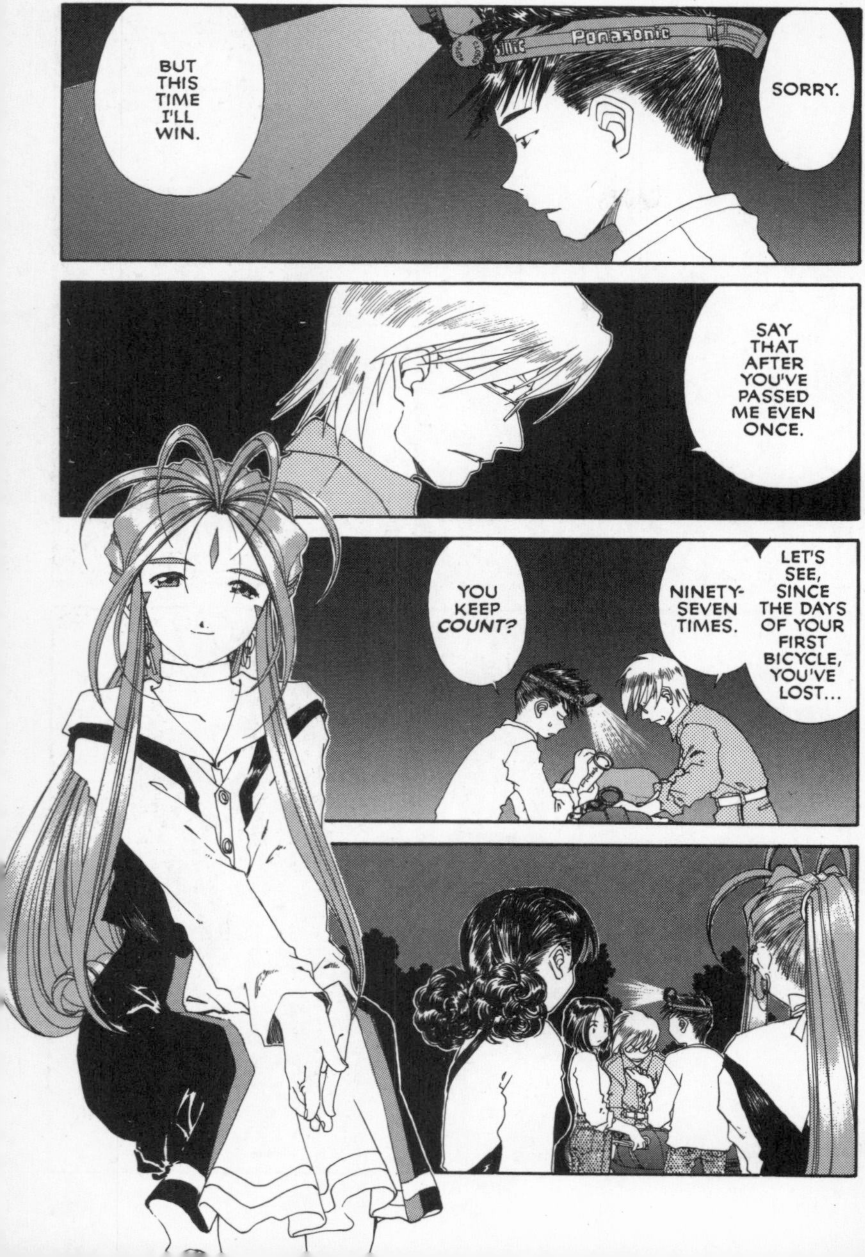
Panasonic
SORRY.
BUT THIS TIME I'LL WIN.
SAY THAT AFTER YOU'VE PASSED ME EVEN ONCE.
LET'S SEE, SINCE THE DAYS OF YOUR FIRST BICYCLE, YOU'VE LOST...
NINETY-SEVEN TIMES.
YOU KEEP *COUNT?*

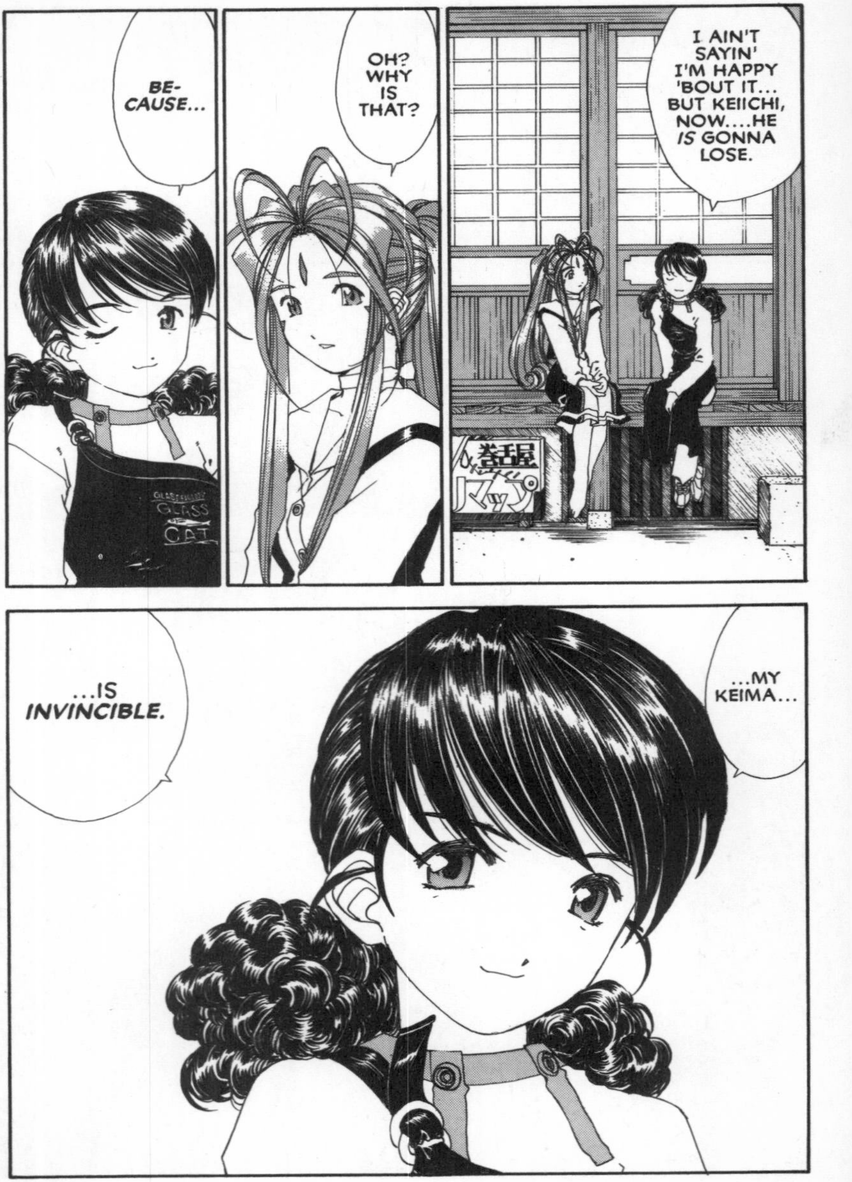
I AIN'T SAYIN' I'M HAPPY 'BOUT IT... BUT KEIICHI, NOW....HE *IS* GONNA LOSE.
OH? WHY IS THAT?
BE-CAUSE...
...MY KEIMA...
...IS **INVINCIBLE.**

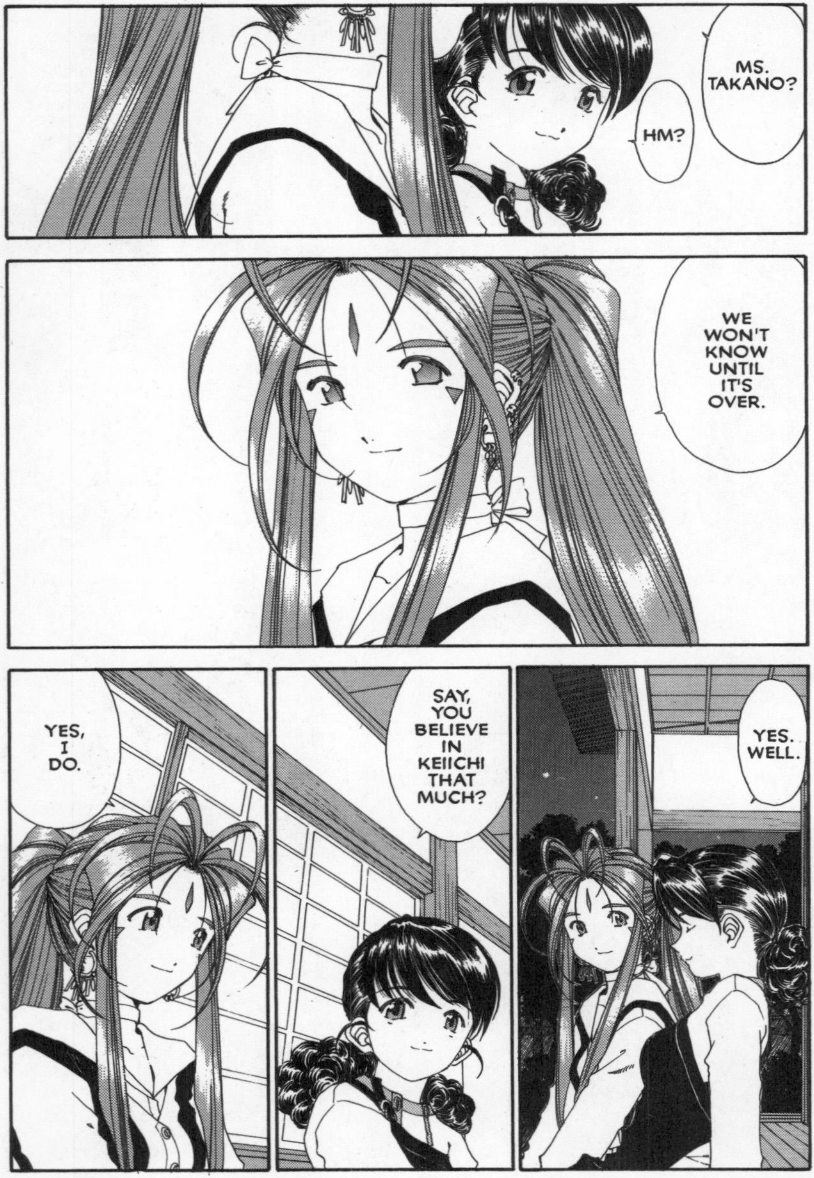
MS. TAKANO?
HM?
WE WON'T KNOW UNTIL IT'S OVER.
YES. WELL.
SAY, YOU BELIEVE IN KEIICHI THAT MUCH?
YES, I DO.

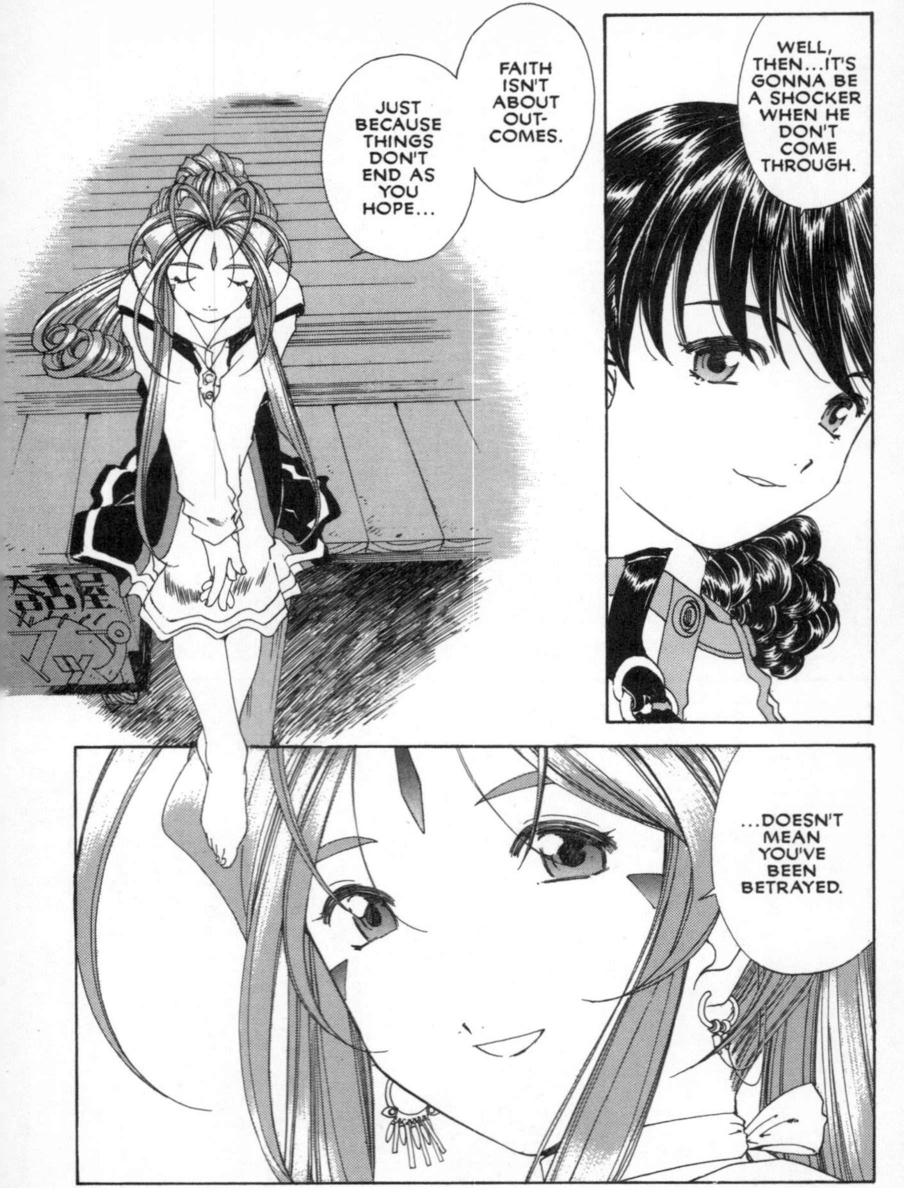
WELL, THEN...IT'S GONNA BE A SHOCKER WHEN HE DON'T COME THROUGH.
FAITH ISN'T ABOUT OUT-COMES.
JUST BECAUSE THINGS DON'T END AS YOU HOPE...
...DOESN'T MEAN YOU'VE BEEN BETRAYED.

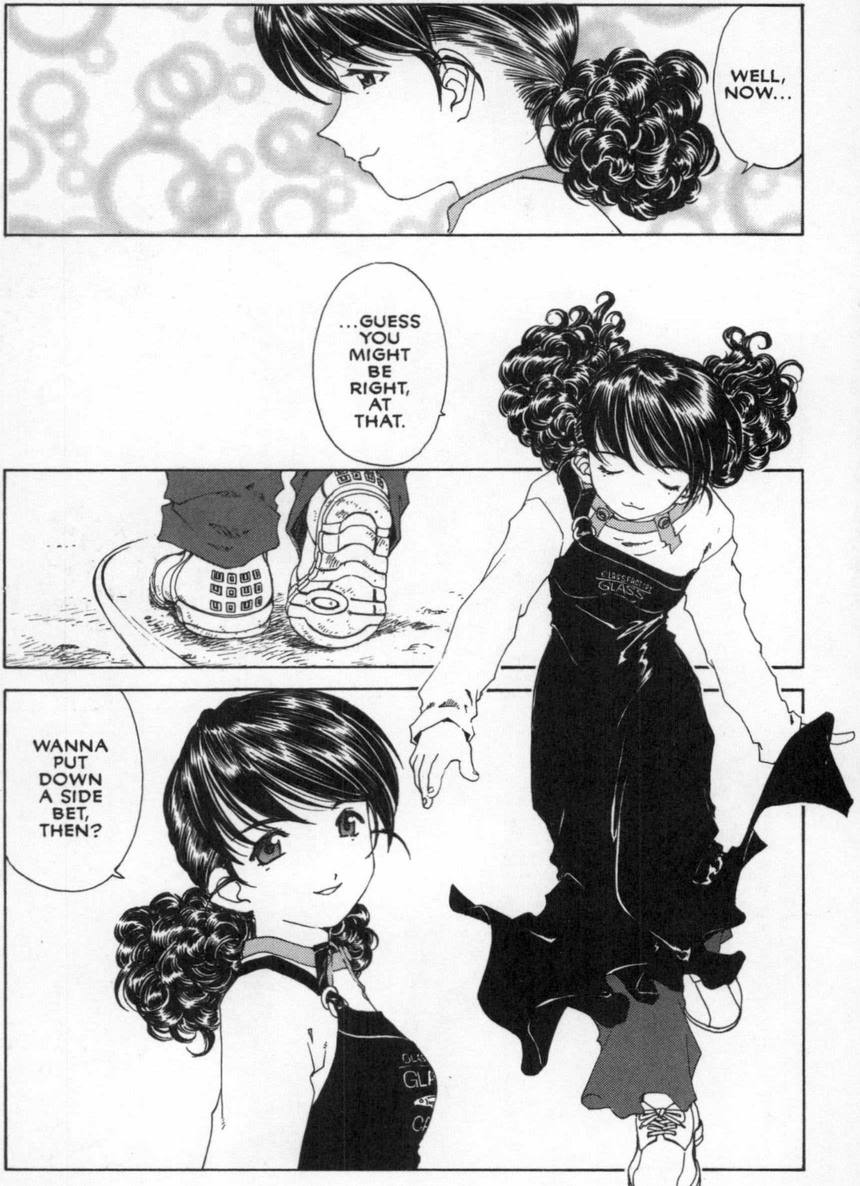
WELL, NOW...
...GUESS YOU MIGHT BE RIGHT, AT THAT.
...
WANNA PUT DOWN A SIDE BET, THEN?

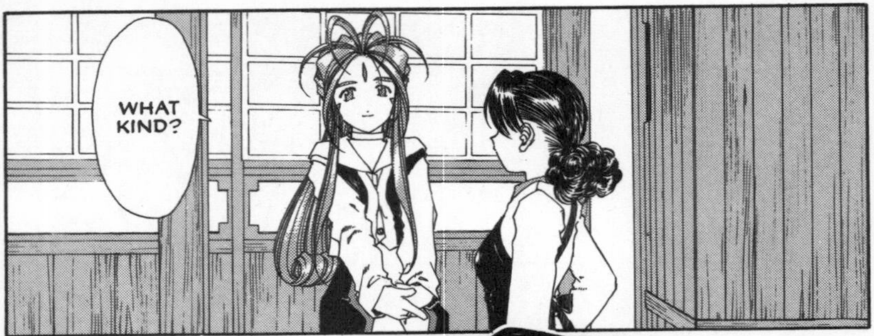
WHAT KIND?

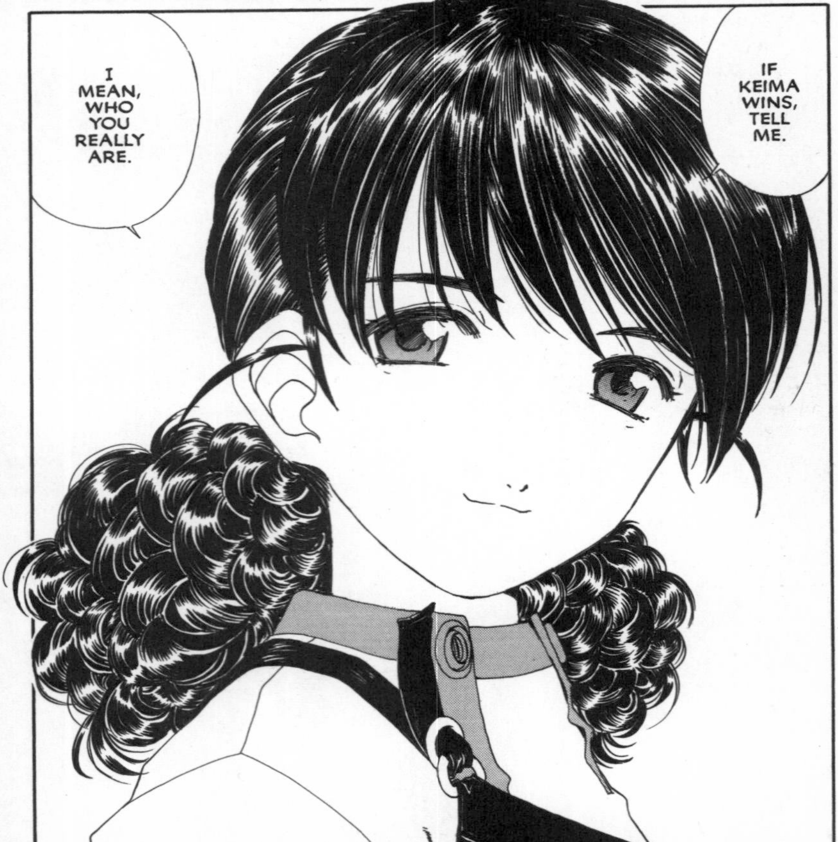
IF KEIMA WINS, TELL ME.
I MEAN, WHO YOU REALLY ARE.

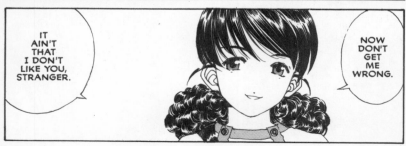

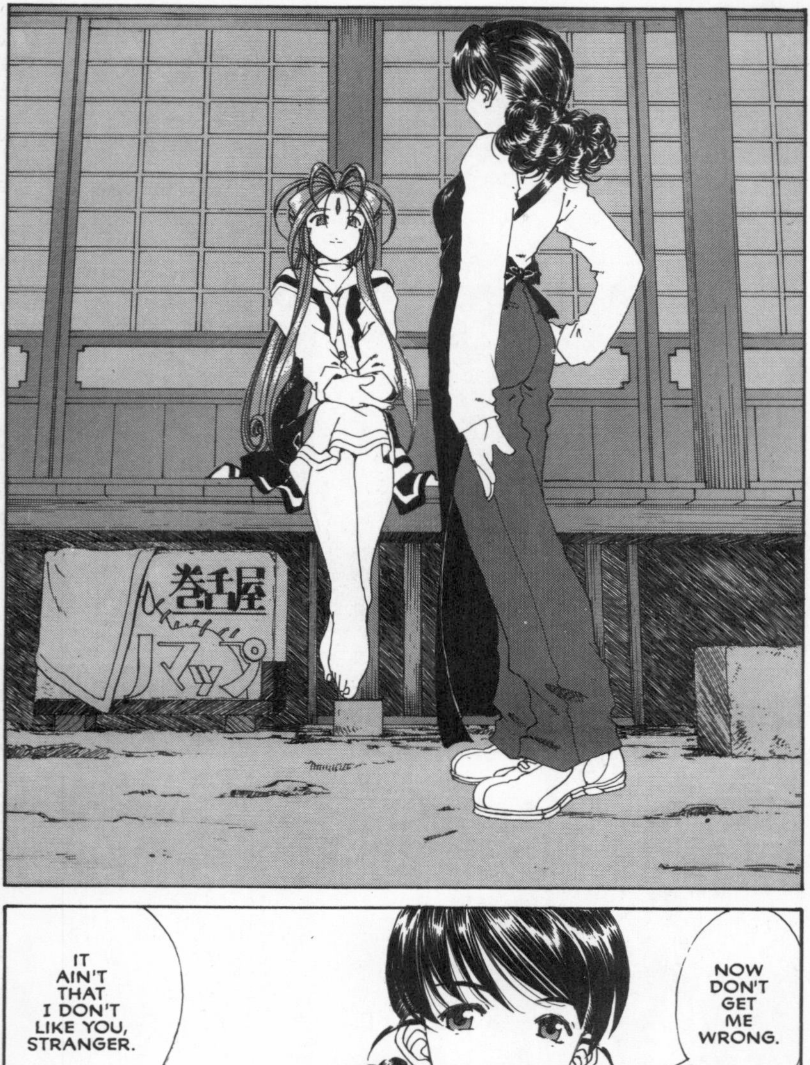
NOW DON'T GET ME WRONG.
IT AIN'T THAT I DON'T LIKE YOU, STRANGER.

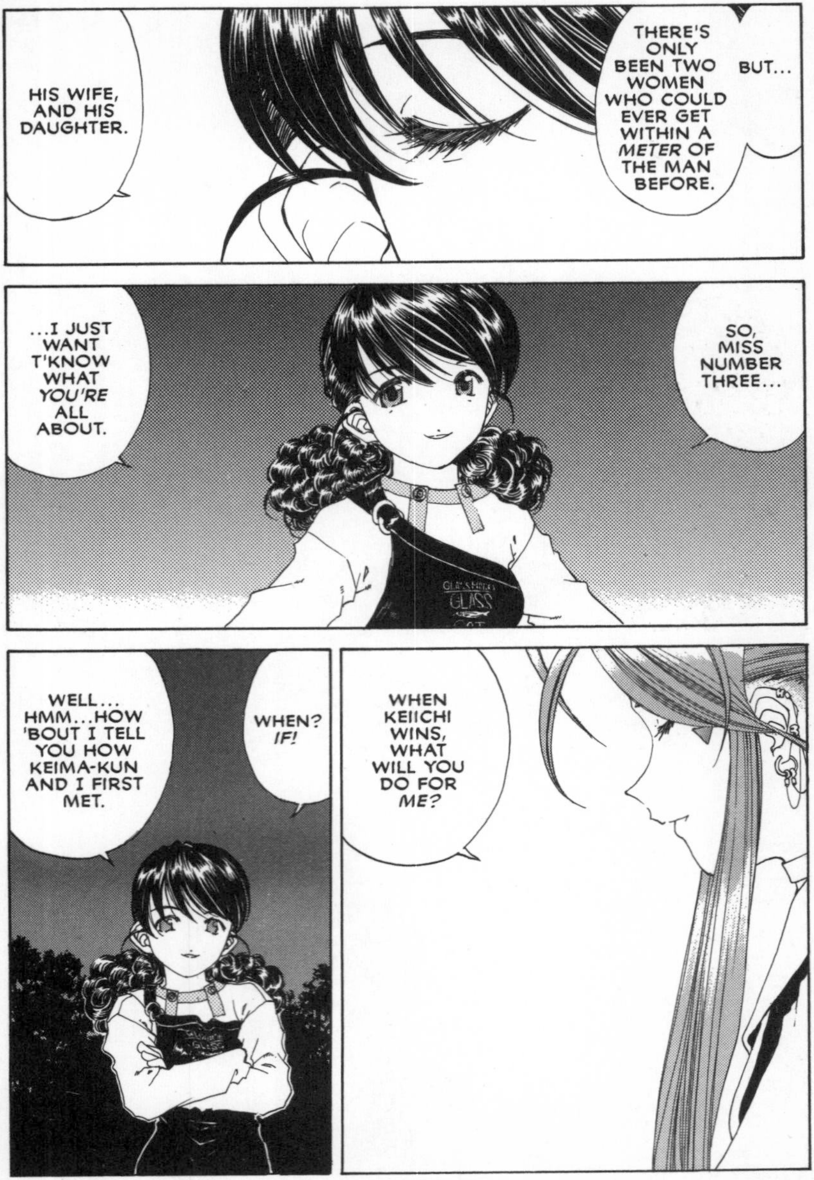
BUT...
THERE'S ONLY BEEN TWO WOMEN WHO COULD EVER GET WITHIN A *METER* OF THE MAN BEFORE.
HIS WIFE, AND HIS DAUGHTER.
SO, MISS NUMBER THREE...
...I JUST WANT T'KNOW WHAT *YOU'RE* ALL ABOUT.
WHEN KEIICHI WINS, WHAT WILL YOU DO FOR *ME?*
WHEN? *IF!*
WELL... HMM...HOW 'BOUT I TELL YOU HOW KEIMA-KUN AND I FIRST MET.

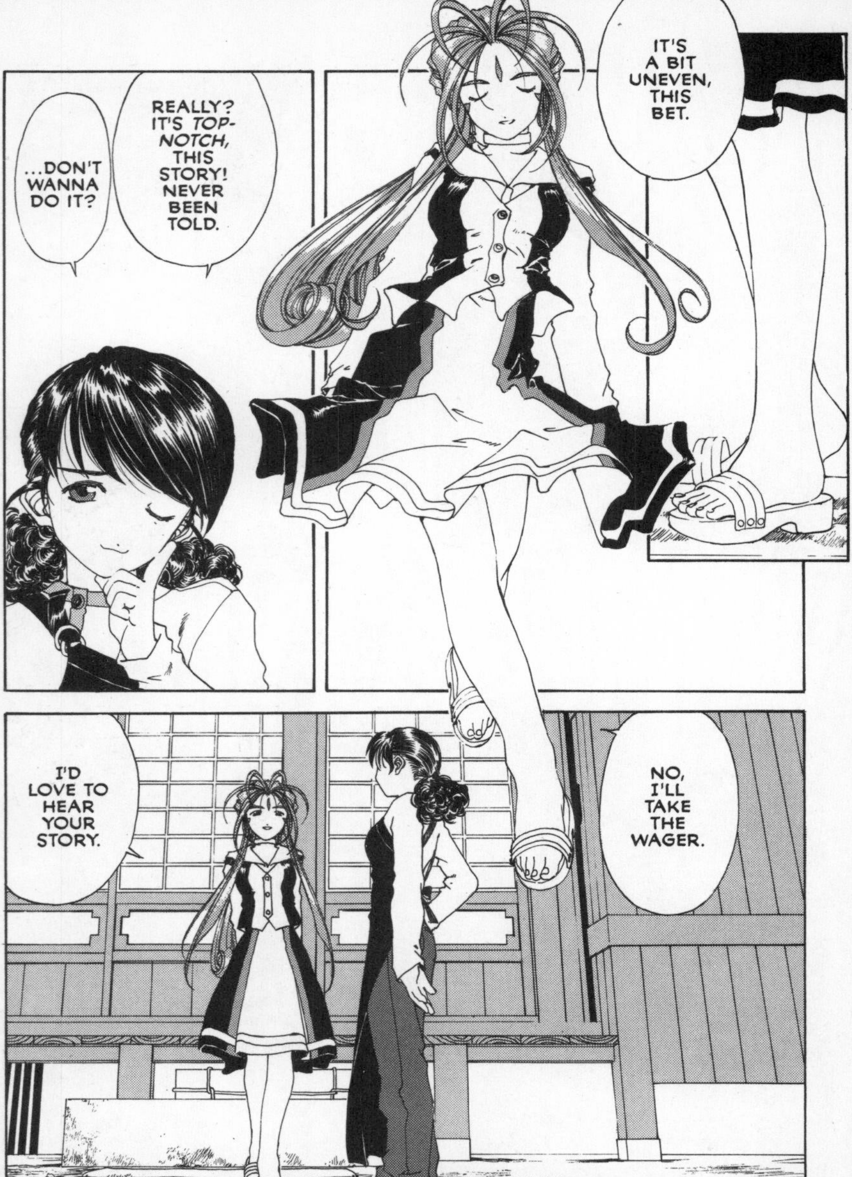
IT'S A BIT UNEVEN, THIS BET.
REALLY? IT'S *TOP-NOTCH,* THIS STORY! NEVER BEEN TOLD.
...DON'T WANNA DO IT?
NO, I'LL TAKE THE WAGER.
I'D LOVE TO HEAR YOUR STORY.

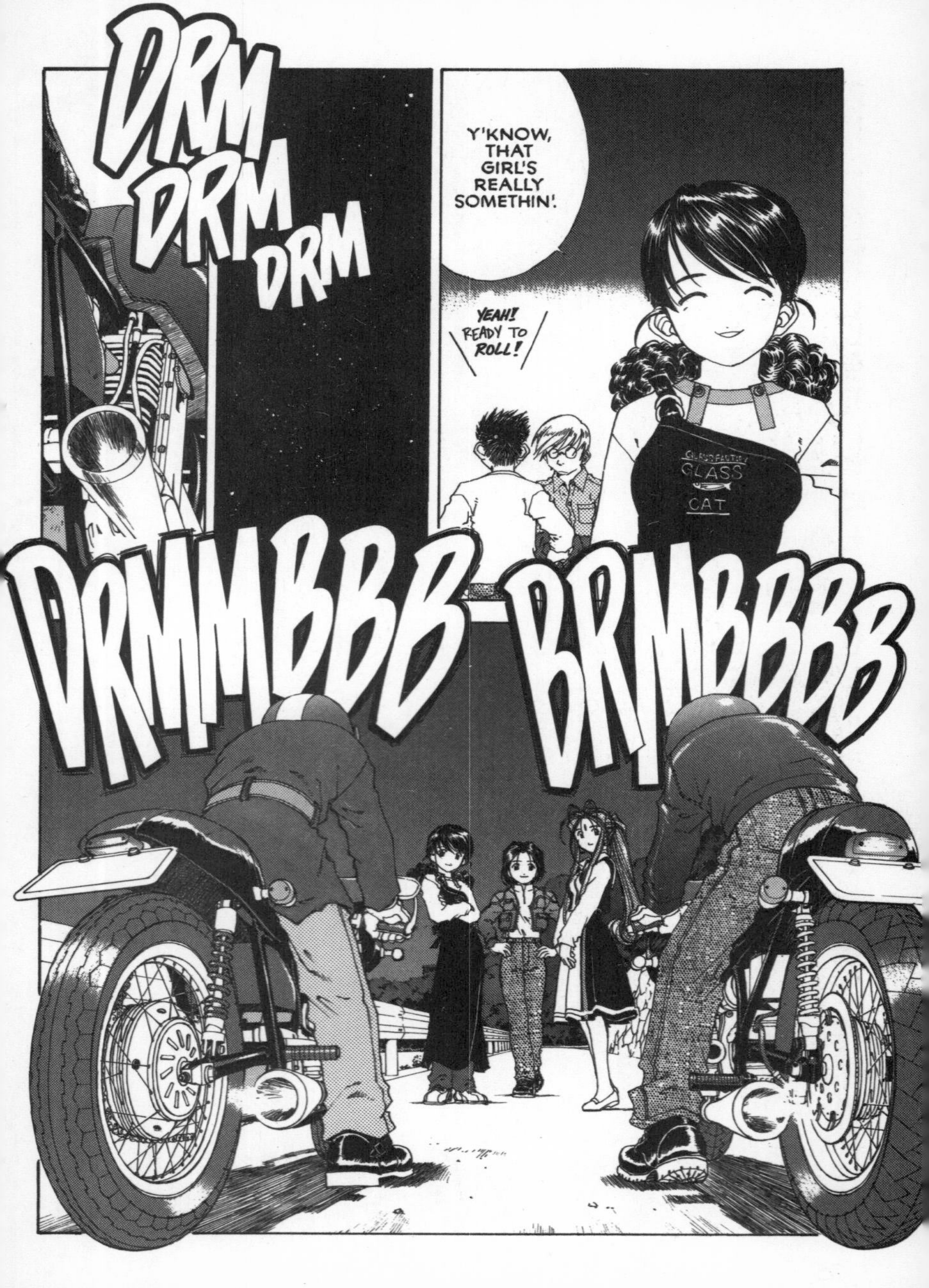
Y'KNOW, THAT GIRL'S REALLY SOMETHIN'.
YEAH! READY TO ROLL!
DRM DRM DRM
BRMBBBB
DRMMBBB

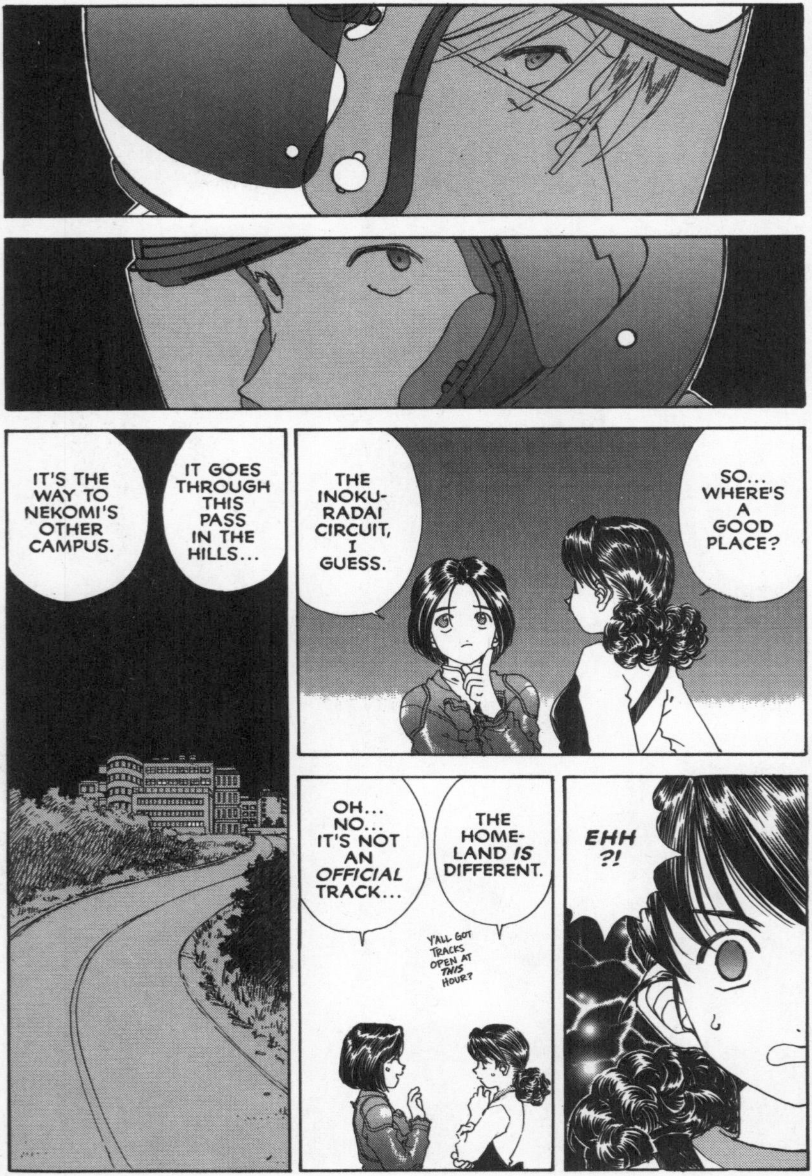
SO... WHERE'S A GOOD PLACE?
THE INOKU-RADAI CIRCUIT, I GUESS.
EHH ?!
THE HOME-LAND IS DIFFERENT.
OH... NO... IT'S NOT AN OFFICIAL TRACK...
Y'ALL GOT TRACKS OPEN AT THIS HOUR?
IT GOES THROUGH THIS PASS IN THE HILLS...
IT'S THE WAY TO NEKOMI'S OTHER CAMPUS.

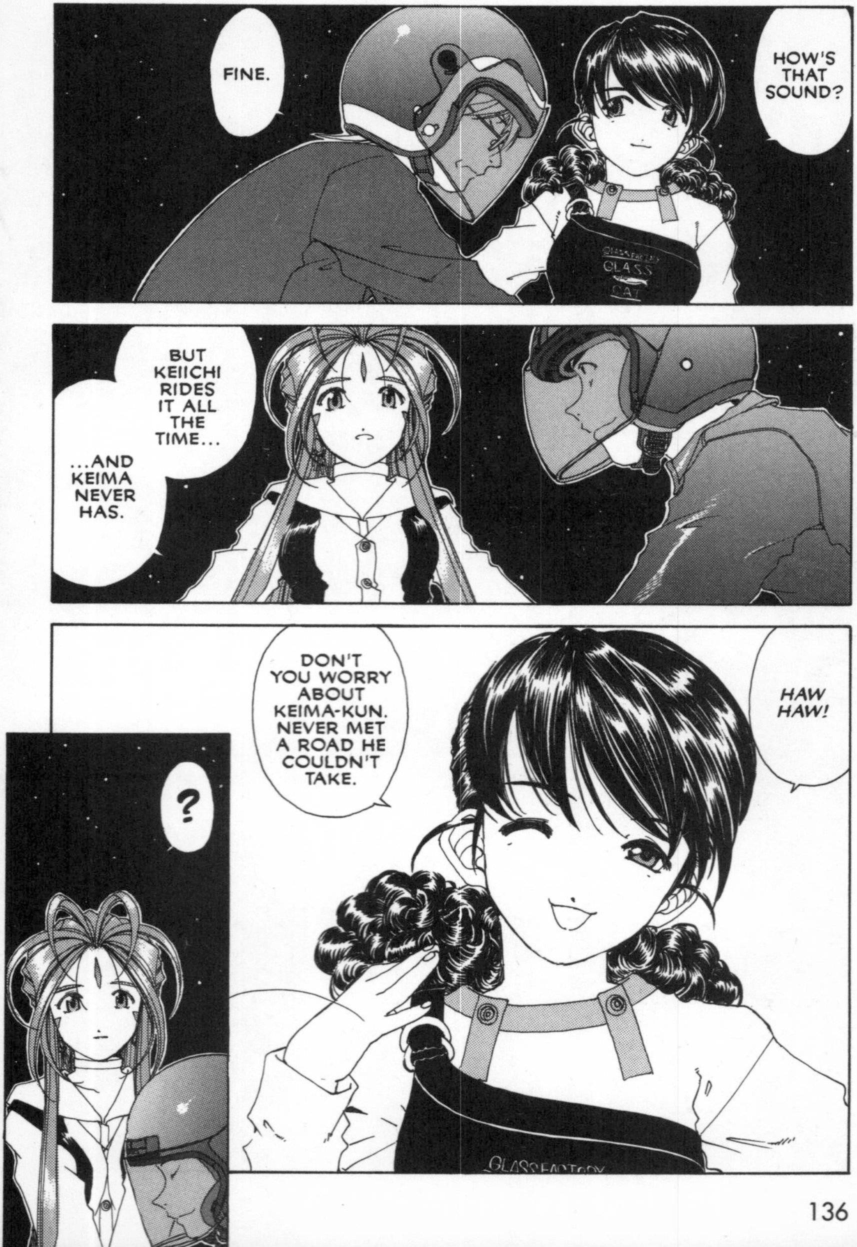
HOW'S THAT SOUND?
FINE.
BUT KEIICHI RIDES IT ALL THE TIME...
...AND KEIMA NEVER HAS.
HAW HAW!
DON'T YOU WORRY ABOUT KEIMA-KUN. NEVER MET A ROAD HE COULDN'T TAKE.
?

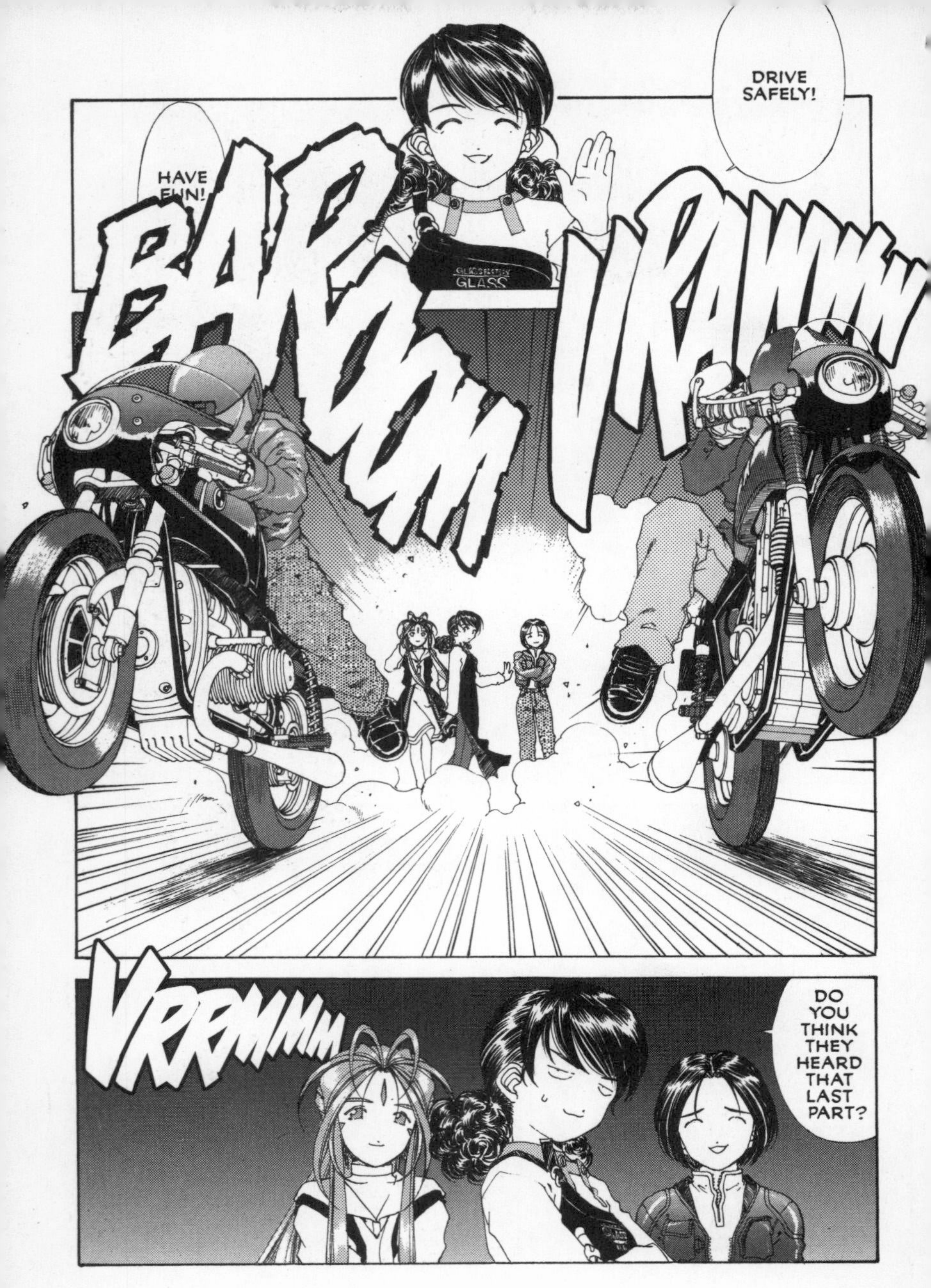
DRIVE SAFELY!
HAVE FUN!
DO YOU THINK THEY HEARD THAT LAST PART?

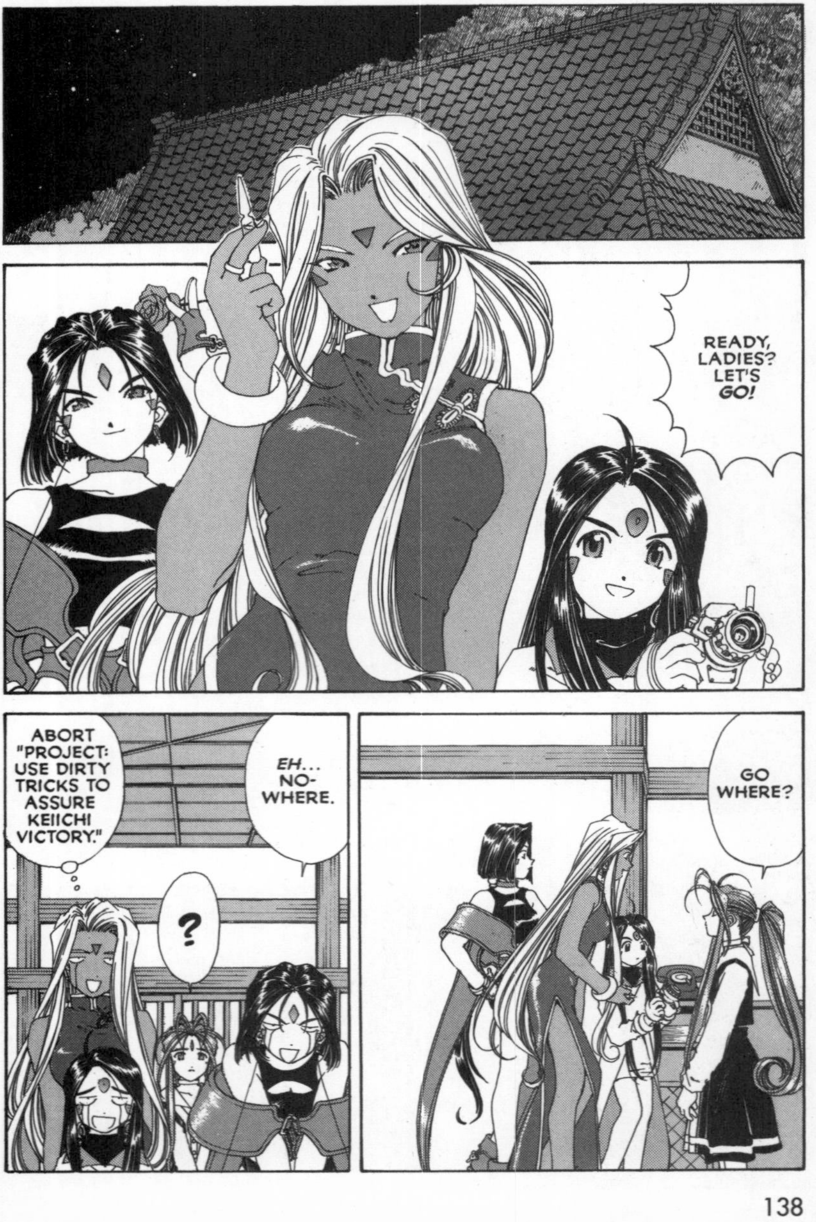

READY, LADIES? LET'S *GO!*
GO WHERE?
EH... NO-WHERE.
ABORT "PROJECT: USE DIRTY TRICKS TO ASSURE KEIICHI VICTORY."
?

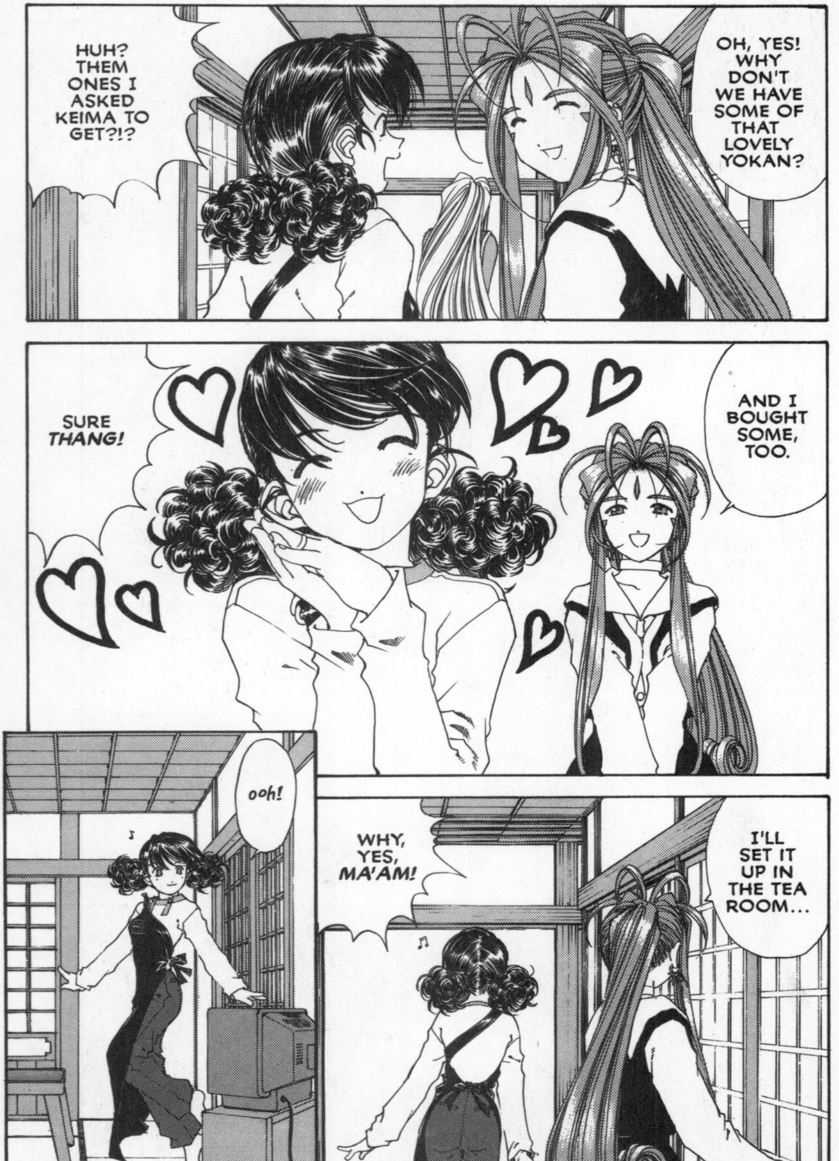
OH, YES! WHY DON'T WE HAVE SOME OF THAT LOVELY YOKAN?
HUH? THEM ONES I ASKED KEIMA TO GET?!?
AND I BOUGHT SOME, TOO.
SURE *THANG!*
I'LL SET IT UP IN THE TEA ROOM...
WHY, YES, *MA'AM!*
ooh!

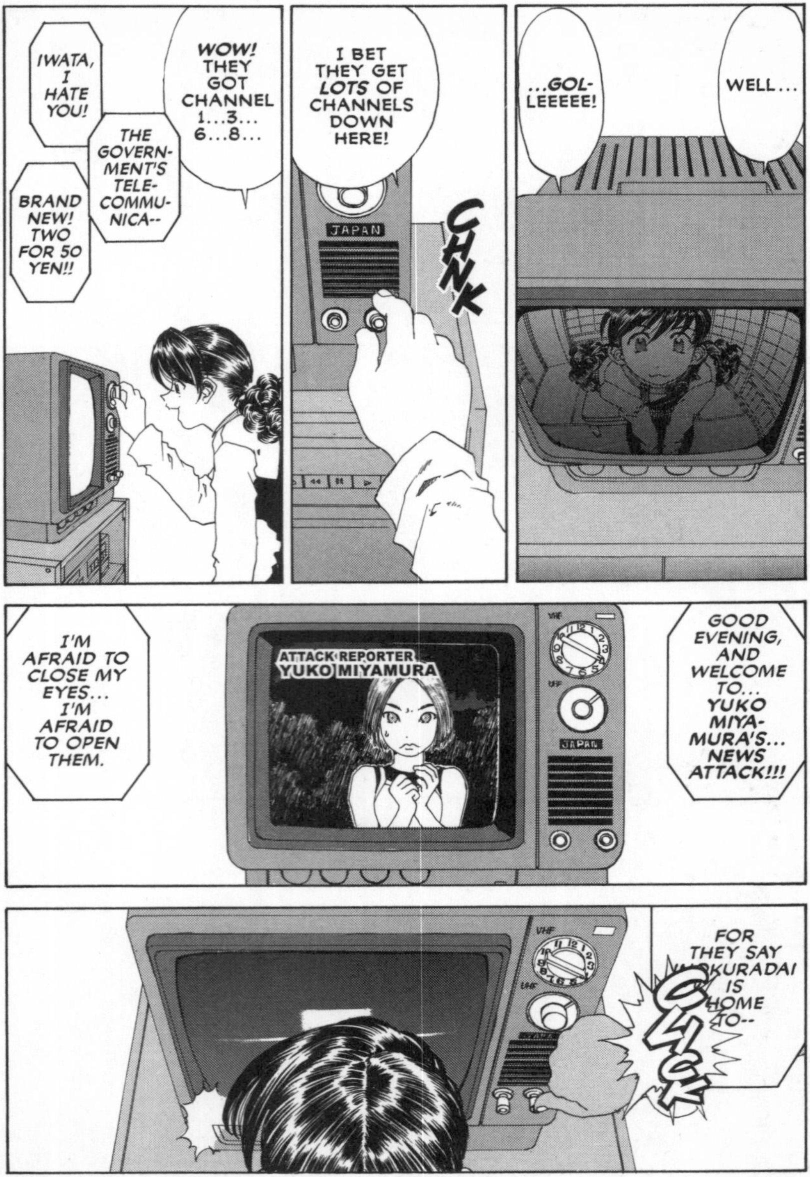
WELL...
...GOL-LEEEEE!
I BET THEY GET LOTS OF CHANNELS DOWN HERE!
CHNK
WOW! THEY GOT CHANNEL 1...3... 6...8...
IWATA, I HATE YOU!
THE GOVERNMENT'S TELE-COMMUNICA--
BRAND NEW! TWO FOR 50 YEN!!
GOOD EVENING, AND WELCOME TO... YUKO MIYAMURA'S... NEWS ATTACK!!!
ATTACK REPORTER YUKO MIYAMURA
JAPAN
I'M AFRAID TO CLOSE MY EYES... I'M AFRAID TO OPEN THEM.
FOR THEY SAY
OKURADAI IS HOME TO--
CLICK

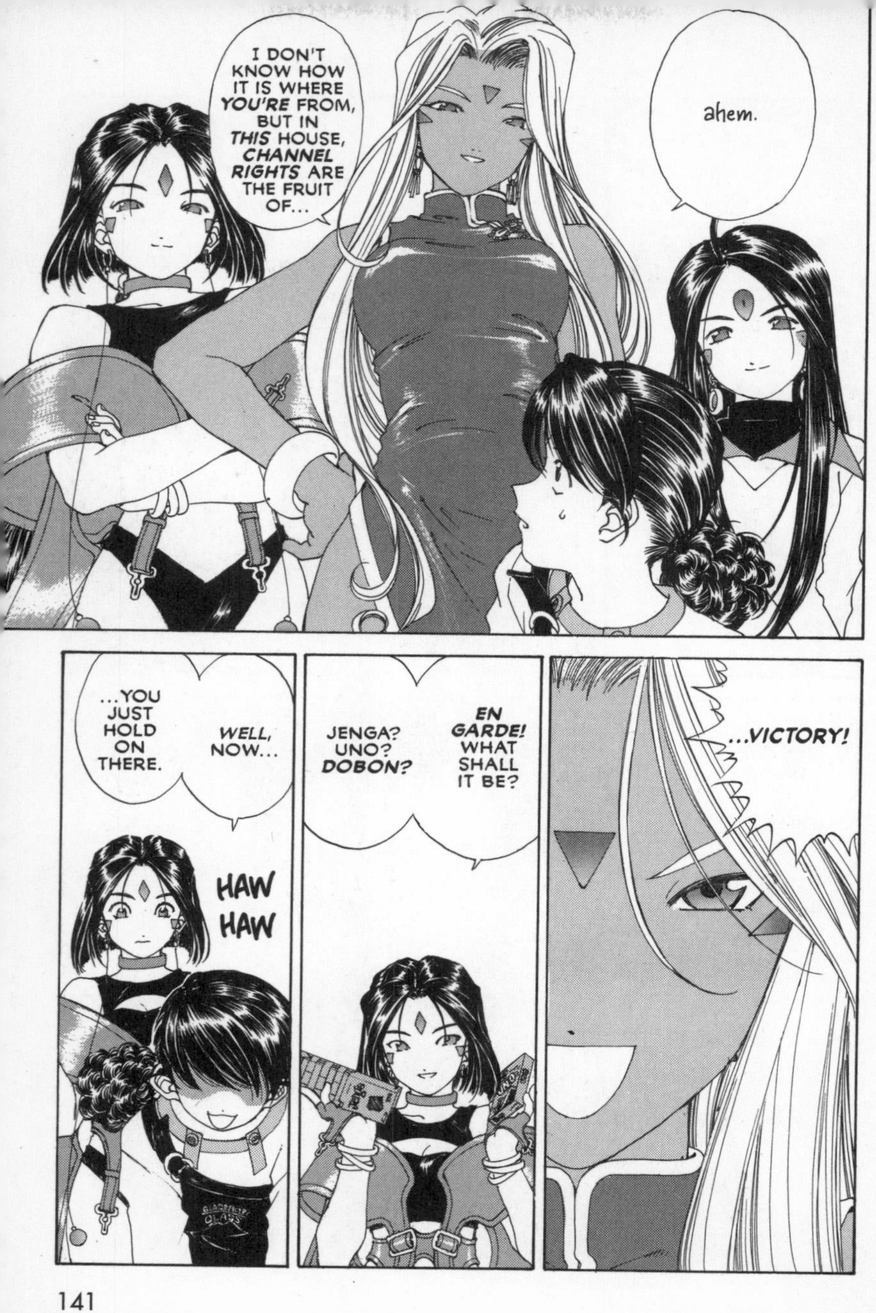
ahem.
I DON'T KNOW HOW IT IS WHERE YOU'RE FROM, BUT IN THIS HOUSE, CHANNEL RIGHTS ARE THE FRUIT OF...
...VICTORY!
EN GARDE! WHAT SHALL IT BE?
JENGA? UNO? DOBON?
WELL, NOW...
...YOU JUST HOLD ON THERE.
HAW HAW

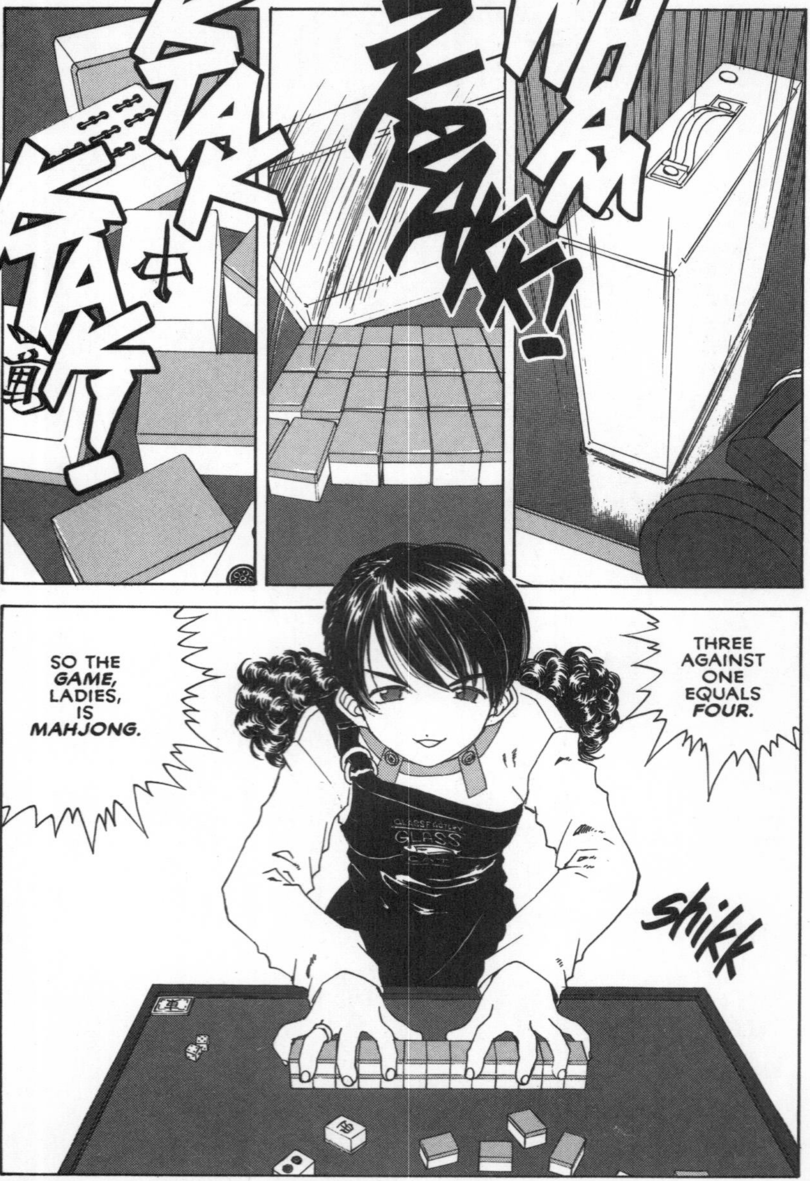
WHAM
SKRAKK!!
KTAK
KTAK!
THREE AGAINST ONE EQUALS FOUR.
SO THE GAME, LADIES, IS MAHJONG.
shikk

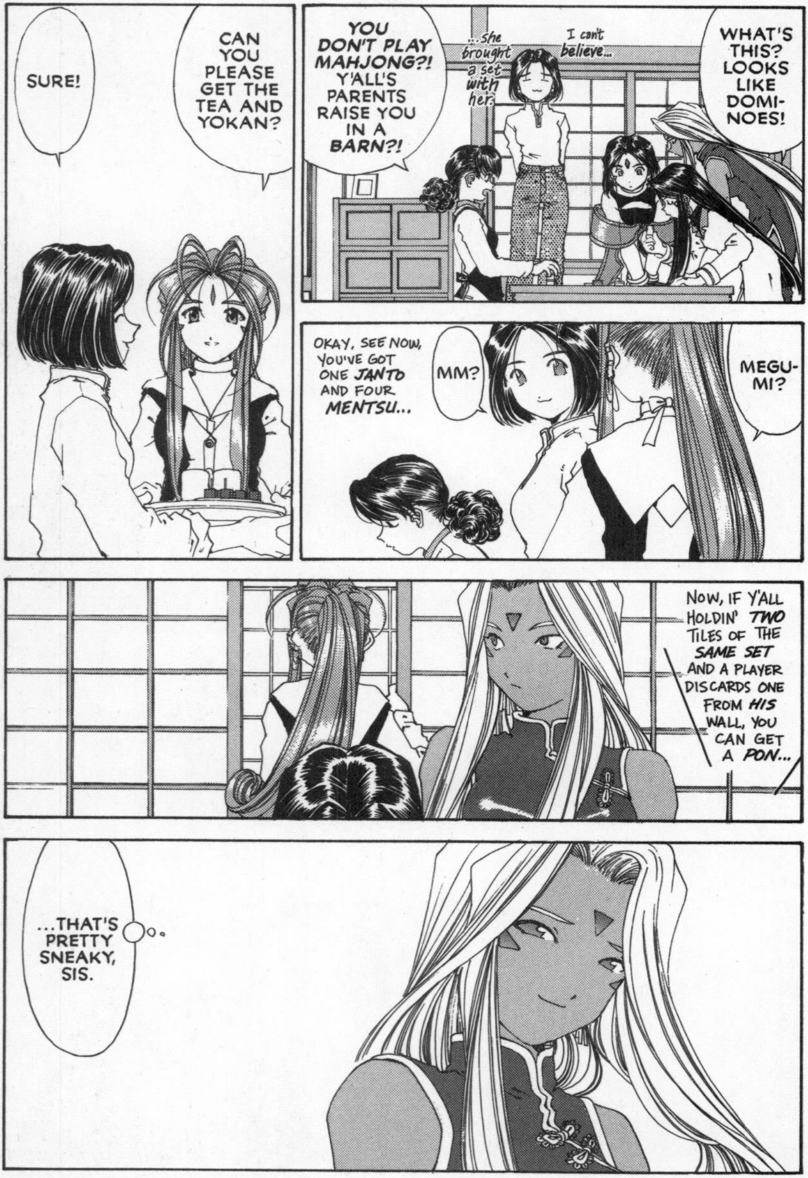
WHAT'S THIS? LOOKS LIKE DOMINOES!
I can't believe...
...she brought a set with her.
YOU DON'T PLAY MAHJONG?! Y'ALL'S PARENTS RAISE YOU IN A BARN?!
MEGUMI?
MM?
OKAY, SEE NOW, YOU'VE GOT ONE JANTO AND FOUR MENTSU...
CAN YOU PLEASE GET THE TEA AND YOKAN?
SURE!
NOW, IF Y'ALL HOLDIN' TWO TILES OF THE SAME SET AND A PLAYER DISCARDS ONE FROM HIS WALL, YOU CAN GET A PON...
...THAT'S PRETTY SNEAKY, SIS.

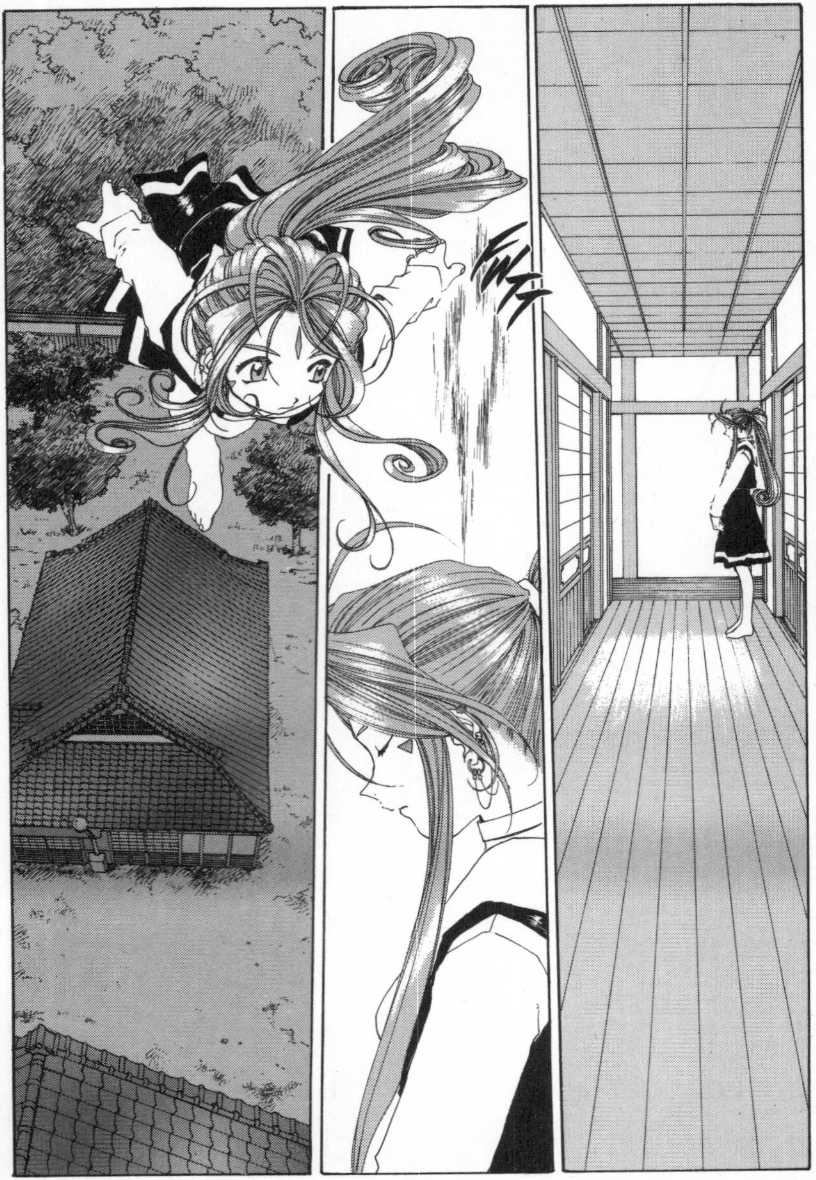

END CHAPTER 147

CHAPTER 148

Let's Dance!

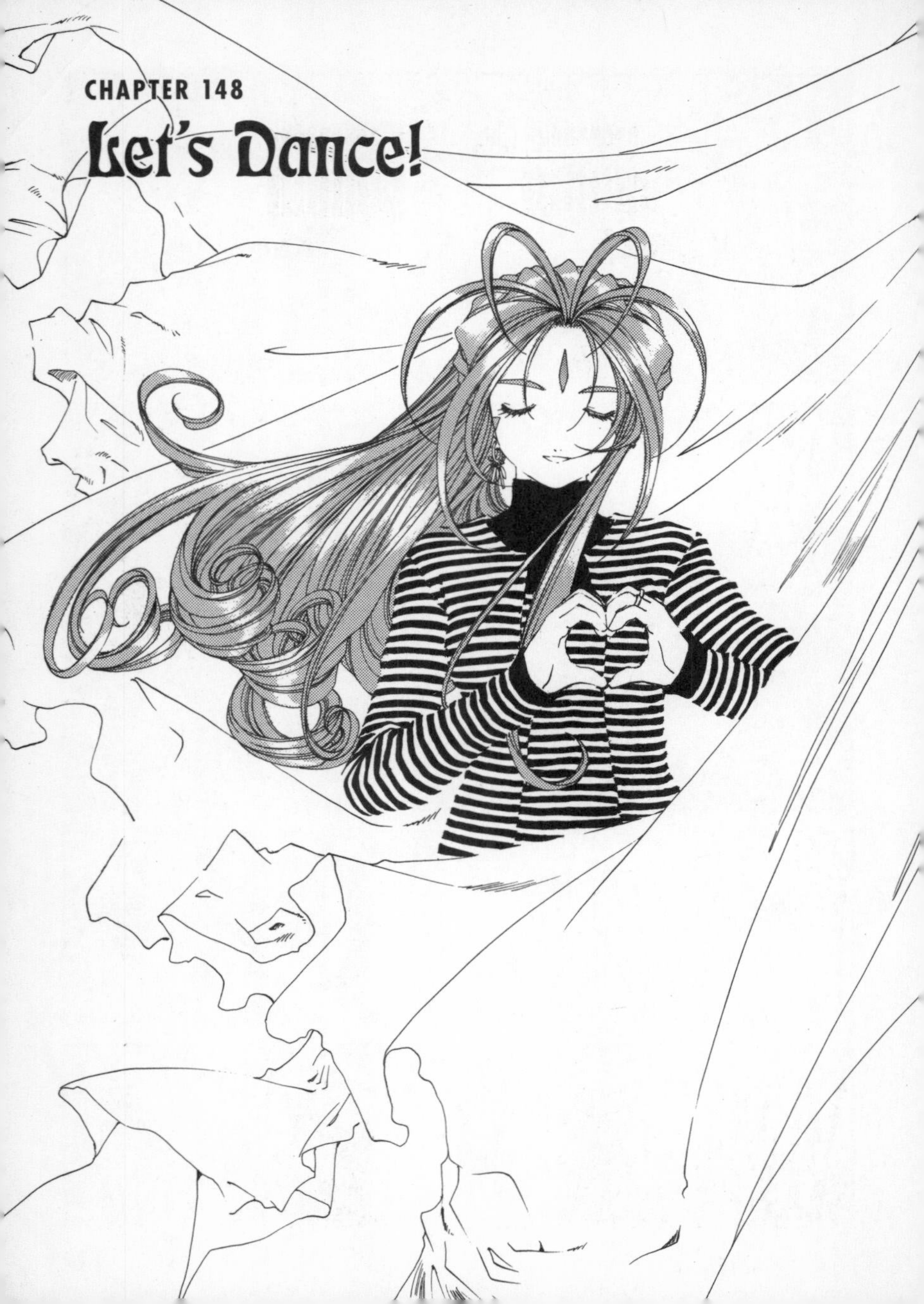

BRMBRMBRM
DRNDRNDRN
YOU PASS ME EVEN *ONCE...*
...YOU WIN.
SOUNDS GOOD.

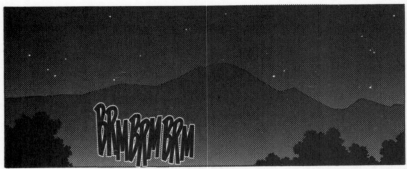

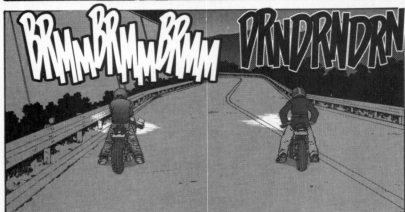

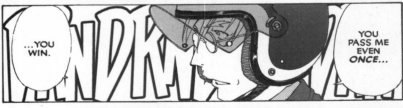

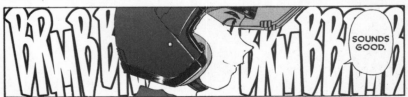

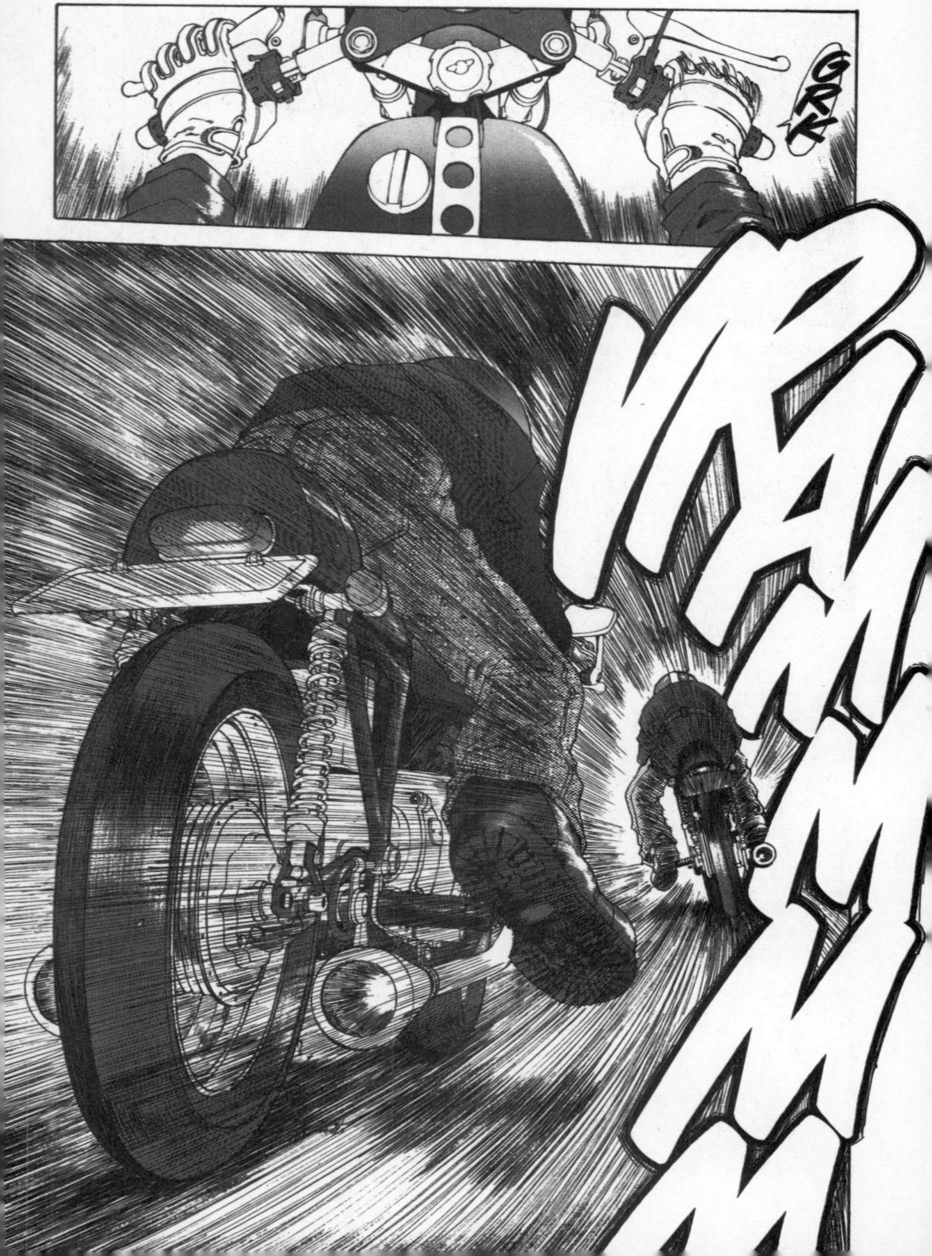
GRK

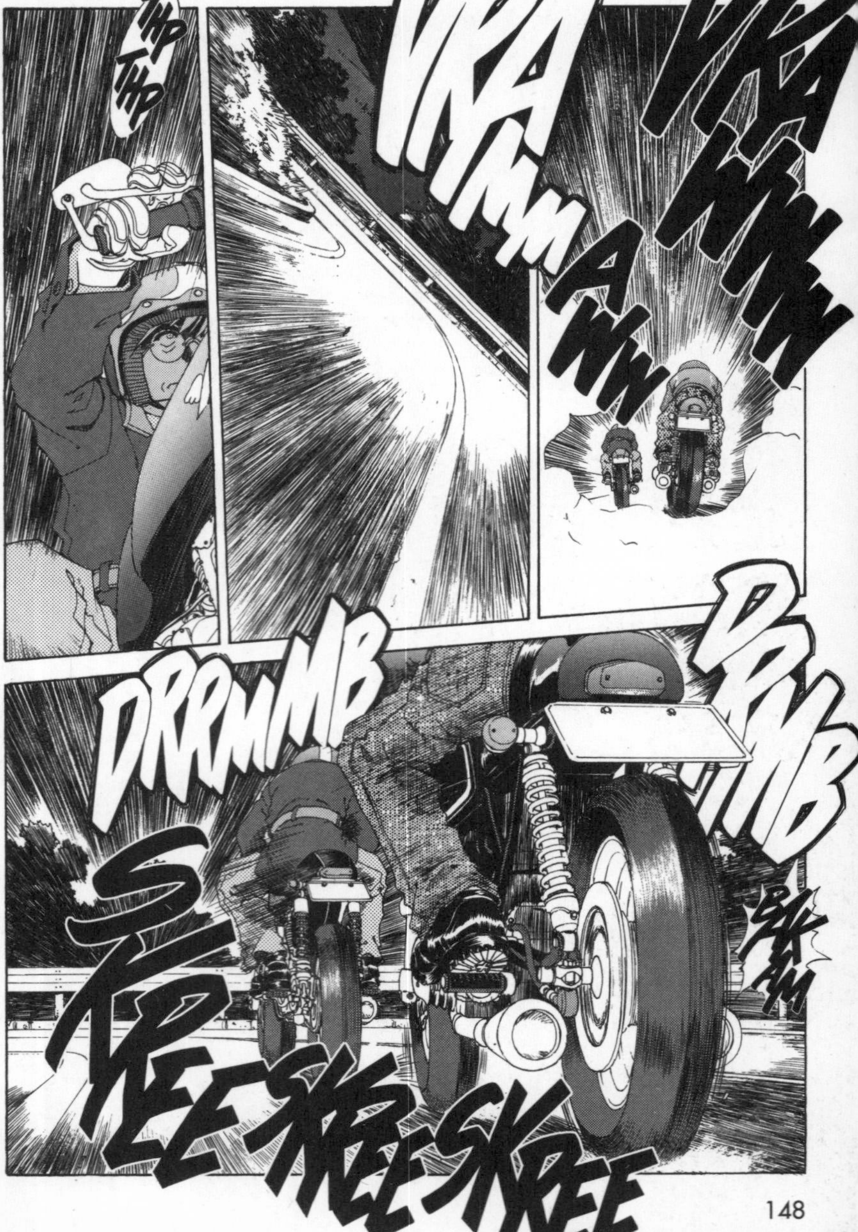
VRA WWWWW
VRA MMM A WW
THP THP
DRMMB
BAKAM
DRRMMB
SKREE SKREE SKREE SKREE

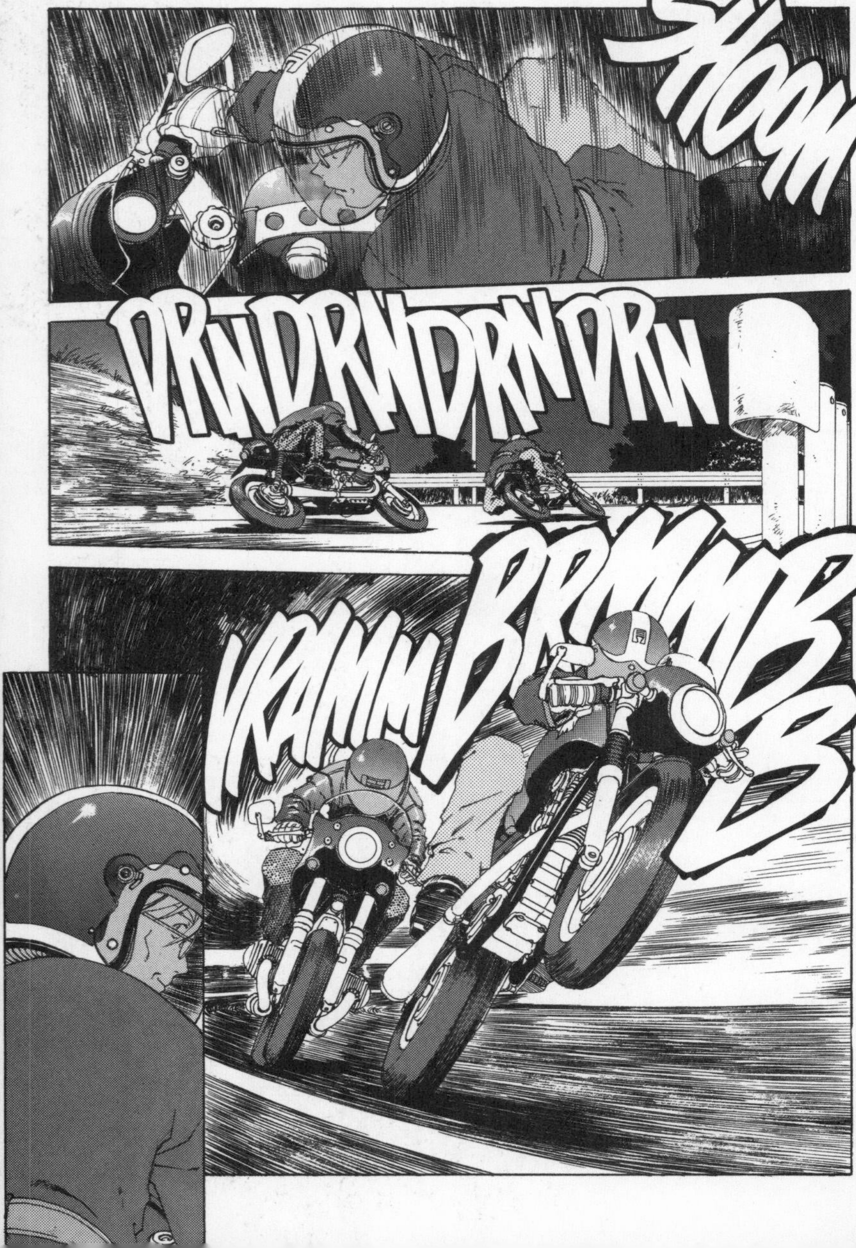
SHOOM
DRNDRNDRN DRN
BRMMBBB
VRAMMM

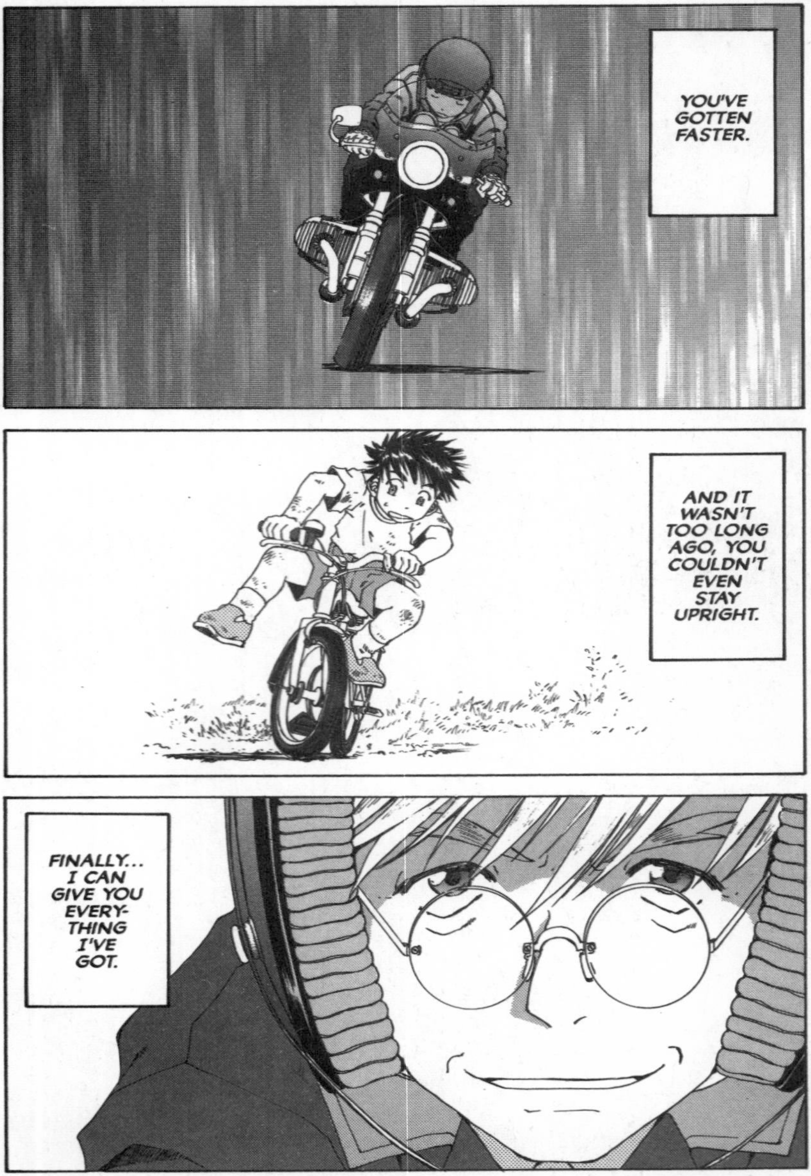
YOU'VE GOTTEN FASTER.
AND IT WASN'T TOO LONG AGO, YOU COULDN'T EVEN STAY UPRIGHT.
FINALLY... I CAN GIVE YOU EVERY-THING I'VE GOT.

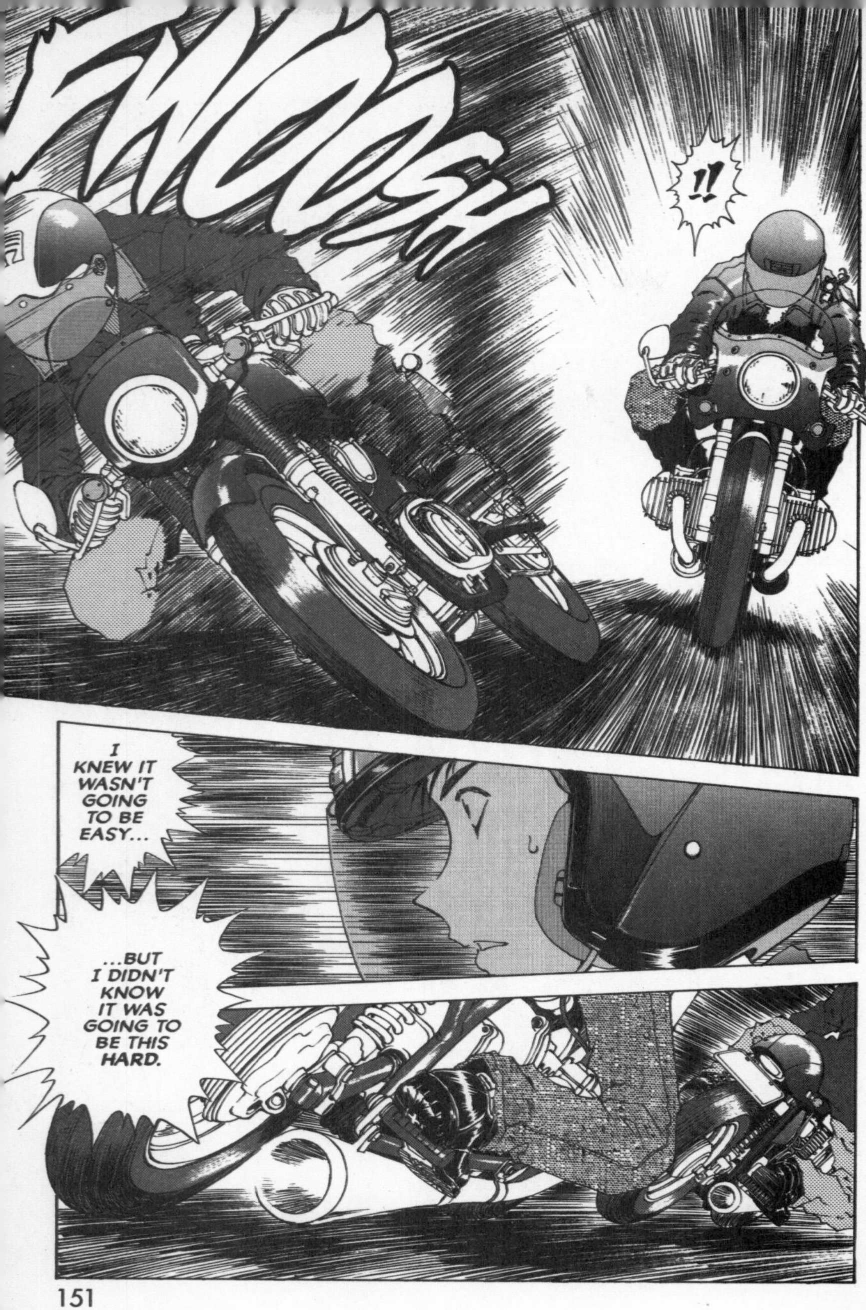
FWOOSH
!!
I KNEW IT WASN'T GOING TO BE EASY...
...BUT I DIDN'T KNOW IT WAS GOING TO BE THIS HARD.

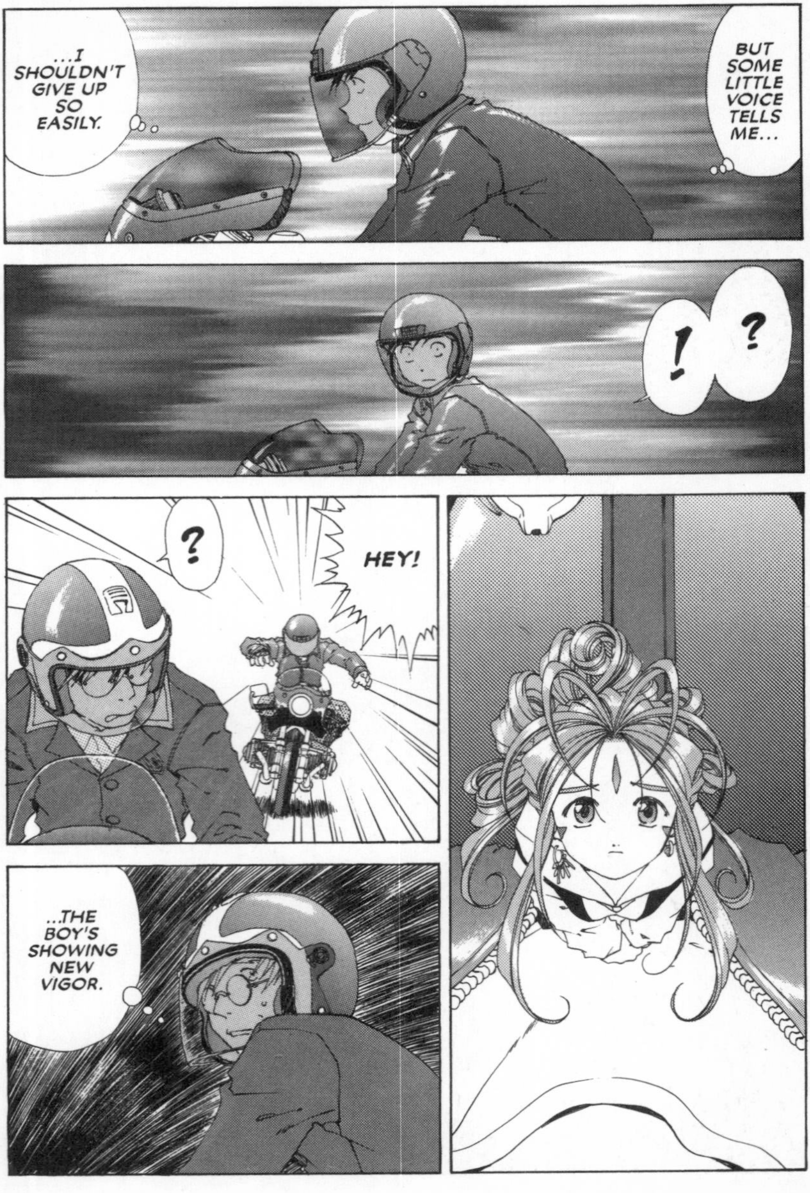
BUT SOME LITTLE VOICE TELLS ME...
...I SHOULDN'T GIVE UP SO EASILY.
! ?
HEY!
?
...THE BOY'S SHOWING NEW VIGOR.

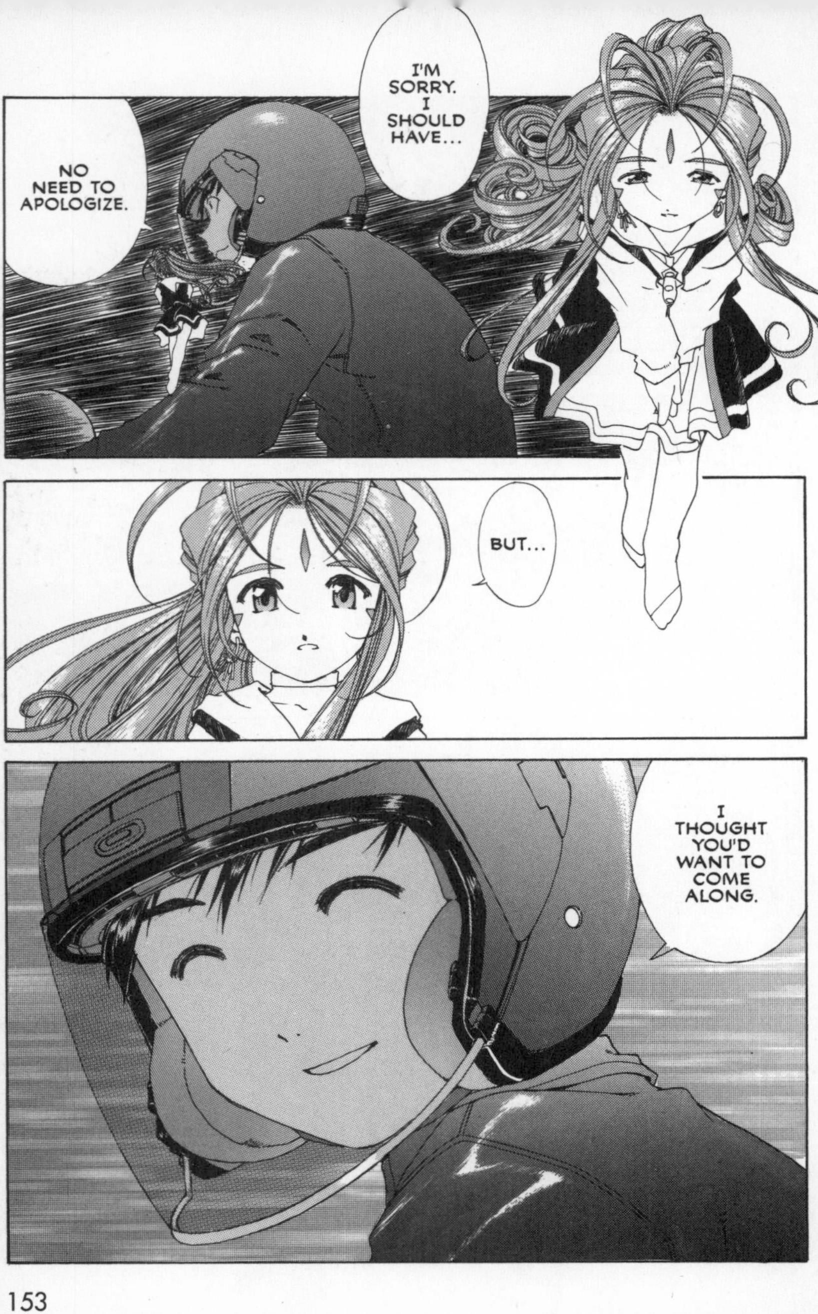
I'M SORRY. I SHOULD HAVE...
NO NEED TO APOLOGIZE.
BUT...
I THOUGHT YOU'D WANT TO COME ALONG.

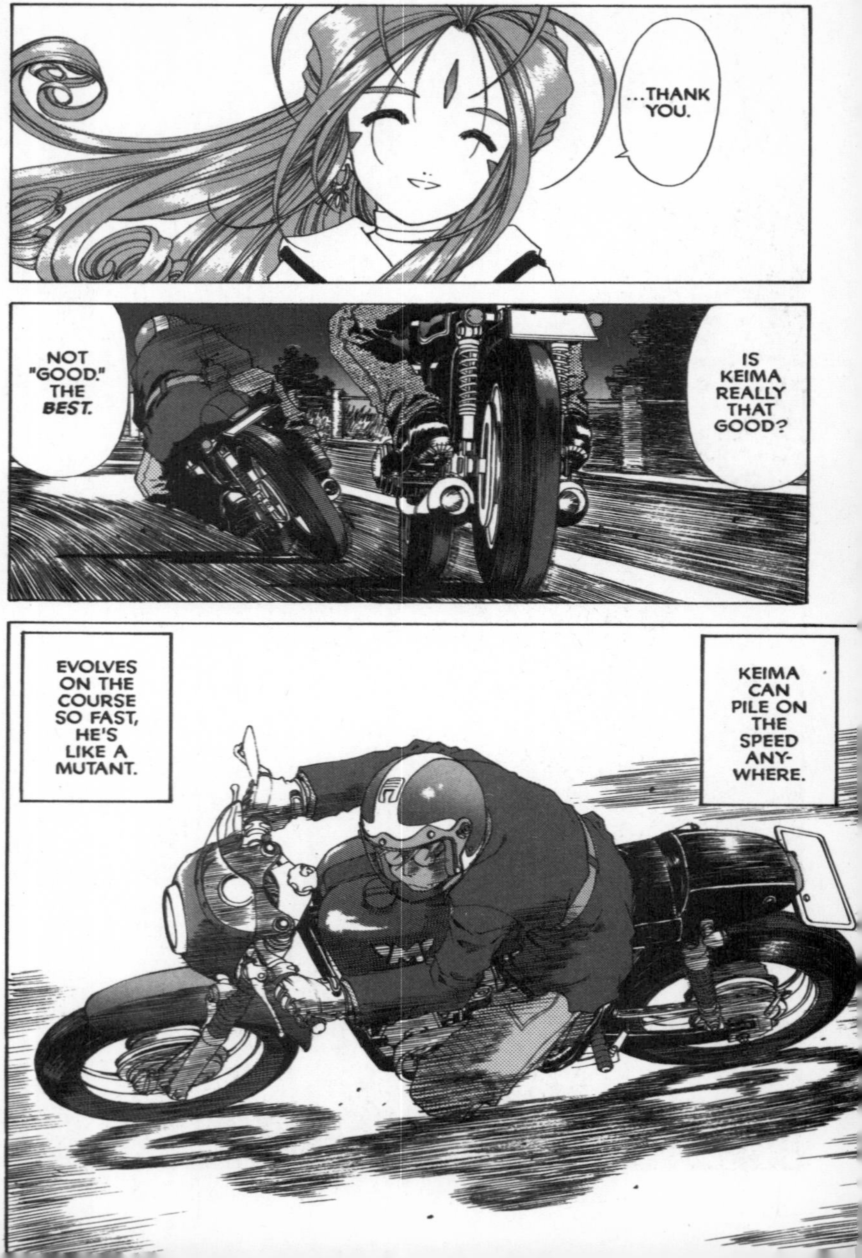
...THANK YOU.
IS KEIMA REALLY THAT GOOD?
NOT "GOOD." THE *BEST.*
KEIMA CAN PILE ON THE SPEED ANY-WHERE.
EVOLVES ON THE COURSE SO FAST, HE'S LIKE A MUTANT.

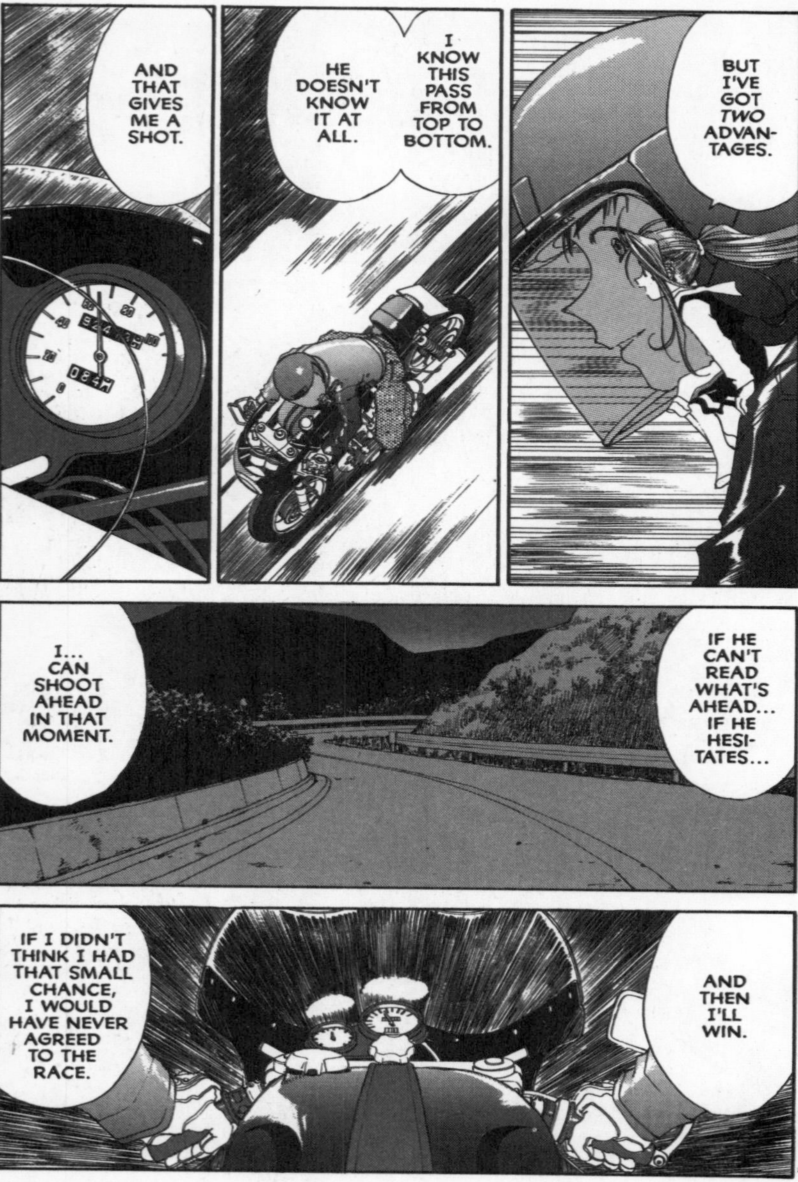
BUT I'VE GOT *TWO* ADVANTAGES.
I KNOW THIS PASS FROM TOP TO BOTTOM.
HE DOESN'T KNOW IT AT ALL.
AND THAT GIVES ME A SHOT.
IF HE CAN'T READ WHAT'S AHEAD... IF HE HESITATES...
I... CAN SHOOT AHEAD IN THAT MOMENT.
AND THEN I'LL WIN.
IF I DIDN'T THINK I HAD THAT SMALL CHANCE, I WOULD HAVE NEVER AGREED TO THE RACE.

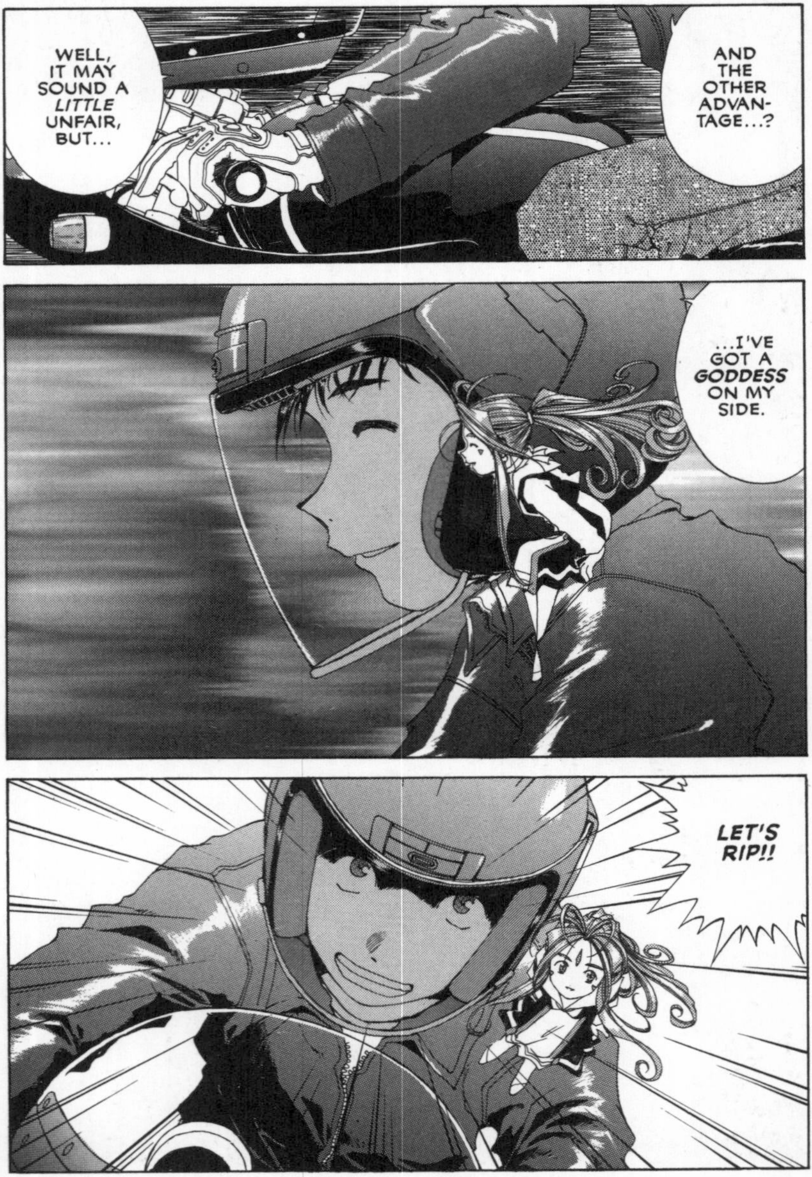
AND THE OTHER ADVANTAGE...?
WELL, IT MAY SOUND A *LITTLE* UNFAIR, BUT...
...I'VE GOT A ***GODDESS*** ON MY SIDE.
LET'S RIP!!

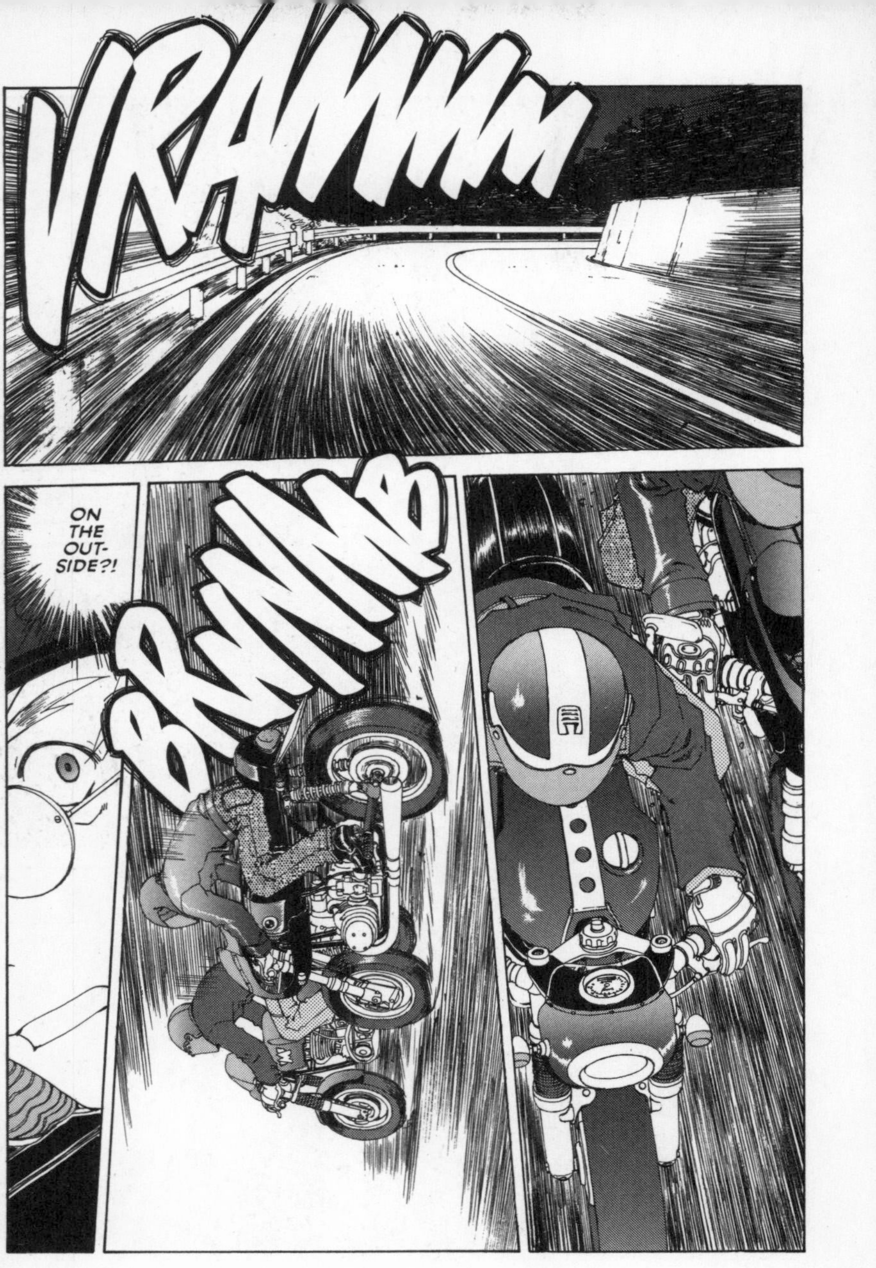
VRAMMM
BRMMMB
ON THE OUT-SIDE?!

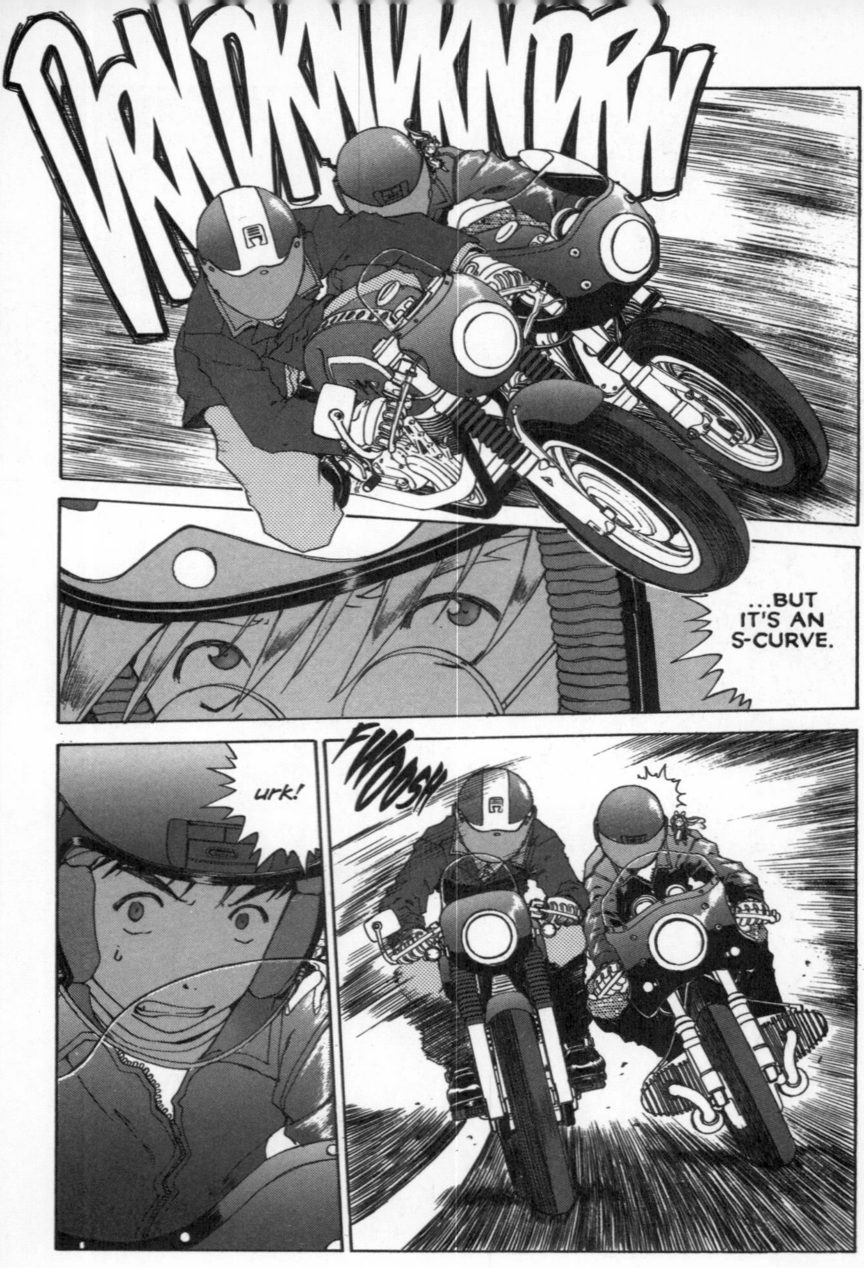
...BUT IT'S AN S-CURVE.
FWOOSH
urk!

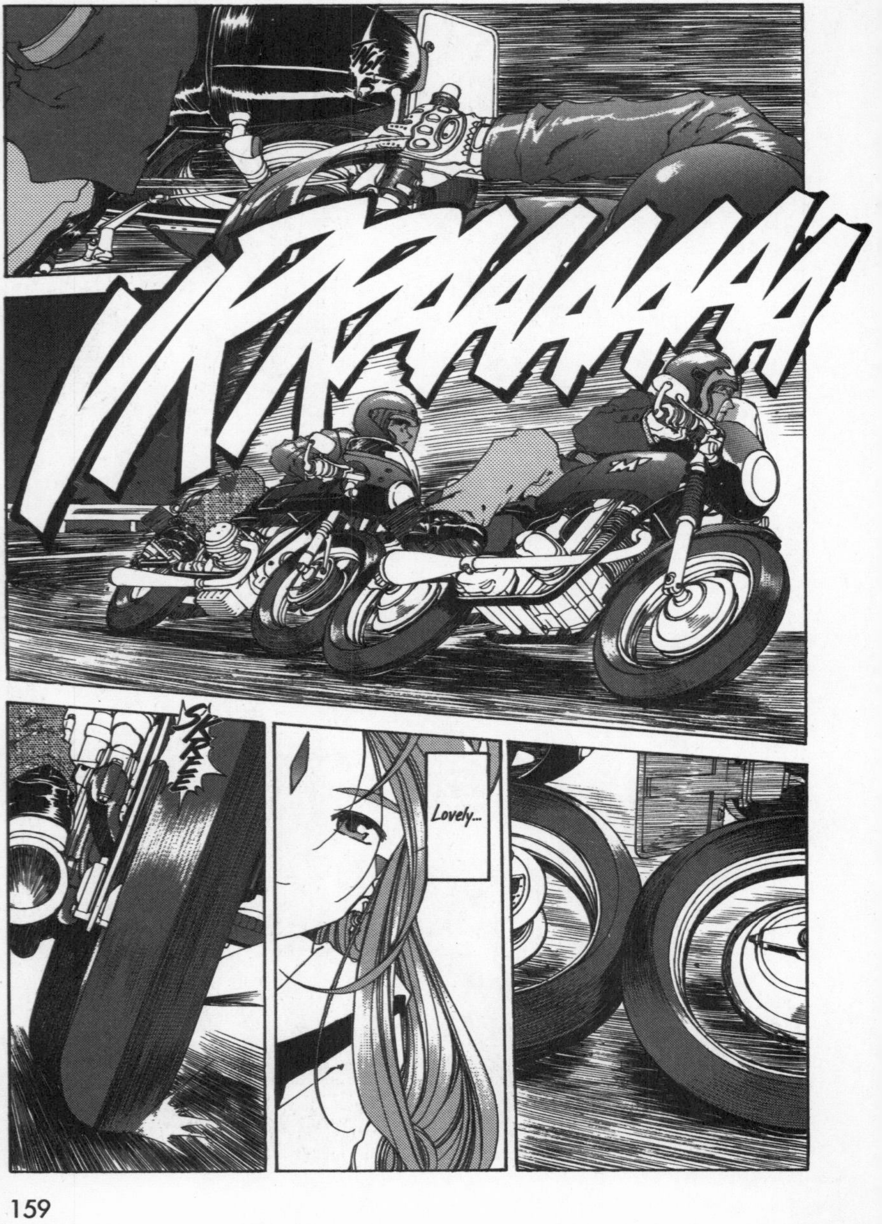
Lovely...
SKREEE

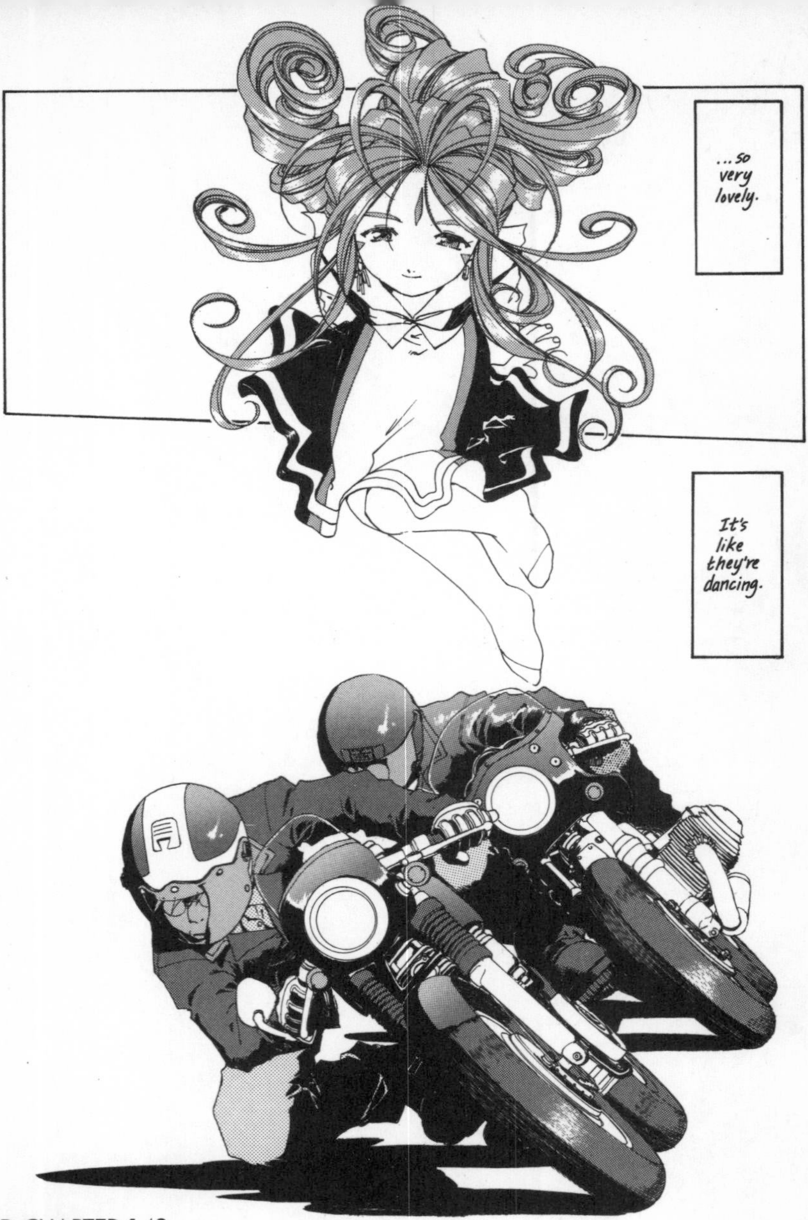
...so very lovely.
It's like they're dancing.

END CHAPTER 148

Continued in
***Oh My Goddess!* Vol. 24**

letters to the

ENCHANTRESS

10956 SE Main Street, Milwaukie, Oregon 97222
omg@darkhorse.com • www.darkhorse.com

NOTE: Full addresses and e-mail addresses will not be printed, unless you ask! All fan artwork, letters, and e-mails submitted become the property of Dark Horse Comics.

7.1: The little "pi pi pi" sounds to be seen among the chicks in the background (of the chicks) are the cheeping noises that baby birds make, as the Japanese hear them. Sometimes this sound is also represented as "piyo piyo," which was the design on Kyoko's trademark apron in *Maison Ikkoku*—see note for 116.4.

7.1.5: If this was one of them authentic manga with unretouched Japanese sound effects and a glossary in 4-point type, you'd get plenty of opportunity from me for labored and pedantic explanations of these things. Don't worry—you can always enjoy this feature in Dark Horse's forthcoming *Mail* and *The Kurosagi Corpse Delivery Service*.

14.3: The translator believes Chihiro was trying to impute that Keiichi's dad is gay. Which brings up an interesting point—if you are a *shonen ai* manga fan, what are you going to do when your favorite characters reach some advanced age, like, I dunno, twenty-two? Are you going to be superficial and stop reading their suggestive adventures? Or are you going to be loyal to them, even if they grow up to look like Keima (now we know where Keiichi gets his tense, worried expression from)?

Remember that the immortal Oscar Wilde was a pioneer of *oyaji ai*.

17.4: I forgot to mention it in the preceding note, but Keima is not gay. Anyway, on this and the next page, Chihiro is obviously having a hard time believing she heard right that Keima drove down from Kushiro. That's because Kushiro is a prefecture (the Japanese equivalent of states—although that's misleading, as they have less autonomy than U.S. states do, and in size they're quite small; for example, Kushiro is only a little larger than Rhode Island) in the northeast of Hokkaido, one of the four main islands that make up Japan. It's almost as far north from Tokyo as you can go and still be in Japan. With a population of 265,000, only one-quarter of one percent of Japan's population lives in Kushiro; you can check out an English-language page on where Keiichi comes from at http://www.kushiro.com/index2.html. Note you can't literally drive straight from Hokkaido to the rest of Japan; it's connected only by a rail tunnel (in fact, the longest one in the world, the Seikan Tunnel—33 1/2 miles long). Presumably Keima took his bike on the train (or took a ferry) and continued his journey from Aomori on the Honshu side.

Since Chihiro doesn't quite grasp Keima's "Incredible Journey," she assumes she misheard, and is straining to find an alternate explanation by thinking of other words that sound like "Kushiro," but are spelled with different kanji. She's straining so hard, in fact, that she's making words up, stringing unrelated kanji together—not unlike those "Asian" tattoos a lot of people get, know what I'm saying? Clockwise from upper right, she comes up with *Ku-Shi-Ro* ("painful death backbone"), *Ku-Shiro* ("longtime representative"), *Kushi-Ro* ("haircomb bribe"), another *Kushi-Ro* ("skewer butterbur"—"skewer" is one of those few kanji that look exactly like what they mean) and finally, another *Ku-Shiro* ("running white").

To be fair, this kind of play on words is pretty common in Japan, but it can be hard on the translator, who notes her own name, Dana Lewis, could be spelled out in Japanese with the kanji "mustard barfing frog of the pomegranate chair." Even people born and raised in Japan have these problems—Chihiro's attempt to draw out the proper kanji (she literally asks Keiichi, "You mean the *kushi* that uses the radical for 'gold' and the *ro* from the *douro*, 'road'?"—which is, finally, correct) in 18.1 is also a common gesture there, like asking someone to spell an unfamiliar name for you. For some reason, "H" manga artists are the worst offenders—they can never just settle for something like a "Dirk Diggler," but glory in strings of kanji with fifteen simultaneous different meanings, probably all wrong.

34.1: Interestingly, Keima calls him "son" here.

50.2: And Bell calls him "father."

51.4: Yokan is a kind of Japanese Jell-O® made out of azuki beans. I've said it before, but I believe that while Japan has developed the comics industry to heights undreamed of here, their own civilization benefited from Western non-bean-based dessert technology.

53: The bangle holding Bell's ponytail has a German motto very appropriate to her character: *Auf Regen folgt Sonnenschein* ("after the rain comes sunshine").

91.3: The sign reads, "Everybody's Tea Room," in case you've been seeing it for years in this manga and wondered what it meant.

115.3: That's what the man said. Is he "breaking the fourth wall"? Perhaps that's why Keiichi is looking very "realistic" here.

115.4: Takano is speaking with a bit of a country accent here. The gift bag is from the fisheries at Todowara, a famous scenic point on Hokkaido's Nemuro peninsula—hence her remark about how the present will only keep a day. Part of the absurdity of the scene is that normal parents, if they wanted to send this kind of gift from home, just would have it mailed overnight.

116.2: Literally, Takano said *amadera*, which is the Japanese term for a Buddhist convent. Such nuns shave their heads just like Buddhist monks, which is probably why they rarely get to be in anime or manga, and all the action roles go to the Catholic nuns, like in *St. Tail, Hellsing, and Chrono Crusade.* Presumably artists feel they can't do much with a bald heroine, whereas with nuns you can have those veils flying around, and, of course, a little bit of hair poking out from underneath for effect. Of course, the irony is that Keiichi *does* live in the temple of a former Buddhist monk (some day that guy is going to come back when the cast least expects it) but you wouldn't exactly call it a place of peace, quiet, and celibacy. Although one out of three ain't bad.

116.4: Although it's supposed to be the early volumes of *OMG!* that drop the

'80s references, Takano is referring here to a classic manga from the creator of *Inu-Yasha*, Rumiko Takahashi's 15-volume *Maison Ikkoku*. Many people consider *Maison Ikkoku* to be Takahashi's most satisfying work, as she took her skills at situation comedy into an everyday (i.e., no aliens, martial arts, or mythic past) background and wrote a love story with a beginning, a middle, and an ending (the editor tugs his collar nervously at the thought *Oh My Goddess!* is now up to Vol. 32). The *Maison Ikkoku* manga ran between 1980 and 1987; the 96-episode anime version from 1986 to 1988. All of the manga and part of the anime are available from Viz Media.

Maison Ikkoku is also the name of the boarding house where the main characters live; the hero, Yusaku Godai, a young man who failed his college entrance exams and is now studying to try again, is in love with the house's manager, Kyoko Otonashi. Takano may have thought Belldandy a good "match" for her, as Kyoko is also a beautiful, mysterious, long-haired young woman. Other tenants of Maison Ikkoku include Mrs. Ichinose, a fat, drunken middle-aged gossip who lives there with her son and (rarely-seen) husband, and Mr. Yotsuya, a Kramer-like man of mystery who knocks a hole in Godai's wall in order to pop in uninvited. Yotsuya knocks a hole in Godai's other wall so he can peep on Ms. Roppongi, a red-headed, hard-drinking, little-wearing bar hostess. I wonder who Takano assigned those roles to?

135.5: For "homeland," Takano uses the old term *naichi* ("inner land"), which during WWII referred to Japan proper, as opposed to the territory overseas Japan occupied as colonies. Of course, the joke here is that she's from Hokkaido, which *is* part of Japan proper.

140.2: Continuing in her hick mode, Takano is amazed at "all" the TV channels you can pick up here as opposed to her hometown. They have cable and DSS in Hokkaido, too, but Takano isn't letting that concern her.

140.4: Yuko Miyamura, born in 1972, achieved fame for her portrayal of Asuka in the original Japanese version of *Neon Genesis Evangelion*. In an essay at the back of Volume Four of the English-language edition of the *Evangelion* manga, Miyamura discusses the role—a performance that (as with several other leading roles in the series) strove for an unusual personal intensity; *The End of Evangelion* won a Japan Academy Award, the only one ever given to a non-Hayao Miyazaki anime. The actress is portrayed here with the hairstyle she wore during a memorable cameo as the TV instructor in the late Kinji Fukasaku's final film, *Battle Royale* (released in December of 2000 in Japan; one month after this story originally ran in *Afternoon* magazine).

141.3: Jenga—from Hasbro—is the tower-building game Urd and Skuld are playing for TV rights in "The Endless Battle, Part One" in *Oh My Goddess!* Vol. 19/20: *Sora Unchained* (the last of the "flopped" series, which story-wise comes immediately before Vol. 21, the first of the "unflopped" series—please see "Letters to the Enchantress" in Vol. 21 for a lengthy explanation ^_^). *Dobon* bears some resemblance to Uno, but is played with a standard deck of cards. Kyoko Ino offers an English-language perspective at: http://www.ii-park.net/~q-dobon/index.html

143.1: The joke here is that proper parents would never teach their daughters a game like mahjong, considered somewhat masculine and "working clarse" (as Student Grant would put it). It further shows how upside down Takano and Keima's universe is. Still more bizarre, mothers in *America* used to teach their daughters mahjong. The game was introduced (with modified rules) to the United States in the 1920s and '30s and was popular in particular among female players for several decades thereafter; many retirees still play this version. You may have heard that there's a whole genre of mahjong manga in Japan, which is true. But like shojo manga, which can pretty much be about anything as long as there's a relationship involved somewhere, all mahjong manga need to keep their cred is to show the occasional game.

When I was in high school in the mid-eighties, I was fortunate that Kinokuniya (at least, the one in San Francisco—BART to Powell St., then the 38 Geary to Japantown) didn't yet shrink-wrap their manga. As you might guess, this policy not only enabled me to scope out them mature-readers titles (most notably Kazuo Koike's *Brothers*, which made my eyes manga-wide) but to browse titles in general.

This was just a few years before companies in North America began to publish manga in English on a regular basis (Dark Horse started doing so in 1988), and, although there were certainly otaku like myself, there wasn't much sense yet of an otaku market for import manga. In those days clerks seemed ever so slightly appalled that *gaijin* knew manga existed; you got the impression they'd much rather have you buy a nice book on Zen gardens or flower arranging. The advantage of all this, though, was that to browse a Reagan-era Kinokuniya was to explore manga as the average Japanese would know it, instead of how the hardcore fan (i.e., otaku), whether Japanese or American, would know it. And that ultimately made for more interesting

discoveries, going away from just the things you know you'll like, to things you didn't even know existed.

Like, well, mahjong manga. At fifteen, just hitting the racks at random, I came across a two-volume series called *Rastapai* (*pai* is a word used in Japanese to refer to the tiles used to play mahjong), written by Karibu Marei (another pen name of Garon Tsuchiya—itself also a pen name—the author of Dark Horse's forthcoming manga *Old Boy*) and drawn by Shin Morimura. The cover certainly wouldn't give you a clue that the manga had anything to do with mahjong—it featured a drawing of the eponymous hero, a grinning Japanese guy in his twenties with good hair, cocking his finger at the audience and sporting black Ray-Bans, which, I was to learn, he never took off. Tom Cruise's wearing them in 1983's *Risky Business* had revived the glasses in a big way—Cruise's "Joel Goodson" character from the movie was the guy you dreamed of being in those years. Being, not doing; this was long before any of that *shonen ai* talk got started about him.

Rastapai is a fairly obscure title today. In fact I don't think anything by Shin Morimura has ever been published in English (his successful boxing saga *Paradise* runs currently in Kodansha's *Young Sunday* magazine), although he reportedly gave great assistance to the launch of the manga *Planetes*, written and drawn by Morimura's former assistant Makoto Yukimura. And it's probably not all that noteworthy a manga in the grand scheme of things. But it was noteworthy to *me*—I'd never seen anything like it before. The story was basically just about this guy who would make some money during the day on construction jobs (we saw as little of that as possible) and by night would get into as many schemes as possible, usually involving women, and always taking breaks to play a little mahjong. He wasn't *exactly* a low-life; he was more like a lower-middle-life. The author of *Rastapai* spelled his pen name with kanji that read "Karibu Marei," but spelled it in English as "Caribu Marley," and given that and the manga's title, it's no surprise the story ended with the hero beamed up one night by space Rastas—floating in midair surrounded by mahjong tiles, still grinning—and still wearing his Ray-Bans.

When I was fifteen, I didn't know you *could* draw a comic about that. What made the biggest impression on me wasn't works of fantasy or science fiction, because I was used to the idea that comics could be about those things. What really grabbed me was the idea of a comic which was about real people in real life—maybe an amped up, surrealistic version of real life, but still real life. In North America comics about "real life" are often seen as efforts toward artistic expression—psychological, confessional, or perhaps political—but these manga were more like really cool TV sitcoms. I didn't know it at the time, but works like *Rastapai* were an expression of the confidence comics have in Japan, where you don't need a big concept or backstory, but a creator can just in effect say, "Okay, so there was this guy who—" It was indicative of the power of manga that I didn't know anything about mahjong before I read *Rastapai*, and didn't know anything about it afterwards, yet the story itself had made a huge impression on me. It's also a reminder of how little categories like "mahjong manga" can really mean, any more than "shojo manga" or "shonen manga." As always, it comes down to the individual story, not necessarily the supposed genre or demographic.

I want to apologize to the people whose letters we received at the last minute, including Olivia Thompson and Benjamin Urrutia (as you know, this column is pre-pared some time before it shows up in the bookstores); it turned out *Letters to the Enchantress* netted more mail this time than the six pages allocated to this volume; but it's good to know its correspondence is growing. We'll do our best to run them next time!

Dear Goddess Office,

Ah! Where to start? This is my first time writing a manga publication, period, much less one that holds the designation as my favorite series in both anime and manga (truthfully, it holds that spot alongside another project Kosuke Fujishima has been involved in [he did many of its character designs—CGH], *Sakura Taisen*). So I'm actually a little apprehensive about just how I'm supposed to sum up my general thoughts about something I appreciate so much, without it coming out more than a little underwhelming in the process.

Well, that impossibility established, I'll get the fan in me out of the way in saying that I definitely love the series in all its forms and I'm really glad that I finally took the plunge and began collecting the manga on which the anime series is based several months back, just prior to Dark Horse's announcement that they would be re-releasing the series in its authentic format. So, while I'm not new to anime (been watching that in some form since Leiji Matsumoto's work was first shown on U.S. shores back in the late '70s/early '80s) or to *OMG!* as a series, I am relatively new to manga itself and it wasn't too long after discovering that my favorite series had thrived in this format for years that I made the rather speedy conclusion that I had darn well better get on board.

As a result, with a handful of volumes already under my belt I'm continually blown away by the masterful work that Kosuke

Fujishima puts to paper in both written and illustrative forms. The characters come out of the work in a way that few others can claim—in any medium—and it's a testament to his talents (and of those surrounding him) across the board that this is the case. I care what happens to Belldandy, Urd, Keiichi, and the others as I've been drawn into the stories, and it's not just a case of appreciating how good this work is on a critical level, but also on a personal one.

Anyhow, with the "fan letter" out of the way I'll be sure to try to write in with more specific comments about future storylines as best I can, and in addition to thanking all of y'all for the hard work that I know you put into the translations, publishing process, etc.—and for Dark Horse's long commitment to the series—I also wanted to thank you for the detailed notes at the end of each volume that explain the historical or cultural relevance of many of the references that are made throughout the Goddesses' adventures. It's very interesting reading (at least, to this history major, and one attempting to learn more and more about the Japanese culture) and I hope y'all will keep it coming!

Until next time then, all the best!

Mr. Kathan D. McCallister
Fort Worth, Texas

P.S. I'll attach a copy of the humble piece of fan art (a manipulated sketch) as a separate attachment as well in the case that my letter doesn't make the cut, feel free to edit it in any way that's helpful, and you have any interest in using it. It's certainly "okay to print." Thanks.

P.P.S. Hope Milwaukie, Oregon is treating a number of y'all well; while away from Texas for a couple of years I lived only a block or two from Dark Horse's headquarters and would often pass its offices while traveling. Stay dry!

I love the expression "all of y'all," especially when the Geto Boys use it. Now, they're from Houston, but Fort Worth is the finest town in that part of Texas. I remember going to see the Soviet Space exhibit there in 1991—the first time the USSR had ever brought an exhibit of that size to America, hauling out a massive amount of capsules, rockets, and other hardware, much of it previously top secret. Unfortunately, the USSR collapsed during the exhibit and I heard that the exhibit and its staff got stuck here; many of the artifacts ended up being auctioned off by Sotheby's.

Not only is that a fine (or as they say in Texas, "fahn") piece of fan art, but, most importantly, you actually sent it in! I don't know why it's so hard to get people to send in their fan art, but I'm hoping that people will take inspiration from this. To paraphrase Bernie Casey in *Flash Gordon*, "May the deed of Mr. McCallister be an example to all the kingdoms of manga!"

—CGH